Cyber Terrorism and Military Preparedness: An International Perspective

Cyber Terrorism and Military Preparedness: An International Perspective

Capt.(Retd.) R.K. Sirohi

PRASHANT PUBLISHING HOUSE
DELHI-110094

Published by :
PRASHANT PUBLISHING HOUSE
C-34, 28 Foota Road, Gali-3,
West Karwal Nagar, Delhi-110094
Phone : 011-22963970, Mob. : 9810396373, 8826258746
e-mail.: prashantpublishinghouse@gmail.com

Cyber Terrorism and Military Preparedness: An International Perspective

First Published 2019

ISBN : 978-93-88526-20-3

PRINTED IN INDIA
Published by Mr. R.K. Jha M/s Prashant Publishing House and Published at H.S. Offset House Press, Delhi.

Preface

Cyberterrorism is the use of the Internet to conduct violent acts that result in, or threaten, loss of life or significant bodily harm, in order to achieve political or ideological gains through threat or intimidation. It is also sometimes considered an act of Internet terrorism where terrorist activities, including acts of deliberate, large-scale disruption of computer networks, especially of personal computers attached to the Internet by means of tools such as computer viruses, computer worms, phishing, and other malicious software and hardware methods and programming scripts.

The presence of terrorist groups on the internet is a relatively new phenomenon, the growth of which has exploded in the past decade. Accurate estimates on the number of active terrorist group's websites vary due to difficulties measuring but, there is a general consensus that in 1996 there was just under 100 websites and to well over 5000 websites today. It is also widely accepted that all Foreign Terrorist Organisation's listed by the U.S. Department of State website have established an online presence of some form.

The menace of cyber terrorism is not the sole responsibility of State and its instrumentalities. The citizens as well as the netizens are equally under a solemn obligation to fight against the cyber terrorism. In fact, they are the most important and effective cyber terrorism eradication and elimination mechanism. The only requirement is to encourage them to come forward for the support of fighting against cyber terrorism. The government can give suitable incentives to them in the form of monetary awards. It must, however, be noted that their anonymity and security must be ensured before seeking their help. The courts are also empowered to maintain their anonymity if they provide any information and evidence to fight against cyber terrorism.

The characteristic of cyber warfare that makes it so uniquely dangerous to the corporate sector is that military power in the cyber domain must be extended through computer networks provided and maintained by non-governmental bodies. The use of these networks for cyberattacks or defense requires the conscription or cooperation of civilian resources. This creates extreme liabilities for the corporations that provide these networks, as they will quickly become the targets of suspicion and possible retaliation from the enemy state. In recent years, both Chinese and American companies have been caught in just this situation.

The Internet is a cheap, fast means of international communication of text, sound or image. In other words, an information resource without political or content boundaries; limited only by the extent to which the information providers are willing to disclose their materials and the fruits of their own writing and research. In the present day, web sites displaying information of all kinds are proliferating. These sites are established and controlled by Internet Service Providers (ISPs) or, sometimes, by the company's information technology department.

Thus cyber security touches practically all activities and all citizens around the globe; it provides tremendous opportunities for enhancing human development as well as achieving better integration in the information society. It also supports wider access to knowledge and education, as well as to the development of policies and strategies.

This is a reference book. All the matter is just compiled and edited in nature, taken from the various sources which are in public domain.

This book is a brief that outlines many of the recent terrorist activities, political objectives, and their use of cyber space. Protecting the organization's infrastructure from cyber-based attacks that are designed to disrupt and/or destroy business operations is becoming increasingly important.

—Editor

Contents

1

Threats and Effect of Cyber Terrorism

THE CONCEPT OF CYBER TERRORISM

Cyber crime and cyber terrorism are both crimes of the cyber world. The difference between the two however is with regard to the motive and the intention of the perpetrator.

While a cyber crime can be described simply as an unlawful act wherein the computer is either a tool or a target or both, cyber terrorism deserves a more detailed definition. One can define cyber terrorism as a premeditated use of disruptive activities or the threat thereof, in cyber space, with the intention to further social, ideological, religious, political or similar objectives, or to intimidate any person in furtherance of such objectives.

Cyber Criminals

Any person who commits an illegal act with a guilty intention or commits a crime is called an offender or a criminal. In this context, any person who commits a Cyber Crime is known as a Cyber Criminal. The Cyber Criminals may be children and adolescents aged b/w 6-18 years, they may be organized hackers, may be professional hackers or crackers, discontented employees, cheaters or even psychic persons.

Kids & Teenagers (age group 9-16 etc.)

This is really difficult to believe but it is true. Most amateur hackers and cyber criminals are teenagers. To them, who have just begun to understand what appears to be a lot about computers, it is a matter of pride to have hacked into a computer system or a website. There is also that little issue of appearing really smart among friends.

These young rebels may also commit cyber crimes without really knowing that they are doing anything wrong. According to the BBC, Teen hackers have gone from simply trying to make a name for them selves to actually working their way into a life of crime from the computer angle. According to Kevin Hogan, One of the biggest changes of 2004 was the waning influence of the boy hackers keen to make a name by writing a fast-spreading virus. Although teenage virus writers will still play around with malicious code, 2004 saw a significant rise in criminal use of malicious programs. The financial incentives were driving criminal use of technology.

Another reason for the increase in number of teenage offenders in cyber crimes are that many of the offenders who are mainly young college students are unaware of its seriousness.

Recently the Chennai city police have arrested an engineering college student from Tamil Nadu for sending unsolicited message to a chartered accountant. The boy is now released on bail. So counseling session for college students has to be launched to educate them on the gravity and consequences emanating from such crimes.

In September, 2005, A Massachusetts teenager pleaded guilty in federal court in Boston for a string of hacking crimes reported to include the February compromise of online information broker Lexis Nexis and socialite Paris Hilton's T-Mobile cellular phone account. The US Court noted that the number of teenage hackers is on the rise and only the lowest 1 percent of hackers is caught.

In the above instance, the judge imposed a sentence of 11 months' detention in a juvenile facility. If he had been an adult, he would have faced charges of three counts of making bomb threats against a person or property, three counts of causing damage to a protected computer system, two counts of wire fraud, one count of aggravated identity theft and one count of obtaining information from a protected computer in furtherance of a criminal act.

This is clearly a deviation from the traditional principles of criminal law.

Organized Hacktivists

Hacktivists are hackers with a particular (mostly political) motive. In other cases this reason can be social activism, religious activism, etc. The attacks on approximately 200 prominent Indian websites by a group of hackers known as Pakistani Cyber Warriors are a good example of political hacktivists at work.

Disgruntled Employees

One can hardly believe how spiteful displeased employees can become. Till now they had the option of going on strike against their bosses. Now, with the increase independence on computers and the automation of processes, it is easier for disgruntled employees to do more harm to their employers by committing computer related crimes, which can bring entire systems down.

Professional Hackers (Corporate espionage)

Extensive computerization has resulted in business organizations storing all their information in electronic form. Rival organizations employ hackers to steal industrial secrets and other information that could be beneficial to them. The temptation to use professional hackers for industrial espionage also stems from the fact that physical presence required to gain access to important documents is rendered needless if hacking can retrieve those.

PRIVACY VIOLATION

The law of privacy is the recognition of the individual's right to be let alone and to have his personal space inviolate. The right to privacy as an independent and distinctive concept originated in the field of Tort law, under which a new cause of action for damages resulting from unlawful invasion of privacy was recognised. *In recent times, however, this right has acquired a constitutional status, the violation of which attracts both civil as well as criminal consequences under the respective laws.* The intensity and complexity of life have rendered necessary some retreat from the world. Man under the refining influence of culture, has become sensitive to publicity, so that solitude and privacy have become essential to the individual. *Modern enterprise and invention have, through invasions upon his privacy, subjected him to mental pain and distress, far greater than could be inflicted by mere bodily injury.* Right to privacy is a part of the right to life and personal liberty enshrined under Article 21 of the Constitution of India. With the advent of information technology the traditional concept of right to privacy has taken new dimensions, which require a different legal outlook. To meet this challenge recourse of Information Technology Act, 2000 can be taken. The various provisions of the Act aptly protect the online privacy rights of the netizens. Certain acts have been categorised as offences and contraventions, which have tendency to intrude with the privacy rights of the netizens. These rights are available against private individuals as well as against cyber terrorists. Section 1 (2) read with Section 75 of the Act provides for an extra-territorial application of the provisions of the Act. Thus, if a person (including a foreign national) contravenes the privacy of an individual by means of computer, computer system or computer network located in India, he would be liable under the provisions of the Act. This makes it clear that the long arm jurisdiction is equally available against a cyber terrorist, whose act has resulted in the damage of the property, whether tangible or intangible.

Secret information appropriation and data theft

The information technology can be misused for appropriating the valuable Government secrets and data of private individuals and the Government and its agencies. A computer network owned by the Government may contain valuable information concerning defence and other top secrets, which the Government will not wish to share otherwise.

The same can be targeted by the terrorists to facilitate their activities, including destruction of property. It must be noted that the definition of property is not restricted to moveables or immoveables alone. In R.K. Dalmia v Delhi Administration the Supreme Court held that the word "property" is used in the I.P.C in a much wider sense than the expression "movable property". There is no good reason to restrict the meaning of the word "property" to moveable property only, when it is used without any qualification. Whether the offence defined in a particular section of IPC can be committed in respect of any particular kind of property, will depend not on the interpretation of the word "property" but on the fact whether that particular kind of property can be subject to the acts covered by that section. Thus, if any person without permission of the owner or any other person who is incharge of a computer, computer system or computer network -

(a) accesses or secures access to such computer, computer system or computer network.

(b) downloads, copies or extracts any data, computer data base or information from such computer, computer system or computer network including information or data held or stored in any removable storage medium;

(c) damages or causes to be damaged any computer, computer system or computer network, data, computer data base or any other programmes residing in such computer, computer system or computer network;

he shall be liable to pay damages by way of compensation not exceeding one crore rupees to the person so affected. The expression "Computer Database" means a representation of information, knowledge, facts, concepts or instructions in text, image, audio, video that are being prepared or have been prepared in a formalised manner or have been produced by a computer, computer system or computer network and are intended for use in a computer, computer system or computer network.

The expression "Damage" means to destroy, alter, delete, add, modify or re-arrange any computer resource by any means. These provisions make it clear that secret information appropriation and data theft by the cyber terrorists will be dealt with punitive sting and monetary impositions.

Distributed denial of services attack

The cyber terrorists may also use the method of distributed denial of services (DDOS) to overburden the Government and its agencies electronic bases. This is made possible by first infecting several unprotected computers by way of virus attacks and then taking control of them. Once control is obtained, they can be manipulated from any locality by the terrorists. These infected computers are then made to send information or demand in such a large number that the server of the victim collapses.

Further, due to this unnecessary Internet traffic the legitimate traffic is prohibited from reaching the Government or its agencies computers.

This results in immense pecuniary and strategic loss to the government and its agencies. It must be noted that thousands of compromised computers can be used to simultaneously attack a single host, thus making its electronic existence invisible to the genuine and legitimate netizens and end users. The law in this regard is crystal clear. If any person without permission of the owner or any other person who is incharge of a computer, computer system or computer network :

(a) introduces or causes to be introduced any computer contaminant or computer virus into any computer, computer system or computer network;

(b) disrupts or causes disruption of any computer, computer system or computer network;

(c) denies or causes the denial of access to any person authorised to access any computer, computer system or computer network by any means;

The shall be liable to pay damages by way of compensation not exceeding one crore rupees to the person so affected. The expression "Computer Contaminant" means any set of computer instructions that are designed -

(a) to modify, destroy, record, transmit data or programme residing within a computer, computer system or computer network; or

(b) by any means to usurp the normal operation of the computer, computer system, or computer network. Thus, distribute denial of services by the cyber terrorists will be tackled by invoking the provisions of sections 43,65 and 66 collectively.

FORMS OF CYBER TERRORISM

It is very difficult to exhaustively specify the forms of cyber terrorism. In fact, it would not be a fruitful exercise to do the same. The nature of cyber terrorism requires it to remain inclusive and open ended in nature, so that new variations and forms of it can be accommodated in the future. The following can be safely regarded as the forms of cyber terrorism applying the definition and the concepts discussed above:

The Roads Ahead

The menace of cyber terrorism can be effectively curbed, if not completely eliminated, if the three sovereign organs of the Constitution work collectively and in harmony with each other. Further, a vigilant citizenry can supplement the commitment of elimination of cyber terrorism.

Legislative Commitment

The legislature can provide its assistance to the benign objective of elimination of cyber terrorism by enacting appropriate statutes dealing with cyber terrorism. It must be noted that to give effect to the provisions of Information Technology Act, 2000 appropriate amendments have been made in the I.P.C, 1860, the Indian Evidence Act, 1872, the Bankers' Books Evidence Act, 1891 and the Reserve Bank of India Act, 1934. On the same lines a new chapter dealing with "Cyber terrorism" can be added to the already existing criminal statues to make them compatible with modern forms of terrorisms. Similarly, a new chapter dealing with cyber terrorism can be incorporated in the Information Technology Act, 2000 by way of its amendment to bring harmonization among various laws. The repealment of POTA and its likely replacement with a new ordinance is an opportunity for the legislature to make the terrorist law effective to deal with cyber terrorism.

Executives Concern

The Central Government and the State Governments can play their role effectively by making various rules and regulations dealing with cyber terrorism and its facets from time to time. The Central Government can, by notification in the Official Gazette and in the Electronic Gazette, makes rules to carry out the provisions of the Information Technology Act. Similarly, the State Government can, by notification in Official Gazette, makes rules to carry out the provisions of the Act. In exercise of the powers conferred by section 90 of the Information Technology Act, 2000 (Central Act 21 of 2000), the Government of Karnataka has made the Information Technology (Karnataka) Rules 2004.

The Rules define "Cyber Café" as premises where the Cyber Café Owner/ Network Service Provider provides the computer services including Internet access to the public. Rule 3 (1) provides that the owner of the Cyber Café shall take sufficient precautions so that computers and computer systems in the Cyber Café are not used for any illegal or criminal activity. Rule 3 (2) mandates that the Cyber Café Owner/Network Service Provider shall not allow any User to use his Computer, Computer System and/or Computer Network without the identity of the User being established before him before use.

The Rule provides that the intending User may establish his Identity by producing any Photo Identity Card issued by any School or College or a Photo Credit Card of any Bank or Passport or Voters Identity Card or PAN Number Card issued by Income-Tax authorities or Photo Identity Card issued by the Employer or Driving License to the satisfaction of Cyber Café Owner.

Rule 4(1) provides that after the identity of the User is established, the owner of the Cyber Café or the manager or the attendant or on his behalf any authorised person managing the Cyber Café shall obtain and maintain the following information in the Log Register for each user: (i) Name of the User, (ii) Age and Sex of the User, (iii) Present residential address of the User, (iv) Log in time, and (v) Log out time. Rule 4 (2) provides that if a User cannot produce any Photo Identity Card to establish his identity to the satisfaction of the Cyber Café Owner/Network Service Provider, he may be photographed by the Cyber Café Owner/Network Service Provider after obtaining his consent using a 'Web Camera' hooked onto one of the computers or computer systems in the Cyber Café and the User shall be explained that his photograph will be taken and stored in the hard disk of the computer, for verification by Law enforcement authorities, whenever required.

This is in addition to the entries made in the log register. The Rule further provides that in case the User does not agree for storing his photograph he shall not be allowed to use any computer, computer system and/or computer network or access to the Internet in the Cyber Café. Rule 4(3) provides that all time clocks in Cyber Cafes must be regularly checked and synchronized with Indian Standard Time (IST).

Rule 4(4) provides that maintaining proper account of the User as explained shall be the responsibility of the Cyber Café Owner/Network Service provider. Rule 5(5) provides that the Log Register and the Photograph of the User shall be maintained by the Cyber Café Owner/Network Service Provider for a minimum period of ONE YEAR and the same shall be provided to Law enforcement agencies as and when required. Rule 4(6) provides that the Cyber Police authorities may on complaint inspect Cyber Cafes at all reasonable time to ensure compliance of these rules.

If any Cyber Café Owner/Network Service Provider fails to maintain Log Register and records he shall be liable for penalties as provided in the Act or any other Law, for the time being in force. These provisions are sufficient to take care of illegal use of cyber café for terrorist activities. Further, the government can also block web sites propagating cyber terrorism. It must be noted that the Indian Computer Emergency Response Team (CERT-In) has been designated as the single authority for issuing of instructions in the context of blocking of web sites. CERT-In has to instruct the Department of Telecommunications to block the web sites after verifying the authenticity of the complaint and satisfying that action of blocking of website is absolutely essential. There is no explicit provision in the IT Act, 2000 for blocking of websites. In fact, blocking is considered to be censorship; hence it can be challenged if it restricts the freedom of speech and expression. But websites promoting hate, contempt, slander or defamation of others, promoting gambling, promoting racism, *violence and terrorism*, pornography and violent sex can reasonably be blocked since all such websites cannot claim the Fundamental Right of free speech and expression. The blocking of such website may be equated to "balanced flow of information" and not censorship. If the blocking of a website is arbitrary, unreasonable and unfair and is based on extraneous and irrelevant materials and reasons, then it would be vulnerable to the attack of unconstitutionality, being in violation of Articles 14, 19 and 21 of the Constitution of India.

Judicial Response

The judiciary can play its role by adopting a stringent approach towards the menace of cyber terrorism. It must, however, first tackle the jurisdiction problem because before invoking its judicial powers the courts are required to satisfy themselves that they possess the requisite jurisdiction to deal with the situation. Since the Internet "is a cooperative venture not owned by a single entity or government, there are no centralized rules or laws governing its use. The absence of geographical boundaries may give rise to a situation where the act legal in one country where it is done may violate the laws of another country. This process further made complicated due to the absence of a uniform and harmonised law governing the jurisdictional aspects of disputes arising by the use of Internet. It must be noted that, generally, the scholars point towards the following "theories" under which a country may claim prescriptive jurisdiction:

(a) a country may claim jurisdiction based on "objective territoriality" when an activity takes place within the country,

(b) a "subjective territoriality" may attach when an activity takes place outside a nation's borders but the "primary effect" of the action is within the nation's borders,

(c) a country may assert jurisdiction based on the nationality of either the actor or the victim,

(d) in exceptional circumstances, providing the right to protect the nation's sovereignty when faced with threats recognised as particularly serious in the international community.

In addition to establishing a connecting nexus, traditional international doctrine also calls for a "reasonable" connection between the offender and the forum. Depending on the factual context, courts look to such factors, as whether the activity of individual has a "substantial and foreseeable effect" on the territory, whether a "genuine link" exists between the actor and the forum, the character of the activity and the importance of the regulation giving rise to the controversy, the extent to which exceptions are harmed by the regulation, and the importance of the regulation in the international community. The traditional jurisdictional paradigms may provide a framework to guide analysis for cases arising in cyberspace. It must be noted that by virtue of section 1(2) read with section 75 of the Information Technology Act, 2000 the courts in India have "long arm jurisdiction" to deal with cyber terrorism.

Vigilant Citizenry

The menace of cyber terrorism is not the sole responsibility of State and its instrumentalities. The citizens as well as the netizens are equally under a solemn obligation to fight against the cyber terrorism. In fact, they are the most important and effective cyber terrorism eradication and elimination mechanism. The only requirement is to encourage them to come forward for the support of fighting against cyber terrorism. The government can give suitable incentives to them in the form of monetary awards. It must, however, be noted that their anonymity and security must be ensured before seeking their help. The courts are also empowered to maintain their anonymity if they provide any information and evidence to fight against cyber terrorism.

CYBER TERRORISM: MASS DESTRUCTION OR MASS DISRUPTION?

Just days after the September 11 terrorist attacks the U.S. Federal Bureau of Investigation began warning the public that the potential for future attacks exist, and among the threats was that of cyber terrorism. The concept is not a new one, such attacks have been taking place between Palestinian and Israeli groups, and between U.S. and Chinese sources, in response to political conflicts. And now, in light of new terrorism and cyber exclusions in insurance policies, commercial insurance buyers are wondering how to protect themselves from the potential threat of today's "hacktivists" becoming tomorrow's cyber terrorists, and weapons of mass disruption turning into weapons of mass destruction.

February 2002 - Al-Qaida, (the notorious terrorist group formed by Osama bin Laden, has not engaged in computer-based attacks in the past. However, in the wake of the World Trade Center (WTC) attacks, bin Laden has suggested that Al-Qaida has the expertise to use computer technology as a weapon, reports Canada's Office of Critical Infrastructure Protection and Emergency Preparedness (OCIPEP).

In response to reports from the FBI about the potential threat of cyber attacks in the wake of September 11, OCIPEP began issuing such advisories, and notes that "retaliatory cyber attacks" against coalition countries, primarily in the form of website defacements had already begun. In late November, the Canadian government helped draft the Council of Europe's Convention on Cybercrime, an international effort to deal with issues of terrorist financing, money laundering and cyber terrorism. The September 11 terrorist attacks changed perceptions of the world's security infrastructure, and the insurance industry's understanding of risk. What had once been inconceivable was now reality and so began the process of imagining the unimaginable in terms of catastrophic risks. Cyber terrorism, a heretofore unconsidered threat, was suddenly put on the world stage amongst a host of new potential threats.

Digital Pearl Harbor

When the U.S. government's new cyber terrorism expert, Richard Clarke, suggested the possibility of a "digital Pearl Harbor", he was greeted with skepticism. The concept of one, large-scale attack on the Internet seems far-reaching, despite the claims of Al Qaida and other Muslim extremist groups who claim to, or are known to, use the Internet as a tool. *That said, there is ample evidence that politically motivated hack attacks are on the rise, notes DK Matai, chairman and CEO of the mi2g intelligence unit, which deals in cyber security.* Tensions between the U.S. and China following the accidental bombing of the Chinese Embassy in Belgrade led to a cyber conflict. In the U.S., key government sites, including the Energy Department, the Interior Department and even the White House were targeted. The Chinese domain, ".cn", and that of Taiwan, ".tw", became the two most defaced domains behind ".com" last year. India (.in) and Pakistan (.pk) saw similar increases in the number of web site defacements due to political tensions (see Charts 1 and 2).

Following NATO air attacks on Serbia in 1999, hackers began to tap into U.S. defense computers and those of other defense related businesses. And, since September 11, several high profile U.S. government sites have been defaced, some bearing the Saudi flag and threatening messages aimed at the U.S. The groups involved, sometimes called "cyber mujihadeens", have hit sites including the U.S. Army Waterways Experiment Station and the National Institute of Health's Human Genome Project.

Striking at .ca: Canada is not immune to the cyber threat, experts say. *Matai points out that the ".ca" domain experienced a similar increase in defacements* *last year, with 215 hits, up from 59 in 2000 and 52 in 1999. He notes that many Canadian sites bear the ".com" domain, as well as ".org" and ".net", also popular targets. Hits are similarly not aimed solely at government sites, he adds. "Admittedly there is some bias of attacks towards high profile sites such as whitehouse.gov or fbi.gov, however more and more attacks are on commercial web sites."*

"The 11 September attack had an even deeper ripple effect: the temporary disruption of the entire U.S. financial and transportation infrastructure," notes the OCIPEP report. "If the terrorists did not fully anticipate these aftershocks, they can see them clearly now. This raises the possibility that those responsible may shift their sights away from primarily symbolic targets, such as heavily populated buildings or sports stadiums, toward critical infrastructures."

There are about 10,000 "serious grade crackers" using original code attack systems, as opposed to what Matai calls "script-kiddies", or hackers who rely on ready-made tools. "In terms of defacement attacks on large corporations, attackers penetrate the systems as multi-level attacks using subterfuge and social engineering," he explains. Criticisms of lax electronic security are still being heard, despite the growing awareness created by large-scale attacks such as the "I Love You" and "Melissa" viruses, and worms like "Nimda" and "Code Red". Criticisms of lax electronic security are still being heard, despite the growing awareness created by large-scale attacks such as the "I Love You" and "Melissa" viruses, and worms like "Nimda" and "Code Red".

"My own opinion is that the potential is there [for cyber terrorists to attack], everyone's networks are so poorly protected, but no one has taken advantage of it," says Chuck Wilmink, director of the Canadian Center for Information Technology Security (CCITS).

A study by the U.S.-based Computer Security Institute reports that 85% of companies admit to having their networks breached in 2000, and 64% acknowledge significant financial losses due to those breaches. A recent report by the U.S. Congress gave two-thirds of American's federal agencies failing grades in cyber security, including the departments of Defense, Justice, Energy and Treasury.

Similarly, in Canada, a 1999 Senate report pointed to the potential for a major cyber attack in Canada, and admitted that the FBI has characterized Canada as a "hacker haven".

Perhaps fortunately, Canada is more often a base for hackers to attack other countries, rather than a target itself. "Canadian hackers have traditionally tended to attack outside of Canada as opposed to within," says Matai. He notes that Canada's quieter political demeanor means that it is less often viewed as a target. ".ca Canadian sites are less vulnerable than .com or .uk because Canada is not seen to be so aggressive on the world stage."

"I really don't think we've ever considered Canada to be at the same threat level (as the U.S.)," says Max London, manager of public affairs for OCIPEP. However, OCIPEP has issued the FBI warnings post-September 11, giving companies advance warning in the event of a cyber attack. Ultimately, London explains, corporations are responsible for their own security systems.

He notes that OCIPEP is aware of "hacktivist" activity in Canada, specifically "around some of the larger meetings", such as the G-8 Summit or World Trade Organization meetings.

However, these are a far cry from the threat by a foreign government or terrorist organization that might harm Canada's critical infrastructure, including systems that support communications, transportation and services such as health care and finance.

With the "increasing dependence and increasing interconnectivity" of such systems comes a greater risk, however. In the past, OCIPEP has been involved in public awareness campaigns around threats including the "Code Red" worm, which was viewed as "a very real threat to the Internet", and has worked with the U.S. National Infrastructure Protection Center (NIPC), an FBI operation, to disseminate infornation. The NPIC issued warnings in mid-October of a potential cyber threat aimed at the U.S. power grid, and yet another aimed at online financial sites.

Insurer Reaction

Canada's insurers have been jumping into the terrorism risk fray since September 11, trying to understand what exposures they might face in the future. Just as no one predicted the events that represent the largest insurance loss in history, there is fear of what other unforeseen risks may lie ahead.

As insurers met through the Insurance Bureau of Canada's (IBC) terrorism task force to discuss the new risk horizon, cyber threats were one possibility on the table, says Anne MacKenzie, assistant vice president, claims technical, at the Dominion of Canada General Insurance Company and a member of the task force.

She adds, however, that they did not top the list of concerns for several reasons, including the notion that terrorists generally tend towards visible, high profile acts. "It's usually physical acts of terrorism," she says. "Terrorists like to put the population at fear." OCIPEP also notes that terrorists have traditionally relied on "bombs over bytes" as the weapon of choice.

Cyber terrorism has not dominated discussion of electronic risks, adds Jennifer Soper, assistant vice president, technology, at St. Paul Canada. Most of the talk seems centered around the major viruses that have plagued companies. This is partly because many companies do not see themselves as targets for such acts. "When you're not in the Fortune 500 or brand name companies, you can get an 'it can't happen to me', almost false sense of security."

She adds that companies often do not discuss the nature of attacks, and still have a "keep it in the closet" attitude about cyber security breaches. The benefit is that this policy of silence denies attackers the desired result of publicity. However, terrorists may soon find that cyber attacks will gain them the same kind of notoriety as physical attacks, MacKenzie adds. "Nothing would scare people more than to learn that terrorists had hacked into government sites".

Exclusions, Exclusions

Commercial insurance buyers are no doubt facing a tough market in the post-September 11 era, although the situation was already beginning to grow bleak prior to the terrorist attacks. Reinsurers had already stated their intention to introduce cyber exclusions into their treaties, leaving insurers to follow suit.

However, insurers assert that cyber or "data" coverage was never really part of commercial general liability (CGL) policies. In light of the potential for differing interpretations (such as the U.S. case of Ingram v. Micro, where it was found that business interruption due to computer failure should be included in CGL policies), more specific wording was added to most policies. "The data exclusion was just a clarification to make sure consumers knew what they were buying, there never was coverage for data," explains MacKenzie. This clarification is apparent in most policies as of yearend 2001, adds Dominion president George Cooke. "Our view is that the wordings don't do anything the old wordings didn't do, they're just clearer."

However, the wordings have left many companies scrambling for coverage, Soper says. "What is available is not widely available." Companies will either have to negotiate coverage as a limited buy-back option in existing policies, or hunt it down as a separate policy from another carrier. "In terms of coverage, if there is anything going on it is on a customer-by-customer level. It has to be." Given the difficulty in quantifying cyber risks, there is no "one size fits all" policy.

Cooke says he is concerned with the lack of cyber coverage available, but acknowledges that insurers simply are not in a position to offer it. "It's a situation that troubles me. But we can't buy coverage [in the reinsurance market], so it's impossible for us to offer it."

September 11 did not help the situation either. He predicts that notwithstanding the terrorist attacks, cyber coverage would have been a top issue for insurers, but given the shift in priorities, insurers were unable to come up with private market capital solutions in advance of yearend commercial policy renewals. "September 11 kind of eclipsed concerns over whether we should be developing new products to deal with cyber risks," says MacKenzie. However, she adds, "we will want to revisit it" in the future.

Overriding Concern

Regardless of new cyber covers, with the current terrorism exclusions being written, any act deemed as "cyber terrorism" would not be covered, as the terrorism exclusion would be overriding. In the wake of September 11, with reinsurers refusing to cover terrorism in their treaties, insurers were forced to either introduce similar exclusions in their policies or to negotiate a deal with the government, which would act as excess of loss reinsurer through a "terrorism pool" arrangement.

By yearend, no such pool had been devised, despite lengthy discussions between IBC representatives and the government. "The nature of the discussions evolved as the market evolved," says Cooke, who is also chair of the IBC. "The decision was taken to wait. It was probably a smart decision."

The U.S. government's inability to come to a solution prior to breaking at the end of the year was among the contributing factors. Cooke recognizes that it was "politically difficult" for the Canadian government to come forward with a solution before the U.S., given the fact that the situation was not of the same scale here. This situation may change as the U.S. House reconvenes in late January. "People have said that the government wasn't prepared to act, but I don't buy that," he adds. "Minister Peterson and the staff in Finance were seriously engaged in discussions and are prepared to act if the need arises."

The need for a solution may not be quite as pressing as originally thought, with renewals moving along despite the lack of a solution, and the fact that many commercial policies on target risks have not yet reached renewal.

However, Cooke still feels a solution is needed. The government has consulted with other associations, most notably the Canadian Bankers Association (CBA), who claim that there is no need for the coverage. "I think they're wrong," Cooke says, but their resistance makes it difficult for insurers to press for a solution. He is most displeased with the view that insurers are looking for a "bail out". "We are not doing an 'Air Canada' here. We're more than prepared to take our pains for our past sins." But without reinsurance coverage in place, it is not economically feasible for insurers to offer the coverage. The terrorism task force was "driven by the sudden recognition that there was now infinite risk and infinite exposure and that wasn't economically sustainable," says MacKenzie. "It [terrorism coverage] isn't anything we could write even if we wanted to."

With no cap on the exposure, insurers would be leaving themselves open to unquantifiable risks, a situation that extends into the domain of cyber terrorism.

CYBERTERRORISM ANGST

The roots of the notion of cyberterrorism can be traced back to the early 1990s, when the rapid growth in Internet use and the debate on the emerging "information society" sparked several studies on the potential risks faced by the highly networked, high-tech-dependent United States. As early as 1990, the National Academy of Sciences began a report on computer security with the words, "We are at risk. Increasingly, America depends on computers. . . . Tomorrow's terrorist may be able to do more damage with a keyboard than with a bomb." At the same time, the prototypical term "electronic Pearl Harbor" was coined, linking the threat of a computer attack to an American historical trauma.

Psychological, political, and economic forces have combined to promote the fear of cyberterrorism. From a psychological perspective, two of the greatest fears of modern time are combined in the term "cyberterrorism." The fear of random, violent victimization blends well with the distrust and outright fear of computer technology. An unknown threat is perceived as more threatening than a known threat. Although cyberterrorism does not entail a direct threat of violence, its psychological impact on anxious societies can be as powerful as the effect of terrorist bombs. Moreover, the most destructive forces working against an understanding of the actual threat of cyberterrorism are a fear of the unknown and a lack of information or, worse, too much misinformation.

After 9/11, the security and terrorism discourse soon featured cyberterrorism prominently. This was understandable, given that more nightmarish attacks were expected and that cyberterrorism seemed to offer al Qaeda opportunities to inflict enormous damage. But there was also a political dimension to the new focus on cyberterrorism. Debates about national security, including the security of cyberspace, always attract political actors with agendas that extend beyond the specific issue at hand—and the debate over cyberterrorism was no exception to this pattern. For instance, Yonah Alexander, a terrorism researcher at the Potomac Institute—a think tank with close links to the Pentagon—announced in December 2001 the existence of an "Iraq Net." This network supposedly consisted of more than one hundred websites set up across the world by Iraq since the mid-nineties to launch denial-of-service (DoS) attacks against U.S. companies (such attacks render computer systems inaccessible, unusable, or inoperable). "Saddam Hussein would not hesitate to use the cyber tool he has. . . . It is not a question of if but when. The entire United States is the front line," Alexander claimed. (See Ralf Bendrath's article "The American Cyber-Angst and the Real World," published in 2003 in *Bombs and Bandwidth*, edited by Robert Latham.) Whatever the intentions of its author, such a statement was clearly likely to support arguments then being made for an aggressive U.S. policy toward Iraq. No evidence of an Iraq Net has yet come to light.

Combating cyberterrorism has become not only a highly politicized issue but also an economically rewarding one. An entire industry has emerged to grapple with the threat of cyberterrorism: think tanks have launched elaborate projects and issued alarming white papers on the subject, experts have testified to cyberterrorism's dangers before Congress, and private companies have hastily deployed security consultants and software designed to protect public and private targets. Following the 9/11 attacks, the federal government requested $4.5 billion for infrastructure security, and the FBI now boasts more than one thousand "cyber investigators."

Before September 11, 2001, George W. Bush, then a presidential candidate, warned that "American forces are overused and underfunded precisely when they are confronted by a host of new threats and challenges—the spread of weapons of mass destruction, the rise of cyberterrorism, the proliferation of missile technology." After the 9/11 attacks, President Bush created the Office of Cyberspace Security in the White House and appointed his former counterterrorism coordinator, Richard Clarke, to head it. The warnings came now from the president, the vice president, security advisors, and government officials: "Terrorists can sit at one computer connected to one network and can create worldwide havoc," cautioned Tom Ridge, director of the Department of Homeland Security, in a representative observation in April 2003. "[They] don't necessarily need a bomb or explosives to cripple a sector of the economy or shut down a power grid." These warnings certainly had a powerful impact on the media, on the public, and on the administration. For instance, a survey of 725 cities conducted in 2003 by the National League of Cities found that cyberterrorism ranked alongside biological and chemical weapons at the top of a list of city officials' fears.

The mass media have added their voice to the fearful chorus, running scary front-page headlines such as the following, which appeared in the *Washington Post* in June 2003: "Cyber-Attacks by Al Qaeda Feared, Terrorists at Threshold of Using Internet as Tool of Bloodshed, Experts Say." Cyberterrorism, the media have discovered, makes for eye-catching, dramatic copy. Screenwriters and novelists have likewise seen the dramatic potential, with movies such as the 1995 James Bond feature, *Goldeneye*, and 2002's *Code*

Hunter and novels such as Tom Clancy and Steve R. Pieczenik's *Netforce* popularizing a wide range of cyberterrorist scenarios.

The net effect of all this attention has been to create a climate in which instances of hacking into government websites, online thefts of proprietary data from companies, and outbreaks of new computer viruses are all likely to be labeled by the media as suspected cases of "cyberterrorism." Indeed, the term has been improperly used and overused to such an extent that, if we are to have any hope of reaching a clear understanding of the danger posed by cyberterrorism, we must begin by defining it with some precision.

What Is Cyberterrorism?

There have been several stumbling blocks to creating a clear and consistent definition of the term "cyberterrorism." First, as just noted, much of the discussion of cyberterrorism has been conducted in the popular media, where journalists typically strive for drama and sensation rather than for good operational definitions of new terms. Second, it has been especially common when dealing with computers to coin new words simply by placing the word "cyber," "computer," or "information" before another word. Thus, an entire arsenal of words—cybercrime, infowar, netwar, cyberterrorism, cyberharassment, virtual warfare, digital terrorism, cybertactics, computer warfare, cyberattack, and cyber-break-ins—is used to describe what some military and political strategists describe as the "new terrorism" of our times. Fortunately, some efforts have been made to introduce greater semantic precision. Most notably, Dorothy Denning, a professor of computer science, has put forward an admirably unambiguous definition in numerous articles and in her testimony on the subject before the House Armed Services Committee in May 2000:

Cyberterrorism is the convergence of cyberspace and terrorism. It refers to unlawful attacks and threats of attacks against computers, networks and the information stored therein when done to intimidate or coerce a government or its people in furtherance of political or social objectives. Further, to qualify as cyberterrorism, an attack should result in violence against persons or property, or at least cause enough harm to generate fear. Attacks that lead to death or bodily injury, explosions, or severe economic loss would be examples. Serious attacks against critical infrastructures could be acts of cyberterrorism, depending on their impact. Attacks that disrupt nonessential services or that are mainly a costly nuisance would not.

It is important to distinguish between cyberterrorism and "hacktivism," a term coined by scholars to describe the marriage of hacking with political activism. ("Hacking" is here understood to mean activities conducted online and covertly that seek to reveal, manipulate, or otherwise exploit vulnerabilities in computer operating systems and other software. Unlike hacktivists, hackers tend *not* to have political agendas.) Hacktivists have four main weapons at their disposal: virtual blockades; e-mail attacks; hacking and computer break-ins; and computer viruses and worms.

A virtual blockade is the virtual version of a physical sit-in or blockade: political activists visit a website and attempt to generate so much traffic toward the site that other users cannot reach it, thereby disrupting normal operations while winning publicity—via media reports—for the protesters' cause. "Swarming" occurs when a large number of individuals simultaneously access a website, causing its collapse. Swarming can also amplify the effects of the hacktivists' second weapon: e-mail bombing campaigns (bombarding targets with thousands of messages at once, also known as "ping attacks"). Maura Conway reported in her essay "Reality Bytes" (*First Monday* 7, no. 11 [November 2002]) on an e-mail bombing campaign launched in July 1997 against the Institute for Global Communications (IGC), a San Francisco–based Internet service provider (ISP) that hosted the web pages of *Euskal Herria* (in English, the *Basque Country Journal*), a publication edited by supporters of the Basque separatist group ETA. The attackers wanted ETA's site removed from the Internet. They bombarded IGC's website with thousands of e-mails, clogging the system, and threatened to attack other organizations using IGC services. IGC pulled the *Euskal Herria* site just a few days later.

The Spanish government was suspected of being behind the e-mail bombing, but the identity of the attackers remains uncertain. Whether or not the suspicion is well founded, it underlines the fact that the hacktivists' tools are widely available and can be as easily employed by governments as by small groups of political activists.

Many cyberprotesters use the third weapon in the hacktivists' arsenal: web hacking and computer break-ins (hacking into computers to access stored information, communication facilities, financial information, and so forth). In her report "Is Cyber Terror Next?" Denning notes that the Computer Emergency Response Team Coordination Center (CERT/CC), a federally funded research and development center operated by Carnegie Mellon University, reported 2,134 cases of computer break-ins and hacks in 1997. The number of incidents rose to 21,756 in 2000 and to almost 35,000 during the first three quarters of 2001 alone. In 2003, CERT/CC received more than half a million e-mail messages and more than nine hundred hotline calls reporting incidents or requesting information. In the same year, no fewer than 137,529 computer security incidents were reported. Given that many, perhaps most, incidents are never reported to CERT/CC or any agency or organization, the actual figures are probably much higher. Moreover, Denning notes that each single incident that is reported involves thousands of victims. This rise in cyberattacks reflects the growing popularity of the Internet, the vast number of vulnerable targets, and the development of sophisticated and easy-to-use hacking tools.

The fourth category of hacktivist weaponry comprises viruses and worms, both of which are forms of malicious code that can infect computers and propagate over computer networks. Their impact can be enormous. The Code Red worm, for example, infected about a million servers in July 2001 and caused $2.6 billion in damage to computer hardware, software, and networks, and the I LOVE YOU virus unleashed in 2000 affected more than twenty million Internet users and caused billions of dollars in damage. Although neither the Code Red worm nor the I LOVE YOU virus was spread with any political goals in mind (both seem to have been the work of hackers, not hacktivists), some computer viruses and worms have been used to propagate political messages and, in some cases, cause serious damage. During the NATO operation to evict Serbian forces from Kosovo, businesses, public entities, and academic institutes in NATO member-states received virus-laden e-mails from a range of Eastern European countries. The e-mail messages, which had been poorly translated into English, consisted chiefly of unsubtle denunciations of NATO for its unfair aggression and defenses of Serbian rights. But the real threat was from the viruses. This was an instance of cyberwarfare launched by Serbian hacktivists against the economic infrastructure of NATO countries.

In February 2000, the sites of Amazon.com, e-Bay, Yahoo, and a host of other well-known companies were stopped for several hours due to DoS attacks. On October 22, 2002, the *Washington Post* reported that "the heart of the Internet network sustained its largest and most sophisticated attack ever." A DoS attack struck the thirteen "root servers" that provide the primary road map for almost all Internet communications worldwide. It caused no slowdowns or outages because of safeguards built into the system, but a longer and more extensive attack could have inflicted serious damage.

Hacktivism, although politically motivated, does not amount to cyberterrorism. Hacktivists do want to protest and disrupt; they *do not* want to kill or maim or terrify. However, hacktivism does highlight the threat of cyberterrorism, the potential that individuals with no moral restraint may use methods similar to those developed by hackers to wreak havoc. Moreover, the line between cyberterrorism and hacktivism may sometimes blur, especially if terrorist groups are able to recruit or hire computer-savvy hacktivists or if hacktivists decide to escalate their actions by attacking the systems that operate critical elements of the national infrastructure, such as electric power networks and emergency services.

THE APPEAL OF CYBERTERRORISM FOR TERRORISTS

Cyberterrorism is an attractive option for modern terrorists for several reasons.

- First, it is cheaper than traditional terrorist methods. All that the terrorist needs is a personal computer and an online connection. Terrorists do not need to buy weapons such as guns and explosives; instead, they can create and deliver computer viruses through a telephone line, a cable, or a wireless connection.
- Second, cyberterrorism is more anonymous than traditional terrorist methods. Like many Internet surfers, terrorists use online nicknames—"screen names"—or log on to a website as an unidentified "guest user," making it very hard for security agencies and police forces to track down the terrorists' real identity. And in cyberspace there are no physical barriers such as checkpoints to navigate, no borders to cross, and no customs agents to outsmart.
- Third, the variety and number of targets are enormous. The cyberterrorist could target the computers and computer networks of governments, individuals, public utilities, private airlines, and so forth. The sheer number and complexity of potential targets guarantee that terrorists can find weaknesses and vulnerabilities to exploit. Several studies have shown that critical infrastructures, such as electric power grids and emergency services, are vulnerable to a cyberterrorist attack because the infrastructures and the computer systems that run them are highly complex, making it effectively impossible to eliminate all weaknesses.
- Fourth, cyberterrorism can be conducted remotely, a feature that is especially appealing to terrorists. Cyberterrorism requires less physical training, psychological investment, risk of mortality, and travel than conventional forms of terrorism, making it easier for terrorist organizations to recruit and retain followers.
- Fifth, as the I LOVE YOU virus showed, cyberterrorism has the potential to affect directly a larger number of people than traditional terrorist methods, thereby generating greater media coverage, which is ultimately what terrorists want.

A Growing Sense of Vulnerability

Black Ice: The Invisible Threat of Cyber-Terror, a book published in 2003 and written by *Computerworld* journalist and former intelligence officer Dan Verton, describes the 1997 exercise code-named "Eligible Receiver," conducted by the National Security Agency (NSA). (The following account draws from "Black

Ice," *Computerworld*, August 13, 2003.) The exercise began when NSA officials instructed a "Red Team" of thirty-five hackers to attempt to hack into and disrupt U.S. national security systems. They were told to play the part of hackers hired by the North Korean intelligence service, and their primary target was to be the U.S. Pacific Command in Hawaii. They were allowed to penetrate any Pentagon network but were prohibited from breaking any U.S. laws, and they could only use hacking software that could be downloaded freely from the Internet. They started mapping networks and obtaining passwords gained through "brute-force cracking" (a trial-and-error method of decoding encrypted data such as passwords or encryption keys by trying all possible combinations). Often they used simpler tactics such as calling somebody on the telephone, pretending to be a technician or high-ranking official, and asking for the password. The hackers managed to gain access to dozens of critical Pentagon computer systems. Once they entered the systems, they could easily create user accounts, delete existing accounts, reformat hard drives, scramble stored data, or shut systems down. They broke the network defenses with relative ease and did so without being traced or identified by the authorities.

The results shocked the organizers. In the first place, the Red Team had shown that it was possible to break into the U.S. Pacific military's command-and-control system and, potentially, cripple it. In the second place, the NSA officials who examined the experiment's results found that much of the private-sector infrastructure in the United States, such as the telecommunications and electric power grids, could easily be invaded and abused in the same way.

The vulnerability of the energy industry is at the heart of *Black Ice*. Verton argues that America's energy sector would be the first domino to fall in a strategic cyberterrorist attack against the United States. The book explores in frightening detail how the impact of such an attack could rival, or even exceed, the consequences of a more traditional, physical attack. Verton claims that during any given year, an average large utility company in the United States experiences about 1 million cyberintrusions. Data collected by Riptech, Inc.—a Virginia-based company specializing in the security of online information and financial systems—on cyberattacks during the six months following the 9/11 attacks showed that companies in the energy industry suffered intrusions at twice the rate of other industries, with the number of severe or critical attacks requiring immediate intervention averaging 12.5 per company.

Deregulation and the increased focus on profitability have made utilities and other companies move more and more of their operations to the Internet in search of greater efficiency and lower costs. Verton argues that the energy industry and many other sectors have become potential targets for various cyberdisruptions by creating Internet links (both physical and wireless) between their networks and supervisory control and data acquisition (SCADA) systems. These SCADA systems manage the flow of electricity and natural gas and control various industrial systems and facilities, including chemical processing plants, water purification and water delivery operations, wastewater management facilities, and a host of manufacturing firms. A terrorist's ability to control, disrupt, or alter the command and monitoring functions performed by these systems could threaten regional and possibly national security.

According to Symantec, one of the world's corporate leaders in the field of cybersecurity, new vulnerabilities to a cyberattack are being discovered all the time. The company reported that the number of "software holes" (software security flaws that allow malicious hackers to exploit the system) grew by 80 percent in 2002. Still, Symantec claimed that no single cyberterrorist attack was recorded (applying the definition that such an attack must originate in a country on the State Department's terror watch list). This may reflect the fact that terrorists do not yet have the required know-how. Alternatively, it may illustrate that hackers are not sympathetic to the goals of terrorist organizations—should the two groups join forces, however, the results could be devastating.

Equally alarming is the prospect of terrorists themselves designing computer software for government agencies. Remarkably, as Denning describes in "Is Cyber Terror Next?" at least one instance of such a situation is known to have occurred:

In March 2000, Japan's Metropolitan Police Department reported that a software system they had procured to track 150 police vehicles, including unmarked cars, had been developed by the Aum Shinryko cult, the same group that gassed the Tokyo subway in 1995, killing 12 people and injuring 6,000 more. At the time of the discovery, the cult had received classified tracking data on 115 vehicles. Further, the cult had developed software for at least 80 Japanese firms and 10 government agencies. They had worked as subcontractors to other firms, making it almost impossible for the organizations to know who was developing the software. As subcontractors, the cult could have installed Trojan horses to launch or facilitate cyber terrorist attacks at a later date.

Despite stepped-up security measures in the wake of 9/11, a survey of almost four hundred IT professionals conducted for the Business Software Alliance during June 2002 revealed widespread concern. (See Robyn Greenspan, "Cyberterrorism Concerns IT Pros," Internetnews.com, August 16, 2002.) About half (49 percent) of the IT professionals felt that an attack is likely, and more than half (55 percent) said the risk of a major cyberattack on the United States has increased since 9/11. The figure jumped to 59 percent among those respondents who are in charge of their company's computer and Internet security. Seventy-two percent agreed with the statement "there is a gap between the threat of a major cyberattack and the government's ability to defend against it," and the agreement rate rose to 84 percent among respondents who are most knowledgeable about security. Those surveyed were concerned about attacks not only on the government but also on private targets. Almost three-quarters (74 percent) believed that national financial institutions such as major national banks would be likely targets within the next year, and around two-thirds believed that attacks were likely to be launched within the next twelve months against the computer systems that run communications networks (e.g., telephones and the Internet), transportation infrastructure (e.g., air traffic control computer systems), and utilities (e.g., water stations, dams, and power plants).

A study released in December 2003 (and reported in the *Washington Post* on January 31, 2004) appeared to confirm the IT professionals' skepticism about the ability of the government to defend itself against cyberattack. Conducted by the House Government Reform Subcommittee on Technology, the study examined computer security in federal agencies over the course of a year and awarded grades. Scores were based on numerous criteria, including how well an agency trained its employees in security and the extent to which it met established security procedures such as limiting access to privileged data and eliminating easily guessed passwords. More than half the federal agencies surveyed received a grade of D or F. The Department of Homeland Security, which has a division devoted to monitoring cybersecurity, received the lowest overall score of the twenty-four agencies surveyed. Also earning an F was the Justice Department, the agency charged with investigating and prosecuting cases of hacking and other forms of cybercrime. Thirteen agencies improved their scores slightly compared with the previous year, nudging the overall government grade from an F up to a D. Commenting on these results, Rep. Adam H. Putnam (R-Fl.), chairman of the House Government Reform Subcommittee on Technology, declared that "the threat of cyberattack is real. . . . The damage that could be inflicted both in terms of financial loss and, potentially, loss of life is considerable."

Such studies, together with the enormous media interest in the subject, have fueled popular fears about cyberterrorism. A study by the Pew Internet and American Life Project found in 2003 that nearly half of the one thousand Americans surveyed were worried that terrorists could launch attacks through the networks connecting home computers and power utilities. The Pew study found that 11 percent of respondents were "very worried" and 38 percent were "somewhat worried" about an attack launched through computer networks. The survey was taken in early August, before the major blackout struck the Northeast and before several damaging new viruses afflicted computers throughout the country.

CYBER SECURITY THREATS IN COUNTER-ATTACKS

Many people have proposed methods of "counter-attack" or "active response" to deal with today's cyber security threats. There is a common belief that traditional approaches to the problem are inadequate. Patching software vulnerabilities is labour intensive, so many people don't do it until there's an attack. The legal system is slow to respond, courts lack the necessary technical expertise, and prosecutions do not occur often enough to deter attacks.

History of Cyber Security

The history of successful counter-attacks in the world of cyber security is a short one. There are an increasing number of papers and publications which make proposals, but concerns over legal issues as well as technical challenges have kept the list of successes small. In Sept. 1998, the Pentagon is reported to have counter-attacked some activists who were doing a Denial of Service attack of the Department of Defense's websites, responding to their requests with an applet which ran on the attackers' machines and forced them to reboot.

In 1999, a California ISP Conxion wrote a script which caused DoS packets sent to the World Trade Organization's website to be sent back to the attackers.

Of course, such an attack would not have worked if the attackers had used what's known as "IP address spoofing", which would have made the packets appear that they came from a different computer from where they did.

In 2001, several defences were created in response to the Code Red II worm. One, called CRclean, if it received a probe from the worm, would make use of a back door which the worm placed on the infected machine to load a neutralizing agent and halt the spread of the worm. But it would also install itself on that machine. Another, called CodeGreen, would actually scan the internet for computers with the IIS vulnerability that allowed CodeRed, then download the patch and place it on the machine, and clean up the back doors.

It is clear that there are serious legal and ethical issues with both of these worms, even the former, which is still a worm even though it only reacts to attacks. In 2003, the Welchia worm was released onto the Internet. Welchia would remove the Blaster worm and patch the vulnerability that Blaster used to spread. However, Welchia also caused severe network congestion.

In late 2004, Lycos Europe got fed up with spammers and launched a popular campaign called "Make Love Not Spam" which attracted over 100,000 users. Users could install a screen saver on their desktop which would send requests to websites which were known to advertise via spam.

This effort was sucessful in causing some of the sites to change locations. (http://www.makelovenotspam.com) Lycos reportedly got around the illegality of DDoS attacks by claiming to only take 95% of the target sites' bandwidth, though, David Dittrich finds this reasoning dubious at best. Lycos ended this campaign in December 2004.

Some companies such as Symbiot Security are currently developing counter attack tools and devices, but there is a lot of skepticism about deployment of devices because of liability concerns.

Cyber Security Incident Response

Counter-attacks are part of the overall process of cyber security incident response. This consists of five stages:

1. Intrusion detection.
2. Identifying the attacker.
3. Defending against the attack.
4. Designing and deploying a counter-attack.
5. Post-conflict investigation and support.

Intrusion Detection: Intrusion detection first identifies if there is an intrusion or intrusion attempt in the network or machine connected to network. Monitoring can be done on the network or on end-hosts. Firewalls and virus scanners also contribute. There are various techniques, such as anomaly detection, and policy-based approaches.

Identifying the Attacker

This very important step towards counter-attack, basically knowing who your enemy is and where is he located. Identifying the attacker can be difficult, since an attacker may use one compromised host to attack another. Also, with today's network architecture it can be quite difficult to locate the real attacker. Packets can be sent with spoofed source addresses, and tracing them through multiple hops and different autonomous systems can be a complicated process. Finding out the specific server and location can be critical in determining what the counter-attack would be.

Defending against the Attack: Before an attack, software patches are used to fix vulnerabillities. More interesting are defences once an attack against a real vulnerability has happened.

Diversions can be set forth to surprise an attacker. Or once the attack has been detected, countermeasures can be put in place to stop further damage.

Also, diversion tactics like Honey Pots can be used to keep the rest of the network safe. The information from these diversions (or information gained during the delays caused by these tactics) can be harnessed to engineer a specific counter-attack.

Designing and Deploying a Counter-Attack: Counter-attacks take a surprising variety of forms. Designing a counter- attack should take into account the following factors: the method of attack; the support of the network infrastructure (*i.e.* are ISPs performing egress filtering); collateral damage; and costs.

Post-Counter-Attack Investigation and Support: In order to aid the post-counter-attack investigation a counter- attack should have inbuilt mechanism to log its trail and its operation history. Ideally, it will also provide a means of discovering the hacker's techniques and identity. The more risk hackers have of being discovered, the less likely they are to go hacking.

Anti-worms

A worm spreads itself by sending out packets which look for certain responses from computers. It will analyse those responses to deduce if it thinks the replying machine has the vulnerability that it exploits. These packets represent a worm's 'signature'. The machine the worm is targeting can detect the signature of the worm and thus know its mode of propagation. An anti-worm is generated, which exploits the same vulnerabilities as the original worm or uses the back doors opened by the original worm. The antiworm would either fix the attacking host, neutralize the worm, or bring it down gracefully, potentially informing the owner. It may also install itself for further propagation.

In addition to the stated goal, an anti-worm adheres to following guidelines to minimize collateral damage:

- It is bug-free and does leave other vulnerabilities that could be exploited further.
- It can be uninstalled gracefully when owner asks for it.
- It makes minimal changes to host that it operates on.
- It should not be able to be used for propagating malicious content.

The countermeasure, or 'Neutralizing Agent' used, can take several forms. For example, it could patch the vulnerability and remove the botnet or worm. Less invasive changes include blocking the port over which the worm sends messages, or using a mutex and rebooting the machine to lock the botnet from being able to execute.

Also, one would have to remove any backdoors left by the worm.

In addition, deployment strategy of the anti-worm will determine its effectiveness and collateral damage it may cause.

- *Active Deployment*: The anti-worm is itself a worm; it propagates across the network by scanning and seeking exploited vulnerabilities. This is the fastest way to remove the original worm from the network, but this also causes the most collateral damage by affecting the network traffic a lot.
- *Passive Deployment*: The anti-worm waits on a host till another host attacks it, and then the anti-worm cures only the attacking host. Collateral damage is bare minimum, but the anti-worm is left behind on the new host.
- *Controlled Deployment*: The anti-worm propagation is control via some statistic of number of infected/vulnerable host to number host it cured. This can be very effective and efficient.
- *IDS base Deployment*: The anti-worm uses the intrusion detection sensors which monitor traffic and may deploy an anti-worm against an attacker. As with passive deployment, collateral damage is limited to computers actively launching attacks, but this is less invasive because it does not leave a worm, it just neutralizes the machine.

Spam

Spam is unsolicited e-mail. A virus is a programme which, when executed, installs malware such as root-kits, key-stroke loggers, etc. These programmes are then used to send sensitive information to the attacker without the user's consent. Both spam and viruses spread through e-mail and require human interaction to activate them. E-mail servers as well as the hosts can detect spam with the help of spam detectors like Symantec's TurnTide. Once the spam is identified one counter attack is achieved by automatic flooding of the Sender Server with bounced e-mails and mail notification to server's administrator. (Even if sender addresses are spoofed, one may be able to identify the last mail server that forwarded a message.)

Botnet

An attacker establishes a botnet by first spreading a virus or worm that takes over the vulnerable hosts. Each worm or virus then calls Home to tell that it has successfully captured the Host. It also establishes a command channel such that the Attacker through the home can control the host. Botnets can be used for DDOS attacks, phishing etc.

Counter-Attack

- Counter-attack involves identifying the attacker by monitoring the compromised Host and intercepting its communication to the Home machine. The Home machine is probably the attacker's base or intermediate node for communication between the host and the attacker base machines. Once that machine is identified, you hack back into that machine bring it down. For hacking back, you can use same techniques as used by the hackers to take control of the attacking machine.

- Taking down the Home machine only removes the attacker for a short duration, the network of compromised hosts still exists. A more effective counter-attack would be to takeover or monitor the command channel for communication between the Home and other compromised hosts. If possible, identify other compromised hosts and fix them or take them down as preventive measure.

THREATS AND COUNTERMEASURES

This chapter analyses Web application security from the perspectives of threats, countermeasures, vulnerabilities, and attacks. The following set of core terms are defined to avoid confusion and to ensure they are used in the correct context.

- *Asset.* A resource of value such as the data in a database or on the file system, or a system resource
- *Threat.* A potential occurrence — malicious or otherwise — that may harm an asset
- *Vulnerability.* A weakness that makes a threat possible
- *Attack (or exploit).* An action taken to harm an asset
- *Countermeasure.* A safeguard that addresses a threat and mitigates risk

This chapter also identifies a set of common network, host, and application level threats, and the recommended countermeasures to address each one. The chapter does not contain an exhaustive list of threats, but it does highlight many top threats. With this information and knowledge of how an attacker works, you will be able to identify additional threats. You need to know the threats that are most likely to impact your system to be able to build effective threat models.

Understanding Threat Categories

While there are many variations of specific attacks and attack techniques, it is useful to think about threats in terms of what the attacker is trying to achieve. This changes your focus from the identification of every specific attack — which is really just a means to an end — to focusing on the end results of possible attacks.

STRIDE

Threats faced by the application can be categorized based on the goals and purposes of the attacks. A working knowledge of these categories of threats can help you organize a security strategy so that you have planned responses to threats. STRIDE is the acronym used at Microsoft to categorize different threat types. STRIDE stands for:

- *Spoofing. Spoofing* is attempting to gain access to a system by using a false identity. This can be accomplished using stolen user credentials or a false IP address. After the attacker successfully gains access as a legitimate user or host, elevation of privileges or abuse using authorization can begin.
- *Tampering. Tampering* is the unauthorized modification of data, for example as it flows over a network between two computers.
- *Repudiation. Repudiation* is the ability of users (legitimate or otherwise) to deny that they performed specific actions or transactions. Without adequate auditing, repudiation attacks are difficult to prove.
- *Information disclosure. Information disclosure* is the unwanted exposure of private data. For example, a user views the contents of a table or file he or she is not authorized to open, or monitors data passed in plaintext over a network. Some examples of information disclosure vulnerabilities include the use of hidden form fields, comments embedded in Web pages that contain database connection strings and connection details, and weak exception handling that can lead to internal system level details being revealed to the client. Any of this information can be very useful to the attacker.
- *Denial of service. Denial of service* is the process of making a system or application unavailable. For example, a denial of service attack might be accomplished by bombarding a server with requests to consume all available system resources or by passing it malformed input data that can crash an application process.
- *Elevation of privilege. Elevation of privilege* occurs when a user with limited privileges assumes the identity of a privileged user to gain privileged access to an application. For example, an attacker with limited privileges might elevate his or her privilege level to compromise and take control of a highly privileged and trusted process or account.

Network Threats and Countermeasures

The primary components that make up your network infrastructure are routers, firewalls, and switches. They act as the gatekeepers guarding your servers and applications from attacks and intrusions. An attacker may exploit poorly configured network devices.

Common vulnerabilities include weak default installation settings, wide open access controls, and devices lacking the latest security patches. Top network level threats include:

Information Gathering

Network devices can be discovered and profiled in much the same way as other types of systems. Attackers usually start with port scanning. After they identify open ports, they use banner grabbing and enumeration to detect device types and to determine operating system and application versions. Armed with this information, an attacker can attack known vulnerabilities that may not be updated with security patches.

Countermeasures to prevent information gathering include:

- Configure routers to restrict their responses to footprinting requests.
- Configure operating systems that host network software (for example, software firewalls) to prevent footprinting by disabling unused protocols and unnecessary ports.

Sniffing

Sniffing or *eavesdropping* is the act of monitoring traffic on the network for data such as plaintext passwords or configuration information. With a simple packet sniffer, an attacker can easily read all plaintext traffic. Also, attackers can crack packets encrypted by lightweight hashing algorithms and can decipher the payload that you considered to be safe. The sniffing of packets requires a packet sniffer in the path of the server/client communication.

Countermeasures to help prevent sniffing include:

- Use strong physical security and proper segmenting of the network. This is the first step in preventing traffic from being collected locally.
- Encrypt communication fully, including authentication credentials. This prevents sniffed packets from being usable to an attacker. SSL and IPSec (Internet Protocol Security) are examples of encryption solutions.

Spoofing

Spoofing is a means to hide one's true identity on the network. To create a spoofed identity, an attacker uses a fake source address that does not represent the actual address of the packet. Spoofing may be used to hide the original source of an attack or to work around network access control lists (ACLs) that are in place to limit host access based on source address rules.

Although carefully crafted spoofed packets may never be tracked to the original sender, a combination of filtering rules prevents spoofed packets from originating from your network, allowing you to block obviously spoofed packets.

Countermeasures to prevent spoofing include:

- Filter incoming packets that appear to come from an internal IP address at your perimeter.

- Filter outgoing packets that appear to originate from an invalid local IP address.

Session Hijacking

Also known as man in the middle attacks, session hijacking deceives a server or a client into accepting the upstream host as the actual legitimate host. Instead the upstream host is an attacker's host that is manipulating the network so the attacker's host appears to be the desired destination.

Countermeasures to help prevent session hijacking include:

- Use encrypted session negotiation.
- Use encrypted communication channels.
- Stay informed of platform patches to fix TCP/IP vulnerabilities, such as predictable packet sequences.

Denial of Service

Denial of service denies legitimate users access to a server or services. The SYN flood attack is a common example of a network level denial of service attack. It is easy to launch and difficult to track. The aim of the attack is to send more requests to a server than it can handle. The attack exploits a potential vulnerability in the TCP/IP connection establishment mechanism and floods the server's pending connection queue.

Countermeasures to prevent denial of service include:

- Apply the latest service packs.
- Harden the TCP/IP stack by applying the appropriate registry settings to increase the size of the TCP connection queue, decrease the connection establishment period, and employ dynamic backlog mechanisms to ensure that the connection queue is never exhausted.
- Use a network Intrusion Detection System (IDS) because these can automatically detect and respond to SYN attacks.

THE THREAT TO CYBER ACTIVISTS

In states where people are not entirely free to speak, the Internet is a vital tool for seeking and imparting information. In Belarus, for example, the Internet is the key source of objective information, as most independent newspapers have been closed down and media is state controlled. The Arab Spring has shown that the Internet can help activists in authoritarian regimes to get organised and exchange views. Furthermore, social media and user-generated content platforms have enabled thousands of bloggers and journalists to publish information and keep the international community focused on the situation in their country. But while the Internet may act as a countervailing force against the power of an authoritarian regime, we must also be aware that the Internet can adversely affect activist movements. The reason for this is that the Internet can strengthen the three most important tools wielded by authoritarian regimes: censorship, surveillance, and propaganda. In particular, censorship and online surveillance threaten the freedom of expression online. In an effort to control the free flow of information, authoritarian regimes have cracked down on cyber activists and have taken significant steps to limit the access to information on the Internet. The reasons why states engage in online censorship and surveillance can be divided into roughly four broad categories, *viz.*, for political gain, to curb civil disorder, to protect national security, and to technically limit the capacity for Internet use.

A number of different tools and mechanisms are currently used by authoritarian regimes to control the online activities of their citizens. These include blocking content, filtering Internet content, and manipulating Internet search results. States have even gone so far as to shut down the Internet and phone services entirely. In other places regimes and their proxies have hacked and sabotaged web sites in order to silence dissenting voices. Furthermore, states may employ online monitoring technologies and hacking tools to eavesdrop on confidential communication. Finally, they can track the digital footsteps of journalists, bloggers and other cyber activists in order to harass them offline through intimidating, arresting or persecuting them, threatening their employment, or ensuring that they disappear.

2

Terrorism using Internet: New Threats Posed by Cyber Terrorism

The presence of terrorist groups on the internet is a relatively new phenomenon, the growth of which has exploded in the past decade. Accurate estimates on the number of active terrorist group's websites vary due to difficulties measuring but, there is a general consensus that in 1996 there was just under 100 websites and to well over 5000 websites today. It is also widely accepted that all Foreign Terrorist Organisation's listed by the U.S. Department of State website have established an online presence of some form.

Only after 9/11 has governmental and public interest really been focussed on terrorists and the internet shown by the large number of articles examining the issue in the media which primarily occurred due to evidence recovered from Al Qaeda computers in Afghanistan, that indicate the Internet was being used to collect intelligence and send encrypted messages. The definition of terrorism used in this document is that of the new academic consensus definition: that terrorism is "a politically motivated tactic involving the threat or use of force or violence in which the pursuit of publicity plays a significant role".

Terrorist Groups use of the Internet

Growth in the use of the internet by terrorist groups is due to the key characteristics of the internet: ease of access which facilitates the possible massive worldwide audiences, few laws when compared to the physical world, little censorship, rapid and 'always on' flow of information, the low cost, anonymity of communication and a multimedia environment. The following is a breakdown of the main purposes that terrorist groups utilise the Internet for:

Cyberterrorism

Directly after 9/11, much was made of the possibilities of a large-scale cyber-terrorism attack by the media. However, several academics in the pending years published papers focusing on the terrorist groups utilize the Internet as it was designed to be; a means to communicate and collaborate, therefore the terrorists have stronger reasons to keep it up and online. Hence the apparently impending large scale cyber-terrorist attack that would cripple the internet has not materialised although Al Qaeda has taken full advantage of this fear.

Publicity and Propaganda

As stated by Dr Maura Conway, terrorism researcher: "Every machine connected to the internet is potentially a printing press, a broadcasting station or place of assembly." The internet is an un-paralleled media suite. Terrorists no longer have to have their messages diluted and edited by the media. Instead they can disseminate information of their choice to aid their causes. In most cases, this is achieved by the terrorists focusing on their grievances in order to justify why they are resorting to terrorist activities. This is usually achieved by the publication of various articles combined with pictures galleries, although this may be supplemented by video and audio files in which the terrorists themselves orally defend their actions. An example of this would be a gallery of atrocities against innocent civilians in Iraq supposedly carried out by foreign forces in order to generate local as well as international support for the terrorists.

In some cases, the terrorists choose to distribute information displaying their acts of violence or relating actions although this is not common. Again, these can be through written articles describing the violence, but are more often videos and pictures. Examples of these would be the pre-mission pictures published on the Tamil Tigers website of the Air Tiger squadron that a few days earlier had carried out its successful inaugural air attack on Sri Lankan governmental forces. A rather more extreme example was the distribution of the beheading of the journalist Daniel Pearl by the terrorist organisation 'The National Movement for the Restoration of Pakistani Sovereignty'.

Data Mining

The Internet is a vast resource of information which anyone can tap into and terrorists are well aware of this. According to Secretary of Defence Donald Rumsfeld, speaking on January 15, 2003, an al Qaeda training manual recovered in Afghanistan tells its readers that: "Using public sources openly and without resorting to illegal means, it is possible to gather at least 80 percent of all information required about the enemy."

The Internet allows access to highly detailed maps, schematics and various other sources of data that would allow terrorists gather information for potential targets. More importantly, once this data has been collated, it is compiled into volumes or "How to" manuals that are distributed between terrorist organisations.

Fund Raising

Terrorist groups have made full use of the Internet's ability to create funds; whether legitimately or otherwise. The main methods that the terrorists achieve this is by: Goods selling: merchandise that is directly related to the terrorist organisation, for example, CDs, DVDs and books from the LTTE.

Website and email based appeals: sending emails to sympathizers who registered interest on a group's website, posting messages on newsgroups/ forums and their own websites that give directions as to how and where donations can be made.

Deception: using seemingly legitimate charities or businesses that unknown to the donator, directs the funds to terrorist organisations. Criminal activity: Illegitimate means of gaining funds that terrorist groups are known to use include credit card fraud, online brokering and gambling.

Recruitment

This section is inherently tied-in with Propaganda. Terrorist organisations are able to monitor users who browse their websites, capture their profile and information about them and if deemed possibly useful to their cause, are contacted. This grooming process starts from when the user begins to absorb the propaganda on the website, for example the often discussed "charismatic" style of delivery that Osama Bin Laden employs on his video messages. Perhaps motivated by this video, the user seeks answers to questions and goes to internet chat-rooms and discussion boards. Possible recruits are spotted by lurking recruiters who through gradual encouragement of discussion of religious issues to gradually including more political discussions. This grooming leads the recruits to become more and more entangled in terrorist related discussions and are led through a maze of private chat-room's until personal indoctrination occurs which is often through the use of the secure software Paltalk.

Communication & Networking

Terrorist groups have changed recently from having a clearly defined hierarchy in the organisations with designated leaders, to having multiple, semi-independent cells with no clear distinct leader in order to allow them to remain hidden. The Internet facilitates communication between cells which allows exchange of information and manuals.

The Internet also assists with internal communication within a cell particularly in relation to the planning of attacks. To avoid being detected and targeted by security forces, Messages are often sent by conspirators through emails which are often sent using public email systems such as Hotmail and Yahoo and may also be sent from public libraries and internet cafes. Chat rooms may also be used for this purpose.

In addition, steganography may be used to hide information embedded within graphic files on websites. Graphic files may also used to send very subtle messages, such as reversing the orientation of a gun graphic may indicate that the next stage of a plan is to proceed. Other methods of concealing instructions and messages may be through the use of coded language, such as that used by Mohamed Atta's final email to the other terrorists who carried out the attacks of 9/11 is reported to have read: The semester begins in three more weeks. We've obtained 19 confirmations for studies in the faculty of law, the faculty of urban planning, the faculty of fine arts, and the faculty of engineering.

This is believed to be in reference to the four targets that the planes were planned to strike; 'architecture' being the World Trade Centre, 'arts': the Pentagon, 'law': the Capitol and 'politics': the White House.

An even more secure method of communication is that which involves using one-time anonymous public email accounts; two terrorists who wish to communicate to open 30 anonymous email accounts whose usernames and passwords are known by each side. To communicate, one terrorist creates a web-based email and instead of sending it, saves it as a draft online. The "recipient" then logs onto this account, reads this message and deletes. The next day, a new account is used; this increases the difficulty of traceability of the users.

The Audiences of the Terrorist Websites

The first group of people that will frequent these websites are current supporters and future supporters. The websites typically include information relative to their activities, their allies, and their competitors. In addition, many websites offer items for sale. The second group of people that will enter these websites will be members of the outside community. In hopes of appealing to people all over the world, many terrorist organizations offer their websites in multiple languages. The websites typically include historical background information and general information about the organization itself. Only some of the websites address the enemy or citizens of a country currently under attack by terrorists. The terrorists hope weaken public support within countries and in some cases will threaten attacks if the government fails to do as they ask.

INTERNATIONAL TERRORISTS USE THE INTERNET

The Internet is used as a prime recruiting tool for insurgents. Extremists use chat rooms, dedicated servers and websites, and social networking tools as propaganda machines, as a means of recruitment and organization, for training grounds, and for significant fund-raising through cyber crime. These websites and other Internet services may be run by international terrorist groups, transnational cyber crime organizations, or individual extremists. YouTube channels and Facebook pages of Taliban and Al Qaeda supporters may radicalise Western-based sympathisers, and also provide a means for communication between these "lone wolf" actors and larger organised networks of terrorists.

The decentralised nature of the Internet as a medium and the associated difficulty in responding to emerging threats can match the franchised nature of terrorist organizations and operations. It is unclear how great a role the Internet plays in coordinating the efforts of a single group or strategy. Many Arabic-language websites are said to contain coded plans for new attacks. Some reportedly give advice on how to build and operate weapons and how to pass through border checkpoints. Other news articles report that a younger generation of terrorists and extremists, such as those behind the July 2005 bombings in London, are learning new technical skills to help them avoid detection by various nations' law enforcement computer technology. Cyber crime has now surpassed international drug trafficking as a terrorist financing enterprise. Internet Ponzi schemes, identity theft, counterfeiting, and other types of computer fraud have been shown to yield high profits under a shroud of anonymity.

According to press reports, Indonesian police officials believe the 2002 terrorist bombings in Bali were partially financed through online credit card fraud. There may be some evidence that terrorist organizations seek the ability to use the Internet itself as a weapon in an attack against critical infrastructures. Also, links between terrorist organizations and cybercriminals may show a desire to hone a resident offensive cyber capability in addition to serving as a means of procuring funds. To some observers, the term "Cyber terrorism" is inappropriate, because a widespread cyberattack may simply produce annoyances, not terror, as would a bomb, or other chemical, biological, radiological, or nuclear explosive (CBRN) weapon. However, others believe that the effects of a widespread computer network attack would be unpredictable and might cause enough economic disruption, fear, and civilian deaths to qualify as terrorism.

At least two views exist for defining the term Cyber terrorism as traditionally understood:

1. *Effects-based*: Cyber terrorism exists when computer attacks result in effects that are disruptive enough to generate fear comparable to a traditional act of terrorism, even if done by criminals other than terrorists.
2. *Intent-based*: Cyber terrorism exists when unlawful, politically motivated computer attacks are done to intimidate or coerce a government or people to further a political objective, or to cause grave harm or severe economic damage.

Propaganda, Recruitment, and Training

In a July 2005 letter to Abu Musab al-Zarqawi, the late leader of Al Qaeda operations in Iraq, senior Al Qaeda leader Ayman al-Zawahiri wrote, "We are in a battle, and more than half of this battle is taking place in the battlefield of the media." Terrorist organizations exploit the Internet medium to raise awareness for their cause, to spread propaganda, and to inspire potential operatives across the globe. Websites operated by terrorist groups can contain graphic images of supposed successful terrorist attacks, lists and biographies of celebrated martyrs, and forums for discussing ideology and methodology. The Quetta Shura Taliban reportedly maintains several dedicated websites, including one with an Arabic-language online magazine, and publishes daily electronic press releases on other Arabic-language jihadist forums.

The As-Shahab Institute for Media Production is Al Qaeda Central's media arm and distributes audio, video, and graphics products online through jihadist forums, blogs, and file-hosting websites.

A recent online English-language terrorist propaganda periodical called *Inspire* appears to have originated from the media arm of a Yemen-based Al Qaeda group and contains articles by Anwar al-Awlaki, an English-speaking, U.S.-born radical imam whose sermonizing rhetoric and calls to action make extensive use of cyberspace. Al-Awlaki has been connected to several terrorist plots, including the attempted Times Square bombing in New York City in May 2010.

Al-Awlaki has also been either directly or indirectly linked to radicalizing Nidal M. Hasan, who allegedly committed the November 2009 shooting at Fort Hood, Texas, and Umar Farouk Abdulmutallab, the Nigerian suspect accused of trying to ignite explosives on Northwest/Delta Airlines Flight 253 on Christmas Day 2009. Faisal Shahzad, a naturalised U.S. citizen from Pakistan, admitted to trying to set off a car bomb in Times Square and said he was inspired by al-Awlaki's online lectures. Some experts question the authenticity of the periodical *Inspire* and its link to Al Qaeda. The effectiveness of violent images used to reach its mainstream target audience is debated, as the violent images may appeal only to a small, self-selected segment of the population. Al-Zawahiri, in a reference to winning the "hearts and minds" of Muslims, noted that "the Muslim populace who love and support you will never find palatable... the scenes of slaughtering the hostages." These websites can also carry step-by-step instructions on how to build and detonate weapons, including cyber weapons. One Web site reportedly carries a downloadable "e-jihad" application, through which a user can choose an Internet target and launch a low-level cyberattack, overwhelming the targeted Web site with traffic in order to deny its service.

The websites may also contain instructions for building kinetic weapons, such as bombs and improvised explosive devices, as well as for conducting surveillance and target acquisition. The Internet can also be used to transmit information and material support for planned acts of terrorism. A recent case involving a U.S. citizen residing in Pennsylvania alleges that a woman using the nickname "JihadJane" posted messages on YouTube and used jihadist websites and chat rooms to plan and facilitate an overseas attack.

Cyber Crime and Fund-raising

Cyber crime has increased in past years, and several recent terrorist events appear to have been funded partially through online credit card fraud. Extremist hackers have reportedly used identity theft and credit card fraud to support terrorist activities by Al Qaeda cells. When terrorist groups do not have the internal technical capability, they may hire organised crime syndicates and cybercriminals through underground digital chat rooms. Reports indicate that terrorists and extremists in the Middle East and South Asia may be increasingly collaborating with cybercriminals for the international movement of money and for the smuggling of arms and illegal drugs. These links with hackers and cybercriminals may be examples of the terrorists' desire to refine their computer skills, and the relationships forged through collaborative drug trafficking efforts may also provide terrorists with access to highly skilled computer programmers.

Cyberattacks

Although terrorists have been adept at spreading propaganda and attack instructions on the web, it appears that their capacity for offensive computer network operations may be limited. The Federal Bureau of Investigation (FBI) reports that cyberattacks attributed to terrorists have largely been limited to unsophisticated efforts such as e-mail bombing of ideological foes, denial-ofservice attacks, or defacing of websites. However, it says, their increasing technical competency is resulting in an emerging capability for network-based attacks.

The FBI has predicted that terrorists will either develop or hire hackers for the purpose of complementing large conventional attacks with cyberattacks. During his testimony regarding the 2007 Annual Threat Assessment, FBI Director Robert Mueller observed that "terrorists increasingly use the Internet to communicate, conduct operational planning, proselytise, recruit, train and to obtain logistical and financial support.

That is a growing and increasing concern for us." In addition, continuing publicity about Internet computer security vulnerabilities may encourage terrorists' interest in attempting a possible computer network attack, or cyberattack, against U.S. critical infrastructure. The Internet, whether accessed by a desktop computer or by the many available handheld devices, is the medium through which a cyberattack would be delivered. However, for a targeted attack to be successful, the attackers usually require that the network itself remain more or less intact, unless the attackers assess that the perceived gains from shutting down the network entirely would offset the accompanying loss of their own communication. A future targeted cyberattack could be effective if directed against a portion of the U.S. critical infrastructure, and if timed to amplify the effects of a simultaneous conventional physical or chemical, biological, radiological, or nuclear (CBRN) terrorist attack.

The objectives of a cyberattack may include the following four areas:

1. loss of integrity, such that information could be modified improperly;
2. loss of availability, where mission-critical information systems are rendered unavailable to authorised users;
3. loss of confidentiality, where critical information is disclosed to unauthorised users; and
4. physical destruction, where information systems create actual physical harm through commands that cause deliberate malfunctions.

Publicity would also potentially be one of the primary objectives for a terrorist cyberattack. Extensive media coverage has shown the vulnerability of the U.S. information infrastructure and the potential harm that could be caused by a cyberattack. This might lead terrorists to believe that even a marginally successful cyberattack directed at the United States would garner considerable publicity.

Some suggest that were such a cyberattack by an international terrorist organization to occur and become known to the general public, regardless of the level of success of the attack, concern by many citizens and cascading effects might lead to widespread disruption of critical infrastructures. For example, reports of an attack on the international financial system's networks could create a fiscal panic in the public that could lead to economic damage.

According to security experts, terrorist groups have not yet used their own computer hackers nor hired hackers to damage, disrupt, or destroy critical infrastructure systems.

Yet reports of a recent disruptive computer worm that has spread through some government networks, including that of the National Aeronautics and Space Administration, have found a possible link to a Libyan hacker with the handle "Iraq Resistance" and his online hacker group "Brigades of Tariq ibn Ziyad," whose stated goal is "to penetrate U.S. agencies belonging to the U.S. Army." References to both the hacker and group have been found in the worm's code. However, this does not provide conclusive evidence of involvement, as e-mail addresses can be spoofed and code can be deliberately designed to implicate a target while concealing the true identity of the perpetrator. The recent emergence of the Stuxnet worm may have implications for what potential future cyberattacks might look like. Stuxnet is thought to be the first piece of malicious software (malware) that was specifically designed to target the computer-networked industrial control systems that control utilities, in this case nuclear power plants in Iran. Although many experts contend that the level of sophistication, intelligence, and access required to develop Stuxnet all point to nation states, not only is the idea now in the public sphere for others to build upon, but the code has been released as well.

An industrious group could potentially use this code as a foundation for developing a capability intended to degrade and destroy the software systems that control the U.S. power grid, to name one example.

FEDERAL GOVERNMENT EFFORTS TO ADDRESS CYBER TERRORISM

A number of U.S. government organizations appear to monitor terrorist websites and conduct a variety of activities aimed at countering them. Given the sensitivity of federal government Programmes responsible for monitoring and infiltrating websites suspected of supporting terrorismrelated activities, much of the information regarding the organizations and their specific activities is deemed classified or law enforcement-sensitive and is not publicly available. The information listed below represents a sampling of what has been publicly discussed about some of the federal government organizations responsible for monitoring and infiltrating jihadist websites.

It should be noted that the actions associated with the organizations listed below could be conducted by employees of the federal government or by civilian contract personnel.

- *Central Intelligence Agency (CIA)*: development, surveillance, and analysis of websites, commonly referred to as honey pots, for purposes of attracting existing and potential jihadists searching for forums to discuss terrorism-related activities.

- *National Security Agency (NSA)*: surveillance of websites and rendering them inaccessible.
- *Department of Defence (DOD):* surveillance of websites focused on discussions of perceived vulnerabilities of overseas U.S. military facilities or operational capabilities and disabling those that present a threat to operations.
- *Department of Justice (DOJ)*: development of polices and guidelines for creating, interacting within, surveilling, and rendering inaccessible websites created by individuals wishing to use the Internet as a forum for inciting or planning terrorism-related activities.
- *Federal Bureau of Investigation (FBI)*: monitoring of websites and analysis of information for purposes of determining possible terrorist plans and threats to U.S. security interests.
- *Department of Homeland Security (DHS)*: monitoring of websites and analysis of information for purposes of determining possible threats to the homeland.

Numerous other federal government organizations have cyber security responsibilities focused on policy development, public awareness campaigns, and intergovernmental and private sector coordination efforts. Information gleaned from the agencies may at times be used to help inform and advise non-federal government entities responsible for safeguarding a geographic area or activity that has been discussed in an online jihadist forum.

Federal Government Monitoring and Response

A number of reasons exist that may provide justification for the federal government to monitor websites owned, operated, or frequented by individuals suspected of supporting international jihadist activity that pose a threat to U.S. security interests.

Such websites may be used for purposes of spreading propaganda, recruiting new members or enticing existing participants, communicating plans counter to U.S. interests, or facilitating terrorist-related activities. Quite often the jihadist websites are the first indicators of extreme elements of the jihadist community identifying a controversial issue for purposes of inciting action harmful to U.S. interests. For example, a recent controversy in the United States about a proposed burning of copies of the Quran on the ninth anniversary of the September 11, 2001, attacks led to increased chatter on international jihadist websites. The FBI reportedly disseminated an intelligence bulletin specifically noting online threats to the pastor and church planning to conduct this event and more general threats to U.S. global interests. When assessing whether to monitor, infiltrate, or shut down a Web site suspected of inciting participants to take harmful actions against U.S. security interests, numerous competing interests should be considered.

First, the federal government would determine whether the Web site is owned by a U.S. corporation and whether U.S. citizens may be participating in the Internet forum. Such a determination is necessary to ensure that proper procedures are adhered to with respect to upholding the rights afforded by the U.S. Constitution's First and Fourth Amendments, in particular.

Second, once it is confirmed that a suspected jihadist Web site is being used to facilitate terrorism-related activities, the national security community may consider the short- and long-term implications of a variety of operational responses. Options include permanently or temporarily shutting down the Web site, passively monitoring the Web site for intelligence-gathering purposes, or covertly engaging the members of the forum with the desire to elicit additional information for purposes of thwarting a potential terrorism-related activity and/or building a stronger criminal case. Different agencies may weigh each option differently, creating a need to achieve interagency consensus prior to action.

DOD has been considering establishing a computer network monitoring database for government and private networks. Organizations would provide information on a voluntary basis, and the data collected would be shared with all participants. However, privacy concerns and questions of DOD's proper role in federal cyber security make the implementation of such a Programme unlikely in the current political climate.

A memorandum of agreement signed in October 2010 between DHS and DOD represents an effort to increase coordination of operations and plans to protect civilian critical infrastructure as well as military networks. The partnership could be used as a means through which DOD would have a greater role in defending privately owned critical infrastructure using the EINSTEIN 2 and 3 network monitoring systems developed by DHS.

Counterpropaganda

In common parlance and in media reporting, the terms "strategic communications," "public diplomacy," "global engagement," "information operations," and "propaganda" are often used interchangeably. This confusion in terms makes it difficult to determine exactly what sorts of programmatic activities are being discussed. There is no overarching definition of strategic communications for the federal government. DOD has defined strategic communication as "focused United States Government efforts to understand

and engage key audiences to create, strengthen, or preserve conditions favorable for the advancement of United States government interests, policies, and objectives through the use of coordinated Programmes, plans, themes, messages, and products synchronised with the actions of all instruments of national power." This term, as defined, describes a U.S. government-wide process, not an organizational structure, capability, or discrete activity within DOD or any other government agency.

As prescribed by the 2009 National Framework for Strategic Communication, the Deputy National Security Advisor for Strategic Communications (DNSA/SC) serves as the National Security Advisor's principal advisor for strategic communications. The Senior Director for Global Engagement (SDGE) is the principal deputy to the DNSA/SC.

Together, they are responsible for ensuring that

- The message-value and communicative impact of actions are considered during decision-making by the National Security Council (NSC) and Homeland Security Council (HSC);
- The mechanisms to promote strategic communication are in place within the National Security Staff (NSS); and
- Similar mechanisms are developed across the interagency.

The DNSA/SC and SDGE are also responsible for guiding and coordinating interagency deliberate communication and engagement efforts, and they execute this responsibility through the NSS Directorate for Global Engagement (NSS/GE) and through the Interagency Policy Committee (IPC) on Strategic Communication. Public Diplomacy (PD) within the State Department is led by the Under Secretary for Public Diplomacy and Public Affairs.

The Department of State distinguishes between Public Affairs (PA), which includes outreach to domestic publics, and PD—which seeks to promote the national interest of the United States through understanding, engaging, informing, and influencing foreign publics, and by promoting mutual understanding between the people of the United States and people from other nations around the world. In DOD, strategic communication-related activities are primarily supported by the integration of three capabilities: Information Operations (IO), and, primarily within IO, Psychological Operations (PSYOP), Public Affairs (PA), and Defence Support to Public Diplomacy (DSPD). Military Diplomacy (MD) and Visual Information (VI) also support strategic communicationsrelated activities.

DOD sees strategic communications as a process to synchronise efforts that:

- Improve U.S. credibility and legitimacy;
- Weaken an adversary's credibility and legitimacy;

- Convince selected audiences to take specific actions that support U.S. or international objectives;
- Cause a competitor or adversary to take (or refrain from taking) specific actions.

Many DOD activities support the State Department's public diplomacy efforts and objectives, which in turn support national objectives. DOD refers to these activities as "Defence Support to Public Diplomacy" (DSPD). Although some reports warn of social media's potential misuse by terrorists, government policies are evolving to embrace the use of tools such as Facebook and Twitter as a means of strategic communications and public diplomacy. On the one hand, social media tools such as Twitter and Facebook can be used by terrorist groups to expand networks and exchange real-time information, enabling operatives to organise and act quickly. These tools can not only spread propaganda, but can also host embedded malicious software in links and applications that can corrupt an unsuspecting user's electronic device.

Based on these security concerns, several services and offices within DOD had banned certain social networking sites from access on their unclassified networks. However, the federal government has begun to embrace using these same tools to allow free access to information, spread democratic values and ideas, and combat the misinformation spread by terrorist groups' media campaigns. In February 2010, DOD issued a directive-type memo (DTM) outlining the department's new social media policy, citing Internet-based capabilities including social networking services as integral to operations.

This policy is due to expire in March 2011; reportedly, there are no plans to develop a replacement policy, nor plans to fill the top positions that were instrumental in creating the social media policy. Some fear that the recent WikiLeaks issue may push the pendulum back Towards more restricted access to Internet-based capabilities and less information sharing between organizations.

Others note that, to date, much of the activity conducted under the current policy has been one-sided, focused on using social network tools to gather information about others, including potential adversaries, rather than to send messages outward in order to shape the information environment. Reportedly, the U.S. Air Force and U.S. Central Command have been developing deceptive identities on the Internet in order to infiltrate chat rooms and other social media using a special software. The U.S., Air Force software contract states that it shall be used to target adversarial sites worldwide without detection, and spokesmen for the U.S. Central Command have stated that it shall not be used to target law-abiding American citizens. Critics of these Programmes point to the potential loss of credibility, a tenet of successful information operations, using the former Office of Strategic Influence (OSI) as an example. Reports that the OSI was planting false news stories into foreign newspapers to gain support for the war in Iraq led many—including the Public Affairs Office—to question the legality of such activity. The OSI was subsequently disestablished.

Department of Defence Offensive Response

Information operations do not refer exclusively to messaging and content; another integrated capability within this area is computer network operations (CNO), which includes cyberattack capabilities, cyber espionage and exploitation, and cyber Defence. The Joint Functional Command Component—Network Warfare (JFCC-NW) and the JFCC—Space and Global Strike (JFCC-SGS) have responsibility for overall DOD cyber security, while the Joint Task Force—Global Network Operations (JTF-GNO) and the Joint Information Operations Warfare Center (JIOWC) both have direct responsibility for Defence against cyberattack.

The DOD focal point for coordinating military information operations is the JIOWC. The JTF-GNO defends the DOD Global Information Grid, while the JIOWC assists combatant commands with an integrated approach to information operations. These include operations security, military information support operations (formerly psychological operations), military deception, and electronic warfare. Many of the specific Programmes under the JIOWC's purview are classified.

The JIOWC also coordinates computer network operations and network warfare with the JTF-GNO and with JFCC-NW. These latter two organizational activities are to fall under the responsibility of the newly formed U.S. Cyber Command (USCYBERCOM), a sub-unified command under U.S. Strategic Command (USSTRATCOM). The commander of USCYBERCOM, General Keith Alexander, also serves as the director of NSA. Traditionally, the NSA mission has been information assurance for national security systems and signals intelligence, and gathering information about potential threats under the Foreign Intelligence Surveillance Act (FISA). The dual-hatted nature of this appointment places this intelligence function alongside the offensive operations command. Information security and cyberwarfare planners in the Pentagon have noted both in doctrine and in informal channels that a good offensive cyber operations capability is the best Defence.

For this reason, USCYBERCOM has integrated the military's defensive computer network operations components with its offensive arm under one joint command. Many of USCYBERCOM's capabilities are unknown, due to the classified nature of offensive cyber operations. There have also been questions in the executive branch and in Congress about what authorities they operate under and how oversight is to be conducted.

A question-and-answer exchange from the Senate Armed Services Committee revealed that DOD had not included cyber operations in its quarterly report on clandestine military activities. Michael Vickers, the nominee for Undersecretary of Defence for Intelligence, reportedly told the committee that those quarterly reporting requirements related only to human intelligence. How USCYBERCOM relates to NSA and how both relate to the private sector, which owns most of the U.S. telecommunications infrastructure, has been a continued subject of discussions.

On the defensive side, although USCYBERCOM is developing plans to defend the.mil domain, there is still no unified federal response policy for coordinating offensive cyber operations at the national level. Yet DOD has been working with DHS and the National Cyber security and Communications Integration Center through Cyberstorm and other exercises to map out a National Cyber Incident Response Plan, which gives a structure for how the federal government might respond in the event of a major cyberattack. At a Reserve Officers Association conference, USCYBERCOM Chief of Staff Major General David Senty said that the sub-unified command might take the lead in defending the nation's military networks as a "supported command" prior to "turning things over" to U.S. Northern Command.

THE INTERNET DOES NOT INCREASE TERRORISM

Terrorists are using the Internet to plot "murder and mayhem," British Prime Minister David Camerondeclared this week, as a parliamentary committee issued a report accusing Internet firms of providing a "safe haven for terrorists." Cameron and the committee were referring specifically to a brutal knife attack that killed British soldier Lee Rigby on a London street in May 2013, but the charge has been levied more broadly as well. Earlier this month, British spymaster Robert Hanniganclaimed that Silicon Valley had created "the command-and-control networks of choice for terrorists." In October, Spanish Secretary of State for Security Francisco Martinez warned that the ruthless ISIS terrorist group now dominating swathes of Syria and Iraq regards the Internet as "an extension of the battlefield," adding that they might be using it to organize an attack in the West using the Ebola virus.

Fortunately, there's good reason to believe these officials wrong. David Benson, a political scientist at the University of Chicago, argues in the summer issue of *Security Studies* that there is very little evidence that the Internet is making terrorism easier to do. While "access to the Internet has increased across the globe," he writes, "there has been no corresponding increase in completed transnational terrorist attacks." Benson defines terrorism as "violence by non-state actors intended to terrorize or frighten a target audience." He focuses on transnational terrorism because the fear of attacks across international borders drives major changes in policy.

The Internet might benefit would-be transnational terrorists by offering anonymity, access to information, and cheap communication, which in turn increases both their capabilities and their ability to network. Anonymity blunts attempts to preempt attacks; information about how to build bombs and carry out attacks is widely available; and cheap communication makes long-distance coordination possible. In theory, all this should make it easier to carry out attacks in other lands.

But as Benson points out, analysts err when they assume that "transnational terrorists have a similar base of support as nationalist or local terror organizations." Local terrorists live among people from whom they can seek support and recruits. They can assess targets in person, and they can meet to research, plan, and prepare using local channels to communicate. Transnational terrorists, by contrast, cannot rely on local support for either recruits or operations.

Benson adds that terrorists are not really all that anonymous, since Internet activity leaves tracks that sophisticated sleuths can follow, and that the availability of bomb-building schematics is no substitute for actual weapons-making experience. Furthermore, governments and other outside groups are adept at monitoring terrorists' communications.

Benson thinks most analysts inflate the Internet's importance because they reason backwards: They look at individual attacks, then assess how the terrorists used the Internet to realize their plans. "Since the Internet is ubiquitous, it would be strange if today's terrorists did not use the Internet, just as it would have been strange if past terrorists did not use the postal service or telephones," Benson notes. The key issue is whether transnational terrorist attacks are *increasing* with the spread of the Internet.

The activities of Al Qaeda have been a focal point for public anxieties, so Benson lists the atrocities committed by Al Qaeda between 1995 and 2011. Using the number of casualties as the benchmark for assessing capabilities, Benson observes that there is a steep reduction in the number of people killed and wounded by Al Qaeda operatives after the attacks on the U.S. embassies in Kenya and Tanzania on August 8, 1998, and the September 11, 2001, barbarity. Benson argues that most of this fall off in effectiveness came as a result of losing their safe havens in Sudan and Afghanistan. Communication and instruction over the Internet is no substitute for face-to-face talk and hands-on training.

After 9/11, various local terrorists groups found value in the Al Qaeda brand and offered to become franchise operations. These franchises include Al-Shabaab in Somalia, Al Qaeda in the Arabian Peninsula (AQAP), and Al Qaeda in the Islamic Magreb (AQIM). Benson excludes Al Qaeda in Iraq and Jemaah Islamiyyah in Indonesia because their operations are almost entirely local. The others are largely local too, and when they do carry out an attack in another country it is usually in a neighboring nation. All of the "transnational" attacks done by the Algeria-based AQIM, for example, have occurred next door—in Morocco, Mauritania, Niger, Mali, and Tunisia.

Some of those countries are practically Internet-free zones. Usage rates in Mali and Niger, for example, are under three percent. Similarly, Internet penetration in Somalia, where Al Shabaab operates, is about 1.5 percent. Attacks are organized by local terrorists who meet and train together face-to-face. "Almost all of [Al Qaeda's] successful attacks following 2005 were completed by local terrorist organizations," Benson observes.

The 2014 Global Terrorism Index notes that 2013 was "the peak year in global terrorist activity not only in the early 21st century, but also for the entire period since 1970," when the statistics in the Index first begin. Deaths from terrorism increased 61 percent, rising from 11,133 in 2012 to 17,958 in 2013. But despite this dismaying increase, "The bulk of terrorist activity in the world is accounted for by militant actors that pursue relatively limited goals in local or regional contexts." Eighty-two percent of the fatalities caused by terrorism in 2013 occurred in just five countries: Iraq, Afghanistan, Pakistan, Nigeria, and Syria. (Internet penetration in those countries is 7.8 percent, 6 percent, 11 percent, 38 percent, and 27 percent, respectively. By contrast, about 87 percent of Americans have access to the Internet.)

The Index further observes that 66 percent of the claimed deaths from terrorism in 2013 are claimed by only four terrorist organizations: ISIL, Boko Haram, the Taliban, and Al Qaeda and its affiliates. Since 2000, only 5 percent of all 107,000 fatalities stemming from terrorist attacks have occurred in OECD countries—and that includes the 2,996 who died on 9/11. Meanwhile, the same Internet used by terrorists is used by governments to gather intelligence.

And as terrorists recruit online, friends and family members use social media to engage and intervene with people at risk of radicalization. So it's not as though all the Internets effects run the same way.

And often what initially looks like a transnational attack might turn out to be local after all. Consider that parliamentary report on Lee Rigby's murder.

The attack was carried out by two British nationals, Michael Adebolajo and Michael Adebowale, of Nigerian heritage. The report notes that Adebowale expressed his desire to kill a British soldier in a single Facebook chat with an extremist thought to be associated with AQAP.

But it adds that the British intelligence agency MI5 "told the Committee that they believe that, while Adebowale and Adebolajo were in contact with other extremists, they planned the murder of Fusilier Lee Rigby without external support, tasking or direction." In other words, the attack was a local action planned locally by local actors, not a transnational plot organized over the Internet.

As Benson argues, exaggerating the Internet's usefulness to terrorism has "egregious costs." Some officials, for example, have been calling for a "kill switch" that would allow the government to shut down the Internet in an emergency. Noting how much Americans depend upon the Net for commerce, communication, medical care, and so forth, Benson points out that "It is difficult to imagine a terrorist attack being as costly as turning off the Internet would be."

But casting the Internet as a "safe haven for terrorists" does give governments another excuse to violate our privacy in the pretense of protecting our security.

TERRORIST ORGANIZATIONS USE THE INTERNET

The Internet is a powerful tool for terrorists, who use online message boards and chat rooms to share information, coordinate attacks, spread propaganda, raise funds, and recruit, experts say. According to Haifa University's Gabriel Weimann, whose research on the subject is widely cited, the number of terrorist sites increased exponentially over the last decade—from less than 100 to more than 4,800 two years ago.

The numbers can be somewhat misleading, however. In the case of al-Qaeda, hundreds of sister sites have been promulgated but only a handful are considered active, experts say. Nonetheless, analysts do see a clear proliferation trend.

Terrorist websites can serve as virtual training grounds, offering tutorials on building bombs, firing surface-to-air missiles, shooting at U.S. soldiers, and sneaking into Iraq from abroad. Terrorist sites also host messages and propaganda videos which help to raise morale and further the expansion of recruitment and fundraising networks. Al-Qaeda's media arm, As-Sahab, is among the most visible. But an entire network of jihadist media outfits has sprung up in recent years, according to a March 2008 study by Daniel Kimmage of Radio Free Europe/Radio Liberty. "The 'original' al-Qaeda led by Osama bin Laden accounts for a mere fraction of jihadist media production," Kimmage writes.

What Constitutes a 'Terrorist Website'?

Defining a terrorist website is as contentious as defining terrorism. Pentagon analysts testifying before Congress have said that they monitor some five thousand jihadi websites, though they closely watch a small number of these—less than one hundred—that are deemed the most hostile.

Terrorist sites include the official sites of designated terrorist organizations, as well as the sites of supporters, sympathizers, and fans, says Weimann. But when websites with no formal terrorist affiliation contain sympathetic sentiments to the political aims of a terrorist group, the definition becomes murky. Hoax sites can also prove a troublesome red herring for monitors of terrorist sites. For instance, in recent years a number of sites sympathetic to the Taliban have proliferated on the web. Frequent site outages, however, make it difficult to track their content and sentiment.

How effective is online terrorist propaganda? Perhaps the most effective way in which terrorists use the Internet is the spread of propaganda. Abu Musab al-Zarqawi's al-Qaeda cell in Iraq has proven particularly adept in its use of the web, garnering attention by posting footage of roadside bombings, the decapitation of American hostage Nick Berg, and kidnapped Egyptian and Algerian diplomats prior to their execution.

In Iraq, experts say terrorist propaganda videos are viewed by a large portion of society, not just those who sympathize with terrorists and insurgents. In addition to being posted online, the videos are said to be sold in Baghdad video shops, hidden behind the counter along with pornography. Evan Kohlmann, an expert in terrorists' use of the Internet, points out that propaganda films are not exclusively made in the Middle East; groups from Bosnia, Afghanistan, and Chechnya have also produced videos. Nor are videos the only form of propaganda. Some jihadi websites have even offered video games in which users as young as seven can pretend to be holy warriors killing U.S. soldiers.

What advantages does the Internet offer terrorists? "The greatest advantage [of the Internet] is stealth," says John Arquilla, professor of defense analysis at the Naval Postgraduate School. "[Terrorists] swim in an ocean of bits and bytes." Terrorists have developed sophisticated encryption tools and creative techniques that make the Internet an efficient and relatively secure means of correspondence. These include steganography, a technique used to hide messages in graphic files, and "dead dropping": transmitting information through saved email drafts in an online email account accessible to anyone with the password.

The Internet also provides a global pool of potential recruits and donors. Online terrorist fundraising has become so commonplace that some organizations are able to accept donations via the popular online payment service PayPal.

Yet some terrorism experts say while the Internet has proven effective at spreading ideology, its use as a planning and tool operational tool is minimal. For instance, the terrorists whoattacked Mumbai in November 2008 could never have carried out their strike if they hadn't received actual training in a physical camp, says terrorism expert Peter Bergen. "We talk about the Internet being important for terrorism, which I think is ridiculous. The people who did the Mumbai attack didn't sit around reading about how to do attacks on the Internet. They actually went to a training camp in Muzaffarabad for several months."

What is cyberterrorism? Cyberterrorism is typically defined as the use of the Internet as a vehicle through which to launch an attack. Terrorists could conceivably hack into electrical grids and security systems, or perhaps distribute a powerful computer virus. "Al-Qaeda operatives are known to have taken training in hacking techniques," Arquilla says, but the likelihood of such a cyber attack seems fairly remote. That said, Western governments have accused state and nonstate actors of infiltrating secure networks, including an alleged breach of a Pentagon system by Chinese hackers in June 2007.

Kohlmann suggests the established definition of cyberterrorism needs to be broadened. He says any application of terrorism on the Internet should be considered cyberterrorism. "There's no distinction between the online [terrorist] community and the real [terrorist] community." As evidence, Kohlmann recounts one extreme instance in which the Iraqi insurgent group Army of the Victorious Sect held a contest to help design the group's new website. According to Kohlmann, the prize for the winning designer was the opportunity to, with the click of a mouse, remotely fire three rockets at a U.S. military base in Iraq.

Are there any prominent online terrorists? Among the most infamous figures to emerge from the world of online terrorism in recent years is "Irhaby 007" ("Terrorist 007"). As a SITE Institute profile explains, Irhaby 007 was celebrated by other online terrorists for his hacking prowess and his ability to securely distribute information. With his assistance, terrorist organizations around the globe were able to expand the reach of their message. Irhaby 007 passed this knowledge along to other online jihadis through web postings such as his "Seminar for Hacking Websites," creating a network of technology-savvy terrorist disciples. In October 2005, Scotland Yard officers in West London arrested 22-year-old Younis Tsouli, whom they later identified as Irhaby 007. Tsouli is awaiting trial on charges that include conspiracy to murder and terrorist fundraising.

Another prominent online terrorist is Abu Maysarah al-Iraqi, who has served as the media representative for al-Qaeda in Iraq leader Zarqawi. Al-Iraqi goes online to claim responsibility for acts of terrorism, post propaganda videos, and issue statements on behalf of Zarqawi, though experts say it is unclear whether al-Iraqi is just one person or several using the same name. Al-Iraqi's current whereabouts are unclear; a March 2007 report from the Iraqi news agency Quds Press, translated by the BBC, indicated that the al-Qaeda spokesman had been released from a Mosul prison.

In November 2008, Ali Hamza Ahmad Suleiman al-Bahlul, al-Qaeda's digital media director, was convicted by a U.S. military tribunal. He is serving a life sentence at Guantanamo Bay.

How do governments respond to terrorists' online activities? There is some debate within the counterterrorism community about how to combat terrorist sites. "The knee-jerk reaction is if you see a terrorist site you shut it down," Kohlmann says, but doing so can cause investigators to miss out on a wealth of valuable information. "You can see who's posting what and who's paying for it," says Michael Kern, formerly a senior analyst at the SITE Institute, a Washington-based terrorist-tracking group. For instance, German officials monitoring online chatter issued early warnings prior to the Madrid train bombings in March 2004.

Shutting down a terrorist website is just a temporary disruption. To truly stop a terrorist site, experts say, the webmaster must be stopped. The ability of the U.S. National Security Agency to monitor such individuals inside the United States has been the subject of a heatedpolitical and legal debate. The United States has tried to prosecute webmasters who run terrorist websites in the West, but has run into opposition from advocates of free speech. "Sites that tell the terrorist side of the story go right up to the brink of civil liberties," Arquilla says. Sami Omar al-Hussayen, a Saudi Arabian graduate student at the University of Idaho, was charged by U.S. officials with supporting terrorism because he served as a webmaster for several Islamic groups whose sites linked to organizations praising terrorist attacks in Chechnya and Israel. Al-Hussayen was acquitted of all terrorism charges by a federal court in June 2004 under the First Amendment. Two months later, Babar Ahmad, a 31-year-old, British-born son of Pakistani immigrants, was arrested in London under a U.S. warrant.

Another approach officials have taken is to create phony terrorist websites. These can spread disinformation, such as instructions for building a bomb that will explode prematurely and kill its maker or false intelligence about the location of U.S. forces in Iraq, intended to lead terrorist fighters into a trap. This tactic must be used sparingly, says Kohlmann, or else officials risk "poisoning a golden pot [of information]" about how terrorists operate.

THE ADVANTAGES OF THE NET FOR AL QAEDA

Al Qaeda's marginalized status vis-à-vis the Western media is partly a consequence of what Phillip Hammond refers to as 'the media war on terrorism'. Bemoaning this 'media siege', al Qaeda as well as other terrorist groups have turned to the Internet as their principal ideological and practical channel of communication. Thus, proliferation of terrorist websites demonstrated an exponential growth from 12 websites in 1998 to over 5,500 in 2007. By its very nature, the Internet is in many ways an ideal arena for activity by terrorist organizations. Most notably, it offers:

- easy access;
- little or no regulation, censorship, or other forms of government control;
- potentially huge audiences spread throughout the world;
- anonymity of communication;
- fast flow of information;
- interactive communication;
- inexpensive development and maintenance of a web presence; and
- a multimedia environment (the ability to combine text, graphics, audio, and video and to allow users to download films, songs, books, posters, and so forth).

Al Qaeda is using the Internet for various purposes, targeting various audiences. Our studies have identified at least eight different uses that can be grouped into two categories: communicative and operational uses. Let us explain and illustrate some of these al Qaeda uses of the Net.

The Communicative Uses

From the communicative perspective, terrorism has often been conceptualized as a form of psychological warfare, and certainly al Qaeda has sought to wage such a campaign through the Internet. For instance, al Qaeda uses the Internet to spread disinformation, to deliver threats intended to instill fear and helplessness, and to disseminate horrific images of recent actions. The Internet—an uncensored medium that carries stories, pictures, threats, or messages regardless of their validity or potential impact—is peculiarly well suited to allowing even a small group to amplify its message and exaggerate its importance and the threat it poses. Since September 11, 2001, al Qaeda has festooned its websites with a string of announcements of an impending "large attack" on U.S. targets. These warnings have received considerable media coverage, which has helped to generate a widespread sense of dread and insecurity among audiences throughout the world and especially within the United States. Interestingly, al Qaeda has consistently claimed on its websites that the destruction of the World Trade Centre has inflicted psychological damage, as well as concrete damage, on the U.S. economy.

Another popular communicative use of the Net is for publicity and propaganda. Until the advent of the Internet, terrorists' hopes of winning publicity for their causes and activities depended on attracting the attention of television, radio, or the print media. The fact that terrorists themselves have direct control over the content of their websites offers further opportunities to shape how they are perceived by different target audiences and to manipulate their image and the image of their enemies. Thus, the most visible part of al Qaeda's online presence involves the spread of propaganda. For its online propaganda al Qaeda is using its media production branch, called As-Sahab Foundation for Islamic Media Publication (As-Sahab means "The Cloud" in Arabic). This organization uses modern technology to produce its video statements to the world, using semi-professional hardware. In addition to being released in Arabic, some published videos come with English or other language subtitles, while more recent productions include videos in English and German. Al Qaeda is also operating online radio and television broadcasting and an additional online production facility—the Global Islamic Media Group (GIMF), an al Qaeda mouthpiece group. Many terrorist groups, among them Hamas and al Qaeda, have undergone a transformation from strictly hierarchical organizations with designated leaders to affiliations of semi-independent cells that have no single commanding hierarchy.

Through the use of the Internet, these loosely interconnected groups are able to maintain contact with one another—and with members of other terrorist groups. The Internet connects not only members of the same terrorist organizations but also members of different groups. For instance, dozens of sites exist that express support for terrorism conducted in the name of jihad. These sites and related forums permit terrorists in places such as Chechnya, Palestine, Indonesia, Afghanistan, Turkey, Iraq, Malaysia, the Philippines, and Lebanon to exchange not only ideas and suggestions but also practical information about how to build bombs, establish terror cells, and carry out attacks. Thus, al Qaeda has became an online "terrorist Internet Service Provider" linking together various elements of the worldwide Jihadist communities. To pursue this objective, bin Laden and his deputy Ayman al Zawahiri set up a unique structure whose essence was to provide a global virtual network linking together thousands of disparate human, financial, military, intellectual and technical resources. Thus al Qaeda became "the Jihad's Franchise", using the Net to link terrorist groups that range from Algeria's "Groupe Islamique Armé" (later becoming GSPC) to Pakistan's "Jaish Muhammad", the Chechen rebels, the Iraqi insurgents or the al Qaeda cells in Lebanon or Indonesia.

Al Qaeda's Cyber-Propaganda

Al Qaeda's propaganda is reacting to every major event, attempting to benefit from disasters or scandals. Even the blackout in the Northeast and Midwest of the United States in the summer of 2003 was used by al Qaeda's communications: Al Qaeda's Abu Hafs Brigades posted online their announcement claiming responsibility for "Operation Quick Lightning in the Land of the Tyrant of this Generation," referring to the blackout. This was the third communiqué by this group: In previous postings they accepted responsibility for the downing of an airplane in Kenya and for the bombing of the Jakarta Marriott Hotel on August 5, 2003. The new communiqué assured readers that the operation "was carried out on the orders of Osama bin Laden to hit the pillars of the U.S. economy" as "a realization of bin Laden's promise to offer the Iraqi people a present." The included text warned, "Let the criminal Bush and his gang know that the punishment is the result of the action, the soldiers of God cut the power on these cities, they darkened the lives of the Americans as these criminals blackened the lives of the Muslim people in Iraq, Afghanistan and Palestine. The Americans lived a black day they will never forget. They lived a day of terror and fear... a state of chaos and confusion where looting and pillaging rampaged the cities, just like the capital of the caliphate Baghdad, and Afghanistan and Palestine were. Let the American people take a sip from the same glass."

Another online channel used to promote the ideological legitimacy of global jihad is the Web site of al Qaeda's Centre for Islamic Studies and Research. This Web site has published the bimonthly virtual magazine *Sawt al-Jihad*, or *The Voice of Jihad*. The new magazine focuses on the use of violence as jihad's only way. The "editorial" by Sheikh Naser al-Najdi entitled "Belief First: They are the Heretics, the Blood of Each of Them Is the Blood of a Dog," calls for the killing of every American: "My fighting brother, kill the heretic; kill whoever's blood is the blood of a dog; kill those that Almighty Allah has ordered you to kill … Bush son of Bush … a dog son of a dog … his blood is that of a dog … Shut your mouth and speak with your other mouth—the mouth of the defender against his attacker. Rhetoric might cause retreat."

Al Qaeda is also targeting women on the Net and attempts to recruit women for terrorist attacks. One of the articles posted on al Qaeda's website, entitled "Umm Hamza, an Example for the Woman Holy Warrior," tells the story of a female martyr, the late Umm Hamza, as told by her husband: "Umm Hamza and Martyrdom: Umm Hamza was very happy whenever she heard about a martyrdom operation carried out by a woman, whether it was in Palestine or Chechnya. She used to cry because she wanted a martyrdom operation against the Christians in the Arabian Peninsula." The article also carries a copy of a letter handwritten by Umm Hamza shortly before her death. On August 26, 2004, al Qaeda launched its online women's magazine called Al- Khansa, named after an early Islamic poetess who wrote eulogies for Muslims who died while fighting the "infidels". The Web site also gives advice on raising children to carry on the Jihad, how to provide first aid for a family member injured in combat and descriptions of physical training women need to prepare themselves for fighting. The main goal of the magazine seems to be teaching women married to Islamists how to support their husbands in their violent war against the non-Muslim world. One of its first articles reads: "The blood of our husbands and the body parts of our children are our sacrificial offering."

THE EMERGING THREAT OF INTERNET BOTS

Network intrusions, data theft using Trojan horses, viruses and worms are among the threats security experts worry about on a regular basis. However, something more dangerous is emerging. Botnets, with their proliferation, sophistication and criminal use are emerging as the number one security threat. The recent arrest of 20-year old Californian man who made $60,000 by selling access to botnets to spammers and hackers is evidence of the growing menace.

A bot is a malicious software programme that invades computer so that it can covertly be controlled by a remote attacker. A bot is seeded by attackers through worms, viruses or other means to exploit desktop and server vulnerabilities. They are then herded into botnets, which can then be controlled from a central command point that can force zombie machines to work together to perform any issued task. Botnets are evolving and getting nastier. Previously, they were controlled exclusively through Internet Relay Chat (IRC) channels, but are now increasingly being manipulated through other means, such as Web, instant messaging or peer-to-peer systems.

Moreover, bots are using rootkits to conceal itself from the user of the machine. "Kernel level rootkits are extremely dangerous as they conceal their malicious code and cannot be removed by most anti-virus or antispyware programmes," says Martin Overton, security specialist at IBM Global Service. "The state of bot technology has reached the point that the state of Web technology has," says Peter Tipett, CTO at Cybertrust, whose security experts found more than 12,000 people contributing to bots or renting out botnets. "Instead of fighting with each other, these guys are working together and posting their code. We are getting a rich set of commands and capabilities used by the bad guys." Apart from evolving as sophisticated security threats, their presence is growing exponentially. Network-security experts identify and shut down botnets with 10 to 100 compromised hosts several times a day. Crackdowns on large botnets with 10,000 or more hosts are rarer, but they still occur weekly, said Johannes Ullrich, chief technology officer for the Internet Storm Center, which detects, analyses, and disseminates information about Internet-related security problems. "Security investigators have even found one botnet of 100,000 computers," Ulrich noted. Research conducted by Symantec found that on average more than 60,000 botnets were activated each day in the first half of this year. They also noted that this is an increase of more than 140 per cent from the previous year's semi-annual count. The following parts discuss how hackers profile and select their victims, attack techniques and their criminal usage and defences home users and system administrators can undertake to mitigate the risk of these attacks.

Profiling and Target Selection

Hackers are diligently profiling hosts and choosing targets that can provide them with longest survivability and carry out large scale attacks, and prevent their detection:

- *High Bandwidth*: One of the most sought after hosts are the machines connected to the Internet using high-bandwidth broadband. This can provide an attacker with an enormous cumulative bandwidth to carry out large scale DDoS attacks on target severs.
- *Availability*: Hosts with broadband connection are always connected to Internet and thus are the most sought after targets. This ensures hackers can carry out attacks round the clock without depending on whims of the users with dial-up connection which may connect to Internet at irregular intervals.

Low User Awareness and Monitoring Capability

Attackers prefer hosts where users have low security awareness and do not have access control mechanism like firewalls installed on their computers. The absence of such defences along with un-patched operating systems create ideal victims for hackers to break into and then install and maintain bots over a long period of time without being identified or traced.

Location

One of the prime goals of these cyber-criminals is to avoid detection after they commit crimes. They achieve this by selecting hosts that are geographically far away from their location. This makes very difficult for law enforcement officers to detect bots back to hackers. Also international prosecution being time consuming, expensive and non-standardised process that varies for each country, unfortunately ends up helping these cyber-criminals to go Scot-free. The typical profile that fits the criteria is that of residential broadband connection that has low or no access control mechanism or university subnets connected to Internet with minimal monitoring, high bandwidth with high availability.

Attack Techniques

Bots generally employ one of several attack methods, but sometimes use multiple techniques to create a network of compromised computers. Some of these approaches are quite sophisticated, such as Phatbot, which can generate a new encryption for itself each time it infects a new system. This makes it difficult for the software to find a common code signature for and thus recognise Phatbot. Director of malicious code for Security Consultancy iDefence, Phatbot has successfully evaded detection by mutating itself from spyware to launch vitriolic DDoS attacks on compromised networks. The following are some of the ways that attackers use to create networks of bots for themselves.

Chat

IRC is the most common used technique, including those in the large Phatbot/Agobot and Sdbot/Robot families as a way to communicate and receive commands from hackers. IRC has a built in mechanism for multicast capabilities which let attackers quickly send commands to all parts of a botnet without writing new code for the bot.

Peer-to-Peer

Many bots take advantage of peer-to-peer communication to infect computers with vulnerabilities. They connect to open-source file sharing technology such as Gnutella and work with the WASTE file-sharing protocol.

WASTE uses a distributed directory rather than a central server which lets bots easily find each other and communicate with one another. They can thus exchange hacker commands or other attack-related information among themselves. An attacker can initiate the process by serving as a peer in P2P network sending commands to one bot, which can then pass them onto the others. Thus, hackers don't have to communicate to bots via IRC multicasting. Decentralised-based bot systems are harder for security officials to trace or shutdown than systems using a single IRC source.

E-mail Attachments/Worms

Many hackers use methods such as e-mail attachments or worms to infect computers. Bots don't replicate or spread on their own, but they can use the worms' functionality to do so. In fact, hackers can spread bots more quickly with worms than with other methods. In addition, Botnets can spread worms faster than worms can spread on their own. The Symantec Security Response team said 2004's Witty worm, which infected and crashed tens of thousands of servers, was probably launched by a botnet. "We saw Witty break out more or less at the same time from a hundred or more machines. The machines were all over the world but they had something in common: they were on our bot list of compromised computers," he noted.

Criminal Use of Bots and Botnets

Bots can serve several purposes both legitimate and illegitimate. One legitimate purpose is to support the operation of IRC channels by conferring special administrative privileges or designated users. However, most of the common uses are criminally motivated for monetary gains or for destructive purposes.

Distributed Denial-of-Service Attacks

A DDoS attack is an attack on a computer system that causes a loss of service to users, typically the loss of network connectivity and services by consuming of the bandwidth of the victim network or overloading the computational resources of the victim's system. Most commonly implemented and often used are TCP SYN and UDP flood attacks. One of the most common uses of DDoS attacks is to wrest control of an IRC channel from its founder and founder's delegates. To take over an IRC channel, attackers conduct a DoS attack against one or more of the network's servers. If they can succeed in downing a server they can split the network into two or more disconnected segments.

If in a given segment there are no users joined to a particular channel of interest, the attacker can join that channel and seize the founder's privileges. Apart from the role in taking over IRC channels, attackers can launch successful DDoS attack against Internet sites. Let us assume if a given botnet has around 15,000 compromised hosts and has an associated bandwidth of 56kbps, a simultaneous attack by the entire botnet would direct almost 850 Mbps at its target – enough to cripple almost all e-commerce sites. These estimates are conservative because most of these compromised machines have cable modem and DSL hosts.

Moreover, because bots are widely distributed within the IP address space, filtering or blocking such DDoS attacks is not easy. At best, it requires cooperation between the target and multiple service providers. DDoS is not just limited to web servers; virtually any service available on the Internet can be a target of such an attack. Higher-level protocols can be used to increase the load even more effectively by using very specific attacks, such as running exhaustive search queries on the victim's web site. Recursive HTTP flooding means that the bots start from a given HTTP link and follow all links on the provided web site in a recursive way. This is also called spidering. Further research also showed that botnets are used to run commercial DDoS attacks against competing corporations. Jay R. Echouafni and Joshua Schictel, alias EMP, ran botnets to send spam and carry out paid DDoS attacks to take a competitor's web site down. Echouafni was indicted on August 25, 2004 on multiple charges of conspiracy and causing damage to protected computers.

Spamming

Some bots enable SOCKS v4/v5 proxy – a generic proxy protocol for TCP/ IPbased networking protocol on a compromised machine which allows them to launch spam attacks. Using bots and thousands of zombies (compromised machines) attackers can send massive amounts of bulk e-mails. These bots can also add special functionality to harvest e-mail-addresses. Harvested e-mail addresses help them to send phishing mail which appears to victims to come from legitimate sources.

Sniffing Traffic

Bots can be used as a packet sniffer to watch for interesting clear-text data passing by compromised machine. The sniffers are mostly used to retrieve sensitive information like usernames and passwords. They can also provide information about other Internet bots if it has been compromised more than once. This allows one to "steal" another's botnet.

Keylogging

If the compromised machine uses encrypted communication channels, then just sniffing the network packets on the victim's computer is useless since, the appropriate key to decrypt the packets is missing. But most bots also offer features to help in this situation. With the help of a keylogger it is very easy for an attacker to retrieve sensitive information. An implemented filtering mechanism further helps in stealing secret data. If the keylogger runs on thousands of compromised machines in parallel, it is easy to imagine how quickly PayPal accounts are harvested.

Spreading New Malware

In most cases, botnets are used to spread new bots. This is very easy since, all bots implement mechanisms to download and execute a file via HTTP or FTP. But spreading an e-mail virus using a botnet is also attractive. A botnet with 10,000 hosts which acts as the starting base for a mail virus allows very fast spreading and thus causes more harm.

The Witty worm, which attacked the ICO protocol parsing implementation in Internet Security System (ISS) products is suspected to have been initially launched by a botnet due to the fact that the attacking hosts were not running any ISS services.

Attacking IRC Networks

Botnets are also used for attacks against Internet Relay Chat (IRC) networks. Popular among attackers is especially the so called "clone attack." In this kind of attack, the controller orders each bot to connect a large number of clones to the victim IRC network. The victim is flooded by a service request from thousands of bots or thousands of channel-joins by these cloned bots. In this way, the victim IRC network is brought down - similar to a DDoS attack.

Manipulating Online Polls/Games

Online polls/games are getting more and more attention and it is rather easy to manipulate them with botnets. Since, every bot has a distinct IP address, every vote will have the same credibility as a vote cast by a real person. Online games can be manipulated in a similar way.

Mass Identity Theft

Often the combination of different functionality can be used for large scale identity theft, one of the fastest growing crimes on the Internet. Phishing e-mails that pretend to be legitimate ask their intended victims to go online and submit their private information. These fake e-mails are generated and sent by bots via their spamming mechanism. These same bots can also host multiple fake web sites pretending to be Ebay, PayPal, or a bank, and harvest personal information. In addition, keylogging and sniffing of traffic can also be used for identity theft.

Defending against Bots and Botnets

Defence against botnet infection and attack can be classified in three stages: prevention, detection and response. These stages need to be treated differently from home and system administrator perspective.

Prevention

The most common way for bots to compromise hosts is by exploiting the known vulnerabilities in the operating system or installed applications. Home users should follow guidelines regarding safe use by updating the installed OS and applications to defend their computers from being infected by attackers. If available, they should activate the auto-patch update facilities included in many popular operating systems and applications. Users should always install the latest version of antivirus software and practice safe handling of common web applications such as web browsers, e-mail, and instant messaging. In addition to this, every system administrator should be given training on online security and privacy issues. A high level of awareness on these issues is the best course in preventing malicious bots from infecting computers. They should implement access control measures and regularly monitor the generated logs on access control/peripheral devices.

Detection

Home users can use Microsoft Antispyware and Antivirus software, which are able to detect and respond to known types of bots, but are not effective for new bots on net. Online resources for scanning a system can also be employed, like the Symantec online security checker which will scan the system for commonly used Trojan ports. In addition to detection techniques used by home users, system administrators can employ network based tools to monitor perimeter defence devices to detect anomalies in Internet traffic. Slow network response, unexpectedly high volumes of traffic, traffic on unusual ports, and unusual system behaviour indicate the presence of malicious software including bots. Tools like network packet sniffers can be used not only to identify but also to isolate the subnet/machine which is generating malicious traffic. Analysis of the logs generated by network sniffer can also be used for finding IRC servers used, the names of the attacker's private channels and authentication keys.

Responses

As soon as the user realises that his/her computer has been compromised, the computer should be physically disconnected from the network. This denies access to the attackers and helps limit the potential damage both to user's own system and to other systems on the Internet. They should immediately update anti-virus software and check OS and application vendor sites for latest patches. If the user stores bank or credit card information on PC, the user should assume them to have been compromised and contact the appropriate organisation. Any passwords or secure data should be no more be used and changed at once. Apart from response measures suggested for the home user, system administrators should isolate infected subnets to prevent the spread of bots. They can asses the damage with the help of a network packet sniffer by identifying the number of machines infected by bots within a subnet. They can assist the incident response team by preserving data on the affected system and relevant system logs like firewalls, mail servers, IDS, DHCP servers, and proxies.

End

Growth of network models like IRC and easily available tools to edit bots has provided attackers, many whom have very limited knowledge of the underlying technology, the ability to create large botnets that are scalable and automated. Sophisticated bots are incorporating encryption and shape-shifting polymorphism in their code, and finding wider uses for rootkits, code that allows a permanent and undetectable presence of computer, to conceal itself from the user of the machine and creating nightmarish scenarios for security experts.

Moreover, hackers are also diligently picking victims with poorly implemented access control mechanisms, minimal monitoring to avoid detection, high bandwidth and software that is easy to infect and that allows for propagation. Bots are creating difficult challenges; nevertheless, users can fight back by proactively following best practices as recommended by the operating system and application vendors to prevent their machines from getting compromised in the first instance.

Some of the reactive methodologies outlined include using packet sniffers, monitoring firewalls and preserving critical logs to help incident response teams track down the attackers.

However, none of these, in isolation are effective. High level security awareness among users and diligent monitoring of the systems are the most effective and real defences against the growing menace of bots. Further, much research is being done at universities and institutions using honeynets to learn about attacker's tools, tactics, and motives, while developing ways to track these criminals. Government should encourage these research efforts as they may provide a future arsenal for law enforcement agencies against bots, the fastest emerging threat on net, which if left unchecked may jeopardise the safety of cyber world in coming years.

CRIME ON THE NET

The Internet is overwhelmingly a power for good. It provides cheap and easy access every moment of every day to a vast reservoir of information and entertainment and it is transforming the nature of commerce and Government. However, with approximately one billion users worldwide accessing almost 75 million Web sites, there is bound to be some offensive, and even illegal, use of the Net.

There is a dark side to the Internet. It would be naïve to deny it and alarmist to exaggerate it. The "British Journal of Criminology" (volume 38, Oxford University Press) contains an article called "Net Crime" by professional criminologist Mike Sutton and IT expert David Mann which claims that people are *"more likely to engage in criminal behaviour online than they are in the physical world"*.

Crime on the Net takes many forms including hacking, viruses, fraud, scams, money laundering, industrial espionage, prostitution, certain forms of gambling, drug use, drug smuggling, suicide assistance, defamatory allegations, cyber stalking, cyber terrorism, actual terrorism.

HACKING

Hacking can take several forms:

- Accessing–entering a network which is intended to be private
- Defacing – changing the content of another person's Web site
- Hijacking – redirecting elsewhere anyone trying to access a particular Web site
- Bombing – overwhelming a site with countless messages to slow down or even crash the server
- Denial of service – running a program which sends thousands of requests to a site simultaneously, frequently from more than one source, so that the relevant server slows down considerably or preferably (from the point of view of the hacker) crashes.

Some Internet users think that hacking is pretty harmless fun and even quite clever, but it can be a serious invasion of privacy and a significant threat to e-commerce. The Information Security Advisory Group estimates that world-wide there are now some 100,000 hackers or crackers (as they prefer to describe themselves). White-hat hackers test computer security at the request of organisations; black-hat hackers act privately to break into systems; and grey-hat hackers straddle both worlds. The hacking of personal computer terminals is actually quite easy because most people use Microsoft software which is notoriously open to abuse. Hackers have developed a program called "The Backdoor" which provides them access to systems running Microsoft Windows. At its most invasive, this would allow a hacker to switch on remotely a microphone or webcam associated with the PC being hacked.

Company computer systems are usually more difficult to hack because they employ protective arrangements such as firewalls. The most serious threats faced by organisations are from insiders or former insiders who have privileged information such as passwords. The most infamous group of hackers – operating since 1994 – is an American team which calls itself "The Cult of the Dead Cow" (CDC). Perhaps the best-known individual hacker is Kevin Mitnick who served five years for five fraud offences related to breaking into the computer systems of several multinational companies including Sub Microsystems and Motorola.

One of the most serious hacking incidents of recent times occurred in February 2000 when distributed 'denial of service' attacks brought down the sites of Yahoo!, CNN, eBay, Buy.com, Amazon, E*Trade, Datek & ZDNet. Subsequently the culprit was found to be a Canadian teenager living in Montreal who was only 15 at the time. He hacked into 75 computers in 52 different networks which he then used to attack 11 Internet sites. Mafiaboy–

as he was dubbed–was eventually sentenced to an eight-month sentence in a Canadian detention centre.

The biggest military computer hacker of all time is said to be a 36 year unemployed computer programmer from north London, Gary McKinnon, who used the handle Solo. He was arrested in March 2002 as a result of allegedly hacking into 92 computer networks operated by NASA and the US military (including two break-ins at the Pentagon).

He has been charged with eight counts of computer fraud and causing damage estimated at nearly $1M. While much hacking is done for so-called 'fun', other forms of hacking are done for more mercenary reasons, especially the obtaining and sale of credit card details. Where on-line trading is concerned, it is not the connection which is particularly insecure but the database which can be hacked into by those with specialist knowledge and criminal intent. Currently the credit card trading centre of the world is St Petersburg in Russia; the buyers tend to be from the Far East; and the victims live predominately in the USA and Europe.

In the UK, following attempts by a hacker to tap into its mailing system, Virgin Net was forced to require some 170,000 of its 800,000 customers to change their passwords. Working from his bedroom on a £700 PC, a Welsh teenager called Raphael Gray manged to hack e-commerce sites to obtain credit card details of some 25,000 Internet shoppers before he was apprehended. In the US, CD Universe refused to pay the $100,000 blackmail demand of a hacker – thought to be from Eastern Europe – who had obtained credit card details of 300,000 of the company's customers, so the hacker posted 25,000 credit card files on the Internet and claimed to have used the details already to obtain money. Another US-based company which has been threatened by a hacker was Bloomberg. The company pretended to be willing to pay the hacker – who was based in Kazakhstan – and arranged a meeting in London where two individuals were arrested.

Western Union closed its web site for five days in September 2001 after a security breach saw hackers access 15,000 records containing credit and debit card details. In February 2003, a hacker gained access to the credit card details of more than 8M Mastercard, Visa, American Express and Discover holders in the US by gaining access to the systems of an undisclosed third party company which processes retailers' payments.

Types of Attacks by Hackers

Hacker is computer expert who uses his knowledge to gain unauthorized access to the computer network. He's not any person who intends to break through the system but also includes one who has no intent to damage the system but intends to learn more by using one's computer. Information

Technology Act 2000 doesn't make hacking per se an offence but looks into factor of mens rea. Crackers on other hand use the information cause disruption to the network for personal and political motives. Hacking by an insider or an employee is quite prominent in present date. Section 66 (b) of the Information Technology Act 2000, provides punishment of imprisonment for the term of 3 years and fine which may extent to two lakhs rupees, or with both

Banks and other financial institutions are threatened by the terrorist groups to use their sensitive information resulting in heavy loss and in turn ask for ransom amount from them. There are various methods used by hackers to gain unauthorised access to the computers apart from use of viruses like Trojans and worms etc.

Therefore if anyone secures access to any computer without the permission of the owner shall be liable to pay damages of one crore rupees under Information Technology Act, 2000. Computer system here means a device including input and output support devices and systems which are capable of performing logical, arithmetical, data storage and retrieval, communication control and other functions but excludes calculators. Unauthorised access under Section 43 of the Information Technology Act 2000 is punishable regardless of the intention or purpose for which unauthorised access to the computer system was made. Owner needn't prove the facto of loss, but the fact of it been used without his authorisation. Case of United States v. Rice would be important in this regard where defendant on the request of his friend (who was been under investigation by IRS officer) tried to find the status of his friend's case by using officer's computer without his consent. Though it didn't cause any damage/loss to the plaintiff (officer) but was convicted by the Jury for accessing the computer system of a Government without his authority and his conviction was later on confirmed. Even if one provides any assistance to the other to gain any unauthorised access to the computer he shall be liable to pay damages by way of compensation of Rupees 1 crore. Does turning on the computer leads to unauthorized access? The mens rea under section 1 of the Computer misuse Act, 1990 comprises of two elements there must be an intent to secure an access to any programme or data held in any computer, and the person must know that he intends to secure an unauthorized access. e.g. When defendants went to his former employee to purchase certain equipments and the sales person was not looking he was alleged to have keyed in certain commands to the computerized till granting himself substantial discount. Though section 1 (1) (a) requires "that second computer must be involved" but the judiciary in the case of R v. Sean Cropp, believed that the Parliament would have intended to restrict the offence even if single computer system was involved.

(A) Computer Viruses: Viruses are used by Hackers to infect the user's computer and damage data saved on the computer by use of "payload" in viruses which carries damaging code. Person would be liable under I.T Act only when the consent of the owner is not taken before inserting virus in his system. The contradiction here is that though certain viruses causes temporary interruption by showing messages on the screen of the user but still it's not punishable under Information Technology Act 2000 as it doesn't cause tangible damage. But, it must be made punishable as it would fall under the ambit of 'unauthorised access' though doesn't cause any damage. Harmless viruses would also fall under the expression used in the provision "to unsurp the normal operation of the computer, system or network". This ambiguity needs reconsideration.

(B) Phishing: By using e-mail messages which completely resembles the original mail messages of customers, hackers can ask for verification of certain information, like account numbers or passwords etc. here customer might not have knowledge that the e-mail messages are deceiving and would fail to identify the originality of the messages, this results in huge financial loss when the hackers use that information for fraudulent acts like withdrawing money from customers account without him having knowledge of it

(C) Spoofing: This is carried on by use of deceiving Websites or e-mails. These sources mimic the original websites so well by use of logos, names, graphics and even the code of real bank's site.

(D) Phone Phishing: Is done by use of in-voice messages by the hackers where the customers are asked to reveal their account identification, and passwords to file a complaint for any problems regarding their accounts with banks etc.

(E) Internet Pharming: Hacker here aims at redirecting the website used by the customer to another bogus website by hijacking the victim's DNS server (they are computers responsible for resolving internet names into real addresses–"signposts of internet), and changing his I.P address to fake website by manipulating DNS server. This redirects user's original website to a false misleading website to gain unauthorised information.

(F) Risk Posed On Banks And Other Institutions: Wire transfer is the way of transferring money from one account another or transferring cash at cash office. This is most convenient way of transfer of cash by customers and money laundering by cyber terrorists. There are many guidelines issued by Reserve Bank of India (RBI) in this regard, one of which is KYC (Know Your Customer) norms of 2002. Main objective of which is to:

(1) Ensure appropriate customer identification, and

(2) Monitor the transaction of suspicious nature and report it to appropriate authority every day bases.

(G) Publishing Pornographic Material In Electronic Form: Section 67 of the Information Technology Act, 2000 in parallel to Section 292 of Indian Penal Code, 1860 makes publication and transmission of any material in electronic that's lascivious or appeals to the prurient interest a crime, and punishable with imprisonment which may extend to 5 years and fine of 1 lakh rupees and subsequent offence with an imprisonment extending to 10 years and fine of 2 lakhs.

Various tests were laid down gradually in course of time to determine the actual crime in case of obscene material published in electronic form on net. Hicklin test was adopted in America in the case of Regina v. Hicklin wherein it was held that "if the material has tendency is to deprive and corrupt those whose minds are open to such immoral influences, and into whose hands a publication of this sort may fall".

In Indian scenario the case of Ranjeet D. Udeshi v. State of Maharashtra the Supreme Court admitted that Indian Penal Code doesn't define obscenity though it provides punishment for publication of obscene matter. There's very thin line existing between a material which could be called obscene and the one which is artistic. Court even stressed on need to maintain balance between fundamental right of freedom of speech and expression and public decency and morality. If matter is likely to deprave and corrupt those minds which are open to influence to whim the material is likely to fall. Where both obscenity and artistic matter is so mixed up that obscenity falls into shadow as its insignificant then obscenity may be overlooked.

In the case of Miller v. California it was held that local community standard must be applied at the time of determination of the offence. As it can traverse in many jurisdictions and can be accessed in any part of the globe. So wherever the material can be accessed the community standards of that country would be applicable to determine the offence of publication of obscene material posted in electronic form. Though knowledge of obscenity under Information Technology Act 2000 and Indian Penal Code may be taken as mitigating factor but doesn't take the case out of the provision.

Section 72 of Information Technology Act, 2000 provides punishment for an unauthorised access or, disclosure of that information to third person punishable with an imprisonment upto 2 years or fine which may extend to 1 lakh rupees or with both. English courts have also dealt with an issue as to what activities would constitute crime under existing legislation, in the case of R. v. Fellows and Arnold it was held that the legislation before the 1994 amendment would also enable computer data to be considered a 'copy of an indecent photograph' and making images available for downloading from the website would constitute material being 'distributed or shown'. Statute is wide enough to deal with the use of computer technology.

(H) Investment Newsletter: We usually get newsletter providing us free information recommending that investment in which field would be profitable. These may sometimes be a fraud and may cause us huge loss if relied upon. False information can be spread by this method about any company and can cause huge inconvenience or loss through junk mails online.

(I) Credit Card Fraud: Huge loss may cause to the victim due to this kind of fraud. This is done by publishing false digital signatures. Most of the people lose credit cards on the way of delivery to the recipient or its damaged or defective, misrepresented etc.

Viruses

Viruses, in the broadest sense, come in three forms:

- Virus: This is a code that attaches itself to a program in a computer and then reproduces itself. It can erase files or lock up a system.
- Worm: This is similar to a virus but does not attach itself to files or programs in a computer. This leaves it free to spread through a network on its own.
- Trojan horse: This is a program that performs malicious actions while pretending to do something else. It is similar to a virus but does not try to reproduce itself.

The first PC virus–the Pakistani Brain virus–appeared in 1986. According to virus experts, as many as 200 new viruses are created every month. According to MessageLabs, in 2000 one in every 790 e-mails contained a virus; in 2001, the figure was one in every 380; and, in 2002, it was one in every 212. In 2002, the top three viruses were Klez.H, Yaha.e and Bugbear. The most prolific virus ever is Klez and MessageLabs estimates that one in every 300 e-mails sent today contains a variation of the Klez virus. However, it is believed that there are around 20,000 different computer viruses in existence, many of them placed on the Internet deliberately to cause confusion or damage.

The threat of new, self-propagating viruses is growing. Melissa, ExploreZip and Ska-Happy99 forward themselves by hijacking a computer's e-mail program which gives them the potential to attack globally in days. The Melissa virus – originated by David Smith in March 1999 and named after one of his favourite strippers – is believed to have cost businesses world-wide an estimated $385 million in damage to their systems. It led to Smith receiving 20 months in prison and a $5,000 fine.

The infamous Love Bug virus of 2000 infected 45 million people in a single day and went on to cause a staggering $8.75 billion in damage. In 2001, we had the SirCam virus which, although more irritating than dangerous, still caused businesses $1.15 billion in damage.

So far, the worst month for viruses has been August 2003. First, Blaster.B (also known as MSBlast) emerged, crashing systems such as that of Air Canada (a couple of weeks later, the FBI arrested an 18 year old American for creating the virus). Then SoBig F arrived which was so prolific that, at its peak, it affected one in every 15 e-mails across the world. Among many systems affected was that of the American railway network which as a result suffered widespread delays. Ironically not all virus warnings relate to actual viruses because, for some reason, there are many hoaxes. Therefore, before passing on a warning of a virus, it is always sensible to check first if the virus is a hoax or not.

Pirating

Digital technology makes it very easy to copy perfectly creative products such as music or films and the Internet provides a free and almost anonymous means of transmitting or exchanging this pirated material around the world. The favoured means of making such material available is peer-to-peer file-sharing applications. Originally the main problem was with music in the form of MP3 files exchanged through sites such as Napster. Now, with the growing availability of broadband connections, the provision of full-length movies can take place in an hour or two through sites such as Movie88.com based in Taiwan. On the music front, some artists are now trying to make it impossible to play new CDs on a PC and therefore make them hard to copy. The Celine Dion CD "A New Day Has Come" has on it the label "Will not play on PC/MAC". On the film front, the Motion Picture Association of America (MPAA) has moved to close sites like Movies88.com.

Illegal Trading

Illegal trading on the Internet uses chatrooms, bulletin boards, newsgroups and Web sites. The arrangements can take various forms:

- A manufacturer with a legitimate order to produce goods for a well-known company can deliberately over-run the volume of the order and sell the excessive items at lower prices in other markets.
- The same goods–such as drugs or drinks–may be sold in different markets at different prices in a process known as 'parallel trading'.

- There is frequently straightforward counterfeiting of well-known brand goods, with 40% of cigarettes and 10% of cosmetics and perfumes sold world-wide believed to be fake.

Brand Intelligence is an Edinburgh-based company employed by businesses to see how their names or brands are being used or abused online. The company uses 'deep searching' techniques to track every part of the Internet except e-mail and instant messenging. Investigations can be complex: goods may be shipped several times before they reach their destination, Web sites offering such goods may be moved frequently, sites may be hidden from search engines using 'robot.txt' files, payments may be to banks in other countries. So it is a technological battle between the illegal traders and the brand owners.

FRAUD ON NET

One of the most common types of fraud on the Internet is designed to trick users of certain sites–notably banks and building socities–into disclosing their passwords or other confidential information needed to access their accounts. A common means of doing this is to e-mail customers advising that it is necesary to check or confirm their password by clicking onto a realistic but fake website and then inputting the confidential information. It is then possible for money to be fraudulently transferred from the individual's account.

In the Autumn of 2003, this type of fraud was perpetrated against UK customers of Barclays, Nat West, Lloyds TSB, Citibank, Halifax and Nationwide. In fact, no bank of financial institution would ever ask a customer to disclose confidential information in this way.

Another type of fraud – which fortunately is not common because of the expert knowledge required – is called 'packet reading'. This involves hackers locating patterns of data, such as credit card digits, intercepting and copying them.

Another practice – known as 'cramming' – involves charging a customer for extra services on top of a service for which they have signed up. A well-known case of this kind involved the company Xpics which ran a network that included a variety of pornography sites and offered a free trial membership on the provision of credit card details allegedly to prove that the customer was over 18. Cancelling the subscription then proved horrendously difficult.

A much more common type of fraud relates to on-line auction trading. This involves a registered seller on an established Web site building up a reputation, then listing for auction items which he does not possess, and finally vanishing with the winning bidders' payments. In August 2000, it was reported that US authorities were investigating a credit card fraud at Flooz.com, one of the best known purveyors of an on-line currency. It was believed that the company had been defrauded of some $300,000 by a ring of credit card thieves operating out of Russia and other parts of Eastern Europe.

In the United States – where currently most online shopping takes place – the National Consumers League runs an Internet Fraud Watch which in 1999 recorded a 38% increase in complaints, with a total consumer loss of $3.2 million. The number one Internet fraud – representing 87% of all reports – was online auction sales, followed by non-action sales of general merchandise, Internet access services, computer equipment/software, and work-at-home plans.

PricewaterhouseCoopers believes that fraudulent e-commerce transactions make up half the annual fraud total in the United States. Concern by banks about online fraud is leading to work on improved security for credit card transactions. Particular attention is being devoted to combating the use of programs, which can be downloaded from the Internet, that can make 'valid' credit card numbers from an algorithm. If these numbers are then used for small virtual purchases, such as access to pornographic sites, there is a fair chance that the transactions will not be checked. Currently the safest sites for e-commerce transactions are those that use Secure Sockets Layer (SSL). In the next couple of years, extra security will come from "smart" cards with microchips embedded in them.

CYBERTERRORISM TODAY AND TOMORROW

It seems fair to say that the current threat posed by cyberterrorism has been exaggerated. No single instance of cyberterrorism has yet been recorded; U.S. defence and intelligence computer systems are air-gapped and thus isolated from the Internet; the systems run by private companies are more vulnerable to attack but also more resilient than is often supposed; the vast majority of cyberattacks are launched by hackers with few, if any, political goals and no desire to cause the mayhem and carnage of which terrorists dream. So, then, why has so much concern been expressed over a relatively minor threat?

The reasons are many. First, as Denning has observed, "cyberterrorism and cyberattacks are sexy right now.... [Cyberterrorism is] novel, original, it captures people's imagination." Second, the mass media frequently fail to distinguish between hacking and cyberterrorism and exaggerate the threat of the latter by reasoning from false analogies such as the following: "If a sixteen-year-old could do this, then what could a well-funded terrorist group do?" Ignorance is a third factor. Green argues that cyberterrorism merges two spheres—terrorism and technology—that many people, including most lawmakers and senior administration officials, do not fully understand and therefore tend to fear. Moreover, some groups are eager to exploit this ignorance. Numerous technology companies, still reeling from the collapse of the high-tech bubble, have sought to attract federal research grants by recasting themselves as innovators in computer security and thus vital contributors to national security. Law enforcement and security consultants are likewise highly motivated to have us believe that the threat to our nation's security is severe. A fourth reason is that some politicians, whether out of genuine conviction or out of a desire to stoke public anxiety about terrorism in order to advance their own agendas, have played the role of prophets of doom. And a fifth factor is ambiguity about the very meaning of "cyberterrorism," which has confused the public and given rise to countless myths.

Verton argues that "al Qaeda [has] shown itself to have an incessant appetite for modern technology" and provides numerous citations from bin Laden and other al Qaeda leaders to show their recognition of this new cyberweapon. In the wake of the 9/11 attacks, bin Laden reportedly gave a statement to an editor of an Arab newspaper claiming that "hundreds of Muslim scientists were with him who would use their knowledge... ranging from computers to electronics against the infidels." Sheikh Omar Bakri Muhammad, a supporter of bin Laden and often the conduit for his messages to the Western world, declared in an interview with Verton, "I would advise those who doubt al Qaeda's interest in cyber-weapons to take Osama bin Laden very seriously. The third letter from Osama bin Laden... was clearly addressing using the technology in order to destroy the economy of the capitalist states."

"While bin Laden may have his finger on the trigger, his grandchildren may have their fingers on the computer mouse," remarked Frank Cilluffo of the Office of Homeland Security in a statement that has been widely cited. Future terrorists may indeed see greater potential for cyberterrorism than do the terrorists of today. Furthermore, as Denning argues, the next generation of terrorists is now growing up in a digital world, one in which hacking tools are sure to become more powerful, simpler to use, and easier to access. Cyberterrorism may also become more attractive as the real and virtual worlds become more closely coupled. For instance, a terrorist group might simultaneously explode a bomb at a train station and launch a cyberattack on the communications infrastructure, thus magnifying the impact of the event. Unless these systems are carefully secured, conducting an online operation that physically harms someone may be as easy tomorrow as penetrating a website is today.

Paradoxically, success in the "war on terror" is likely to make terrorists turn increasingly to unconventional weapons such as cyberterrorism. The challenge before us is to assess what needs to be done to address this ambiguous but potential threat of cyberterrorism—but to do so without inflating its real significance and manipulating the fear it inspires. Denning and other terrorism experts conclude that, at least for now, hijacked vehicles, truck bombs, and biological weapons seem to pose a greater threat than does cyberterrorism. However, just as the events of 9/11 caught the world by surprise, so could a major cyberassault. The threat of cyberterrorism may be exaggerated and manipulated, but we can neither deny it nor dare to ignore it.

ASSESSING THE RISKS OF CYBER TERRORISM, CYBER WAR AND OTHER CYBER THREATS

Cyber-warfare conjures up images of information warriors unleashing vicious attacks against an unsuspecting opponent's computer networks, wreaking havoc and paralyzing nations. This a frightening scenario, but how likely is it to occur? What would the effects of a cyber attack be on a potential opponent?

Cyber attacks, network security and information pose complex problems that reach into new areas for national security and public policy. This paper looks at one set of issues – those related to cyber-terrorism and cyber attacks on critical infrastructure and their implications for national security. Cyber-terrorism is "the use of computer network tools to shut down critical national infrastructures (such as energy, transportation, government operations) or to coerce or intimidate a government or civilian population."

The premise of cyber terrorism is that as nations and critical infrastructure became more dependent on computer networks for their operation, new vulnerabilities are created – "a massive electronic Achilles' heel." A hostile nation or group could exploit these vulnerabilities to penetrate a poorly secured computer network and disrupt or even shut down critical functions.

Much of the literature on cyber-terrorism assumes that the vulnerability of computer networks and the vulnerability of critical infrastructures are the same, and that these vulnerabilities put national security at a significant risk. Given the newness of computer network technology and the rapidity with which it spread into economic activity, these assumptions are not surprising. A closer look at the relationships between computer networks and critical infrastructures, their vulnerability to attack, and the effect on national security, suggests that the assumption of vulnerability is wrong. A full reassessment is outside the scope of this paper, but a brief review suggests that while many computer networks remain very vulnerable to attack, few critical infrastructures are equally vulnerable. A reassessment of the cyber threat has four elements. First, we need to put cyber-warfare and cyber-terrorism in the historical context of attacks against infrastructure. Strategies that emphasize attacks on critical civil infrastructures have discussed for more than eighty years. Second, we need to examine cyber attacks against a backdrop of routine infrastructure failures.

There is extensive data on power outages, flight delays and communications disruptions that occur normally and the consequences of these routine failures can be used to gage the effect cyber-warfare and cyber-terrorism. Third, we need to measure the dependence of infrastructure on computer networks and the redundancy already present in these systems.

Finally, for the case of cyber-terrorism, we must consider the use of cyber-weapons in the context of the political goals and motivations of terrorists, and whether cyber-weapons are likely to achieve these goals. A preliminary review of these factors suggests that computer network vulnerabilities are an increasingly serious business problem but that their threat to national security is overstated. Modern industrial societies are more robust than they appear at first glance. Critical infrastructures, especially in large market economies, are more distributed, diverse, redundant and self-healing than a cursory assessment may suggest, rendering them less vulnerable to attack. In all cases, cyber attacks are less effective and less disruptive than physical attacks. Their only advantage is that they are cheaper and easier to carry out than a physical attack.

Infrastructure as Target

Cyber-terrorism is not the first time a new technology has been seized upon as creating a strategic vulnerability. While the match between theories of cyber-warfare and air power is not precise, a comparison of the two is useful. In reaction to the First World War, European strategists like Douhet and Trenchard argued that aerial bombing attacks against critical infrastructure well behind the front lines would disrupt and cripple an enemies' capacity to wage war. Their theories were put to the test by the U.S. Army and Royal Air Forces during World War II in strategic bombing campaigns aimed at destroying electrical power, transportation and manufacturing facilities. Much of the first tranche of literature on cyber attacks resembles in many ways (and owes an unspoken debt to) the early literature on strategic bombing.

A key document for understanding how attacks on infrastructure affect societies is the Strategic Bombing Survey conducted by the United State during and after World War II. During the war, Britain and America launched thousands of heavy bombers that dropped millions of tons of high explosives on Germany, seeking to cripple its infrastructure, destroy its industrial base and break the will of the population to continue the war. Early theorists of air warfare had predicted that such an onslaught would paralyze or cripple the target. What the survey found, however, is that industrial societies are impressively resilient. Industrial production actually increased for two years under the bombing and it was not until ground forces occupied Germany that resistance ceased:

As the air offensive gained in tempo, the Germans were unable to prevent the decline and eventual collapse of their economy. Nevertheless, the recuperative and defensive powers of Germany were immense; the speed and ingenuity with which they rebuilt and maintained essential war industries in operation clearly surpassed Allied expectations. Germany resorted to almost every means an ingenious people could devise to avoid the attacks upon her economy and to minimize their effects....

The mental reaction of the German people to air attack is significant. Under ruthless Nazi control, they showed surprising resistance to the terror and hardships of repeated air attack, to the destruction of their homes and belongings, and to the conditions under which they were reduced to live. Their morale, their belief in ultimate victory or satisfactory compromise, and their confidence in their leaders declined, but they continued to work efficiently as long as the physical means of production remained.... The U.S. found similar results from aerial bombardment during the Vietnam War. Counter-intuitively, the effect of aerial attack was often to harden and increase popular support for continued resistance. The advent of nuclear weapons (and perhaps large precision-guided munitions) gave air power the ability to disrupt civil infrastructures needed to achieve the visions of Douhet, Trenchard or Mitchell, but cyber attacks do not pose the same level of lethality.

One of the Strategic Bombing Survey's conclusions was that "The German experience showed that, whatever the target system, no indispensable industry was permanently put out of commission by a single attack. Persistent re-attack was necessary." However, cyber attacks are likely to be single attacks. Once a hacker has gained access and the damage done, the target usually responds quickly to close off the vulnerability that allowed that line of attack and to bring systems back on line. Cyber attackers would continually need to exploit new vulnerabilities and new tactics to ensure sustained disruption. Cyber attacks also seldom if ever produce physical damage that requires time-consuming repairs.

'Routine' Failure versus Cyber Attack

Critical infrastructure protection creates a new set of problems for national security. Different actors are involved. The focus is on civilian and commercial systems and services. Military force is less important. The scope of these new problems depends on how we define national security and how we set thresholds for acceptable damage. From a legal or public safety perspective, no country will accept even a single attack on infrastructure or interruption of services. If the goal is to prevent cyber-attacks from costing a single day of electric power or water service, we have set a very high standard for security. However, from a strategic military perspective, attacks that do not degrade national capabilities are not significant. From this perspective, if a cyber-attack does not cause damage that rises above the threshold of the routine disruptions that every economy experiences, it does not pose an immediate or significant risk to national security.

It is particularly important to consider that in the larger context of economic activity, water system failures, power outages, air traffic disruptions and other cyber-terror scenarios are routine events that do not affect national security. On a national level, where dozens or even hundreds of different systems provide critical infrastructure services, failure is a routine occurrence at the system or regional level, with service denied to customers for hours or days. Cyber-terrorists would need to attack multiple targets simultaneously for long periods of time to create terror, achieve strategic goals or to have any noticeable effect. For most of the critical infrastructure, multiple sustained attacks are not a feasible scenario for hackers, terrorist groups or nation states (particularly for nation states, where the risk of discovery of what would be universally seen as an act of war far outweigh the limited advantages gained from cyber attacks on infrastructure).

Weapons of Mass Annoyance

A detailed examination of some of the scenarios for attacks on critical infrastructures helps place cyber-attacks more accurately in a strategic or national security context. For example, dams used for water storage and for power generation are often cited as a likely target for cyber attack. The Washington Post recently wrote that unnamed "U.S. analysts" believe that "by disabling or taking command of the floodgates in a dam, for example, or of substations handling 300,000 volts of electric power, an intruder could use virtual tools to destroy real-world lives and property."

In the United States, the water supply infrastructure would be an elusive target for cyber attack. There are 54,064 separate water systems in the U.S. Of these, 3,769 water systems serve eighty one percent of the population and 353 systems served forty-four percent of the population. However, the uneven spread of diverse network technologies complicates the terrorists' task. Many of these water supply systems in the U.S., even in large cities, continue to rely on technologies not easily disrupted by network attacks. There have been cases in the U.S. when a community's water supply has been knocked out for days at a time (usually as a result of flooding), but these have produced neither terror nor paralysis. A cyber terrorist or cyber warrior would need to carry out a sustained attack that would simultaneously disrupt several hundred of these systems to gain any strategic benefit.

Assuming that a terrorist could find a vulnerability in a water supply system that would allow him to shut down one city's water for a brief period, this vulnerability could be exploited to increase the damage of a physical attack (by denying fire fighters access to water).

In general, a cyber attack that alone might pass unnoticed in the normal clutter of daily life could have useful multiplier effects if undertaken simultaneously with a physical attack. This sort of simultaneous combination of physical and cyber attacks might be the only way in which cyber weapons could be attractive to terrorists. The American Waterworks Association assessment of the terrorist threat to water supplies placed "physical destruction of the system's components to disrupt the supply of water" as the most likely source of infrastructure attack.

Comparing aerial and cyber attacks on hydroelectric dams helps provide a measure for cyber-threats. Early in World War II, the Royal Air Force mounted a daring attack on dams in the Ruhr, a chief source of electrical power for German industry. The raid was a success, the dams breached by bombs and, for a period of time, the electrical supply in the region was disrupted.

A comparable cyber attack occurred when a young hacker reportedly gained access to the computer controls for a dam in the U.S. Southwest, but did not disrupt service or cause physical damage.

In neither attack was the damage or the reduction in electrical power paralyzing. Of the two, the cyber attack was less effective in that it caused no physical damage and could be classed more as an annoyance than a threat. The aerial attack resulted in physical damage that needed to be repaired. The only advantage of a cyber attack is that it is less expensive - a teen-ager and a desktop computer rather than valuable aircrews and expensive aircraft.

Many analyses have cyber-terrorists shutting down the electrical power system. One of the better cyber security surveys found that power companies are a primary target for cyber attacks and that seventy percent of these companies had "suffered a severe attack" in the first six months of 2002. The U.S. electrical power grid is a desirable target, but it is a network of multiple, redundant systems that are used to routine system failure and disruption. The national electrical grid is a highly interconnected system of over 3,000 public and private utilities and cooperatives. These 3,000 electrical power providers use a variety of different information technologies to operate their controls for power generation and transmission. A hacker or even a large group of hackers would need to find vulnerabilities in multiple systems to significantly disrupt the power supply and even then, an attack might only disrupt service for a few hours.

The North American Electric Reliability Council, an industry group formed after the 1965 New York blackout, has been working with the Federal government since the 1980s to improve the security of the electrical system and to develop rapid responses to large outages. In Congressional testimony, NERC officials have said that in the last few years, neither viruses nor Distributed Denial of Service attacks against the U.S. electrical system have interrupted service. While industry sources can paint an over-optimistic picture at times, it remains true that falling trees have caused many electric system disruptions while cyber attacks have caused none. A risk assessment by the Information Assurance Task Force of the National Security Telecommunications Advisory Committee concluded "Physical destruction is still the greatest threat facing the electric power infrastructure. Compared to this, electronic intrusion represents an emerging, but still relatively minor, threat." The U.S. has already run a large-scale experiment on the effects of disrupting electrical power supplies, thanks to California's experience with 'deregulation' last year. California's efforts to de-regulate the electrical power market resulted in months of blackouts and rolling brownouts across the state. Deregulation was a more powerful 'attack' on the electrical infrastructure than anything a cyber-terrorist could mount. There was clearly economic cost to the California regulatory event, but it was not crippling nor did it strike terror into the hearts of Americans. Similarly, power outages across the country in 1999 affected millions of people and cost electrical power customers millions of dollars in lost business and productivity. These outages were the result of increased electricity use prompted by sustained high summer temperatures. In contrast to California's State government or hot weather, the number of blackouts in U.S. caused by hackers or cyber-terrorists remains zero.

Interference with national air traffic systems to disrupt flights, shut down air transport and endanger passenger and crews is another frequently cited cyber-threat. We are not yet at a stage where computer networks operate aircraft remotely, so it is not possible for a cyber-attacker to take over an aircraft. Aircraft still carry pilots who are trained to operate the plane in an emergency. Similarly, the Federal Aviation Authority does not depend solely on computer networks to manage air traffic, nor are its communications dependent on the Internet. The high level of human involvement in the control and decision making process for air traffic reduces the risk of any cyber attack. In a normal month storms, electrical failures and programming glitches all ensure a consistently high level of disruption in air traffic. Pilots and air traffic controllers are accustomed to unexpected disruptions and have adapted their practices to minimize the effect. Airlines and travelers are also accustomed to and expect a high degree of disruption in the system. In the United States, it is normal for 15,000 to 20,000 flights to be delayed or cancelled every month. A cyber attack that degraded the air traffic system would create delays and annoyance, but it would not pose a risk to national security.

The FAA has 90 major computer systems and nine different communications networks. These networks rely on elderly equipment and use proprietary software that make them difficult for outsiders to hack. This may explain why the few reported attacks have not affected air traffic. In one reported incident, a young hacker interrupting local phone service in a New England, cutting off a regional airport's control tower and the ability to turn on runway lights. Although the interruption lasted six hours, there were no accidents at the airport. In other cases, FAA headquarters computer networks have been penetrated, allowing hackers to make public unpublished information on airport passenger screening activities, and in another case, a hacker was able to enter an FAA mail server. None of these cases resulted in any disruption to flight. Ironically, modernization could actually increase FAA vulnerability if greater attention is not given to security.

A recent attack on the Internet illustrates the nature of vulnerabilities from cyber attack. For a one-hour period in October 2002, unknown parties launched a Distributed Denial of Service attack on the thirteen 'root servers' that form the basis of the domain names system that governs Internet addresses. Eight of the thirteen servers were forced off-line because of the attacks. The attack itself was invisible and without effect on Internet users. The attack on the DNS system did not noticeably degrade Internet performance. Most DNS data needed for the daily operation of the Internet is stored locally and updated daily. Very few requests require assistance from the root servers. Additionally, the presence of thirteen servers (of which five were not affected by the attack) gives a degree of redundancy that suggests that if there are vulnerabilities to the Internet, the DNS servers are not one of them. In contrast to the DNS attack, shortly after it occurred thousands of Internet customers in the western United States experienced serious delays when their service provider had routing problems due to programming errors. Unlike the attack, this DNS failure actually disrupted service, but it had no effect on national security.

While the Internet may have a few points of failure that offer the possibility for system-wide disruption, it was designed to be a robust, distributed communications network capable of continuing operations after a strategic nuclear exchange. Packet switching and Internet protocols were developed to allow communications to be maintained even when some nodes in the network were eliminated and the Internet itself was designed to automatically route around damage to allow for continued communications. Additionally, computer networks rely on a backbone of high capacity telecommunications systems that are relatively secure from cyber-attack. The introduction of new communications technologies also enhances survivability. Wireless and satellite communications also provide some redundancy for landline systems. Most industrial countries now have access to three or four different modes of communications, making the system considerably more robust than it was a decade ago. Increased use of ultra wideband and mesh radio networks will also increase redundancy and survivability against cyber attack in communications networks.

The 911 emergency response system, a specialized communications network that relies on local telephone service, is also a favorite target for theorists of cyber-terrorism, but like other infrastructures, it is a robust target. The U.S. for example, does not use a single 911 system in but instead has several thousand local systems using different technologies and procedures. No 911 system in a major city has been hacked. It might be possible to send a flood of email messages instructing people to call 911 for important information and thus overload the system (this was the technique used in the 1997 U.S. cyber exercise "Eligible Receiver"). This sort of technique usually works only once - but made in conjunction with a bombing or other physical attack they could act as a 'force multiplier' for a terrorist event.

Manufacturing and economic activity are increasingly dependent on computer networks, and cyber crime and industrial espionage are new dangers for economic activity. However, the evidence is mixed as to the vulnerability of manufacturing to cyber attack. A virus in 2000 infected 1,000 computers at Ford Motor Company. Ford received 140,000 contaminated e-mail messages in three hours before it shut down its network. E-mail service was disrupted for almost a week within the company. Yet, Ford reported, "the rogue program appears to have caused only limited permanent damage. None of its 114 factories stopped, according to the automaker. Computerized engineering blueprints and other technical data were unaffected. Ford was still able to post information for dealers and auto parts suppliers on Web sites that it uses for that purpose." Companies now report that the defensive measures they have taken meant that viruses that were exceptionally damaging when they first appeared are now only "nuisances."

Cyber attacks are often presented as a threat to military forces and the Internet has major implications for espionage and warfare. Information warfare covers a range of activities of which cyber attacks may be the least important. While information operations and information superiority have become critical elements in successful military operations, no nation has placed its military forces in a position where they are dependent on computer networks that are vulnerable to outside attack. This greatly limits the effectiveness of cyber weapons (code sent over computer networks). The many reports of military computer networks being hacked usually do not explain whether these networks are used for critical military functions. It is indicative, however, that despite regular reports of tens of thousands of network attacks every year on the Department of Defence, there has been no degradation of U.S. military capabilities.

For example, while there were many attack against U.S. military computer networks during operations in Kosovo, these attacks did not result in sorties being cancelled or in a single casualty. Similarly, a foreign power that used cyber-weapons to try to prevent a carrier battle group from leaving the U.S. would be unlikely to succeed. A recent attack by a British hacker neither compromised classified information nor disrupted military operations. A Rand study conducted for the U.S. Air Force on military operations and information vulnerabilities noted "while most of the current topical interests has focused on the newer, trendier threats to information systems, particularly computer hacking and associated disruption and manipulation...our analysis showed that some of the "old-fashioned" threats pose a greater danger...."

CYBER-CRIME AND LEGAL PROBLEMS OF USAGE NETWORK THE INTERNET

The most significant social changes during the last decades have occurred in the sphere of new social relations - informational. The essence of transfer from the industrial to informational society is the aggregate of processes related to automated processing, search, storage and transmission of increasing flow of information into all spheres of social life.

This has increased the need in legal regulation of relationship in the sphere telecommunication systems in order to speed up the processes of informatization of Ukrainian society and catching up to other countries.

Together with the development of global Internet network and formation of new economic technologies (trading through virtual stores, broker operations, cyber-banks, etc.) the new types of crime have appeared (cyber-crime). Cyber-crime and its sequences are the new form of anti-social behavior, which only recently has been acknowledged as phenomenon, which is dangerous for safety and normal functioning of the society. According to the domestic and foreign specialists' assessments, the resolution of the problems of prevention and investigation of crimes of this type is rather complicated task for the law enforcement agencies, because only 10% of disclosed crimes in the sphere of computer information can be detected in time, and 90% are detected accidentally. The indicated data evidences high level of latency of such types of crimes. The state and commercial structures affected are not inclined to announce the sequences of such acts. Partially, this is confirmed by statistic data in our country. According to the data of the Department of Operative Information of MIA of Ukraine in 1997 under the article 198. On Violation of the Work of Automated Systems» of the Criminal Code of Ukraine (CC) 12 criminal cases were opened, and in 1998 - 15. The indicated data witnesses complication of this category of crimes investigation, as well as imperfection of organization-legal protection of information in computer systems.

Term "cyber-crime" is young and created by combination of two words: cyber and crime. The term "cyber" means the cyber-space (terms "virtual space", "virtual world" are used more often in literature) and means (according to the definition in "New hacker vocabulary" by Eric S. Raymond) the informational space modeled through computer, in which defined types of objects or symbol images of information exist – the place where computer programs work and data is processed. The term "cyber-crime" is not by chance put in quotes and its further use requires certain explanation. The thing is, that cyber-crime is not covered by CC of Ukraine currently in force, therefore this term will be used without quotes as social phenomenon well-known all around the world.

From the moment of announcement of Ukraine state independence the national system of the laws and normative legal acts is being created for legal regulation of social informational relationship and informatization process, taking into account the speed of its development and penetration into different spheres of social activity.

In order to regulate the informational relationship on the state level it is necessary to determine the most important legal norms of its participants acts, including preventing and combating the offences, related to use of the global Internet network. In turn, this conditioned the necessity of separating and establishing the section in the national law, named today as "computer law", which goal is to implement the state policy in the conditions of stabilization and development of the country's informatization: creation of information resources, their turn over and distribution, consuming, storage and protection, etc.

Term "computer law" appeared in industrially developed countries in the middle of our century in connection with wide introduction of calculation machinery means and other related technical means into different spheres of social activity, private life and formation of the relationship, which appear in the production process and using of new information technologies.

The appropriate legislation is developed quite quickly, trying to take into account the development of the computer technology and telecommunication systems, but, naturally, is not catching up due to reasonable conservatism, which anticipates appearing of new legal mechanisms upon accumulation of certain "critical mass" of legal relationship requiring regulation.

In Ukraine similar legislation is named "legislation in the sphere of informatization", which covers — according to different assessments — from 50 to 250 normative acts (including acts providing for creation of branch or specialized automated systems).

Analysis of domestic normative-legal base directed to regulation of the relationship in the sphere of informatization and endurance of information protection, allows to conclude that it is on its initial stage. The regime of legitimacy is also on the stage of establishing in this sphere of normative – legal regulation. The establishment of legitimacy regime in this case means the aggregation of socially conditioned processes related to development and adoption of legal norms as well as implementing means for its accurate and steady execution and adherence.

For further analysis of these problems, let's consider certain legal aspects of using global Internet network. In contemporary conditions Internet is catalyst for many negative phenomenon, the social danger of which requires additional attention and research. Besides that, if consider Internet from legal point of view, we can conclude that the subjects of these new social relations face the range of legal issues, which require prompt resolution. Among basic generally theoretic issues, it is necessary to determine the problems of network jurisdiction, legal relations between the subjects, which distribute and consume information within the network, as well as the problem of determining the time and place of action within Internet.

Analyzing the mechanisms of Internet action and ways of presenting and distributing information the unique special legal problems appear, which does not have any analog. First of all, these are problems of electronic commerce regulation. They include concluding contracts through Internet, advertising, problem of Internet entrepreneurs' taxation, etc.

The next group of legal problems is copy right problems, which appear when the issues of using information or referring to information received through the network are interpreted by different ways under Ukraine legislation and legislation's of other foreign countries.

The trade marks issue is also disputable, including well-known dilemma: trade mark – domain name, as well as the issue of abuses upon domain registrations (cybersquatting). Currently, a lot of court cases are opened (in

Western countries) on this network problem. Very important Internet problem is to define the liability of providers and site owners for content of information, located on their servers. Several countries have already adopted certain specific normative acts regulating such relationship, and law enforcement practice has obvious national differentiation, which is contradictory to international character of the Internet.

Another group of legal relationship reflecting peculiarity of the problem is many-sided issues of information protection, which include coding, data access protection, privacy protection. This group is related to issues of moral and censorship (of private and network social groups, as well as state and organizations).

It can, therefore, be concluded that currently in Ukraine and in the entire world as well, the new branch of the law is being established – the law of using the global informational Internet network.

Of course, the objects of legal regulation of Internet are, first of all, social relationships related to copy right, patent right, trade marks and personal non-property rights, to the extent to which the information, located in the Internet can affect it, then, the objects of legal regulation are other property relationship, realized through Internet (for instance, those, related to international contracts conclusion or settlements of international disputes through Internet) — all of it, to our opinion, can be determined as information, which use is regulated by the law.

The detailed description of the objects of legal regulation in the Internet is the same as list of all types of social relationship realized through Internet.

Nowadays, when people realize the importance of possession of accurate and actual information for the work in any sphere, the information industry related to modern information technologies is coming foreground. Using Internet now it is possible to get access to official as well as scientific resources through official sites.

The Organization of United Nations and European Union provide direct access to officially published documents of these organizations, information notes and bulletins, not depending on where the user is located. Teleconferences open absolutely new opportunities to exchange opinions and obtain information directly from the source in the regime of real time.

There is now new branch of production – information industry, which is developed according to general rules, but also has certain peculiarities. Besides that, generally accepted human rights and freedoms, which do not depend on pertaining to certain country, are becoming more important as well as endurance of these human rights.

As practice shows, in Ukraine there is lack of attention to the issues of legal regulation of using the telecommunication systems in general and the Internet related law in particular.

This is conditioned by low level of development of technical communication means, telecommunication infrastructure and enterprises of this sphere. However, the interest to this branch of the law is continuously increasing together with willing to implement and use new information technologies.

The legal relationship in the sphere of telecommunication is new and quite wide term. This sphere is regulated by the state law as well as international norms. Upon development of technique, the information systems of different states start to contact each other and, therefore, the part of international legal regulation should increase, so the international cooperation is necessary in the sphere of transmission and distribution of information.

The issue of legal regulation of telecommunication systems using occupies one of the important places abroad. As an example, let's consider the Internet pages (as of today they are the most accessible object for research) the general, popular, as well as specific legal resources, always contain telecommunication section.

Article 19 of the General Declaration of Human Rights provides for freedom of search, obtaining and distribution of information and ideas by any means and not depending on state borders.

Meaning of this provision is difficult to overestimate. Recently, when information technologies provide more opportunities, the people's need in information becomes as much important as need in property and other benefits.

That is why the provisions of Declaration should be considered as starting point for international regulation of relationship, connected to transmission of the information between the states. The main task of the international legal regulation in this sphere is organization of cooperation between the states and coordination of their efforts in global information exchange.

In order to resolve many issues of the international legal regulation in this sphere, it is necessary to conduct the scientific research of the telecommunication systems international law problems when as an aggregate of legal principles, norms and rules regulating the relationship between the states and international organizations.

The issue of the international legal regulation of telecommunications in its nature and content is an integral part of the international law. It is created by the subjects of the international law in accordance to general rules of creation of international law norms taking into account the peculiarities of the new information technologies and information exchange needs of the society.

Legal regulation of telecommunications is quite wide term, which is used in different scientific spheres, sometimes in different meanings. However, for international legal regulation it is necessary to give general meaning of telecommunication systems. On our opinion, the definition given in the Law of Ukraine "On the National Informatization Program" is appropriate: information – telecommunication system includes high-speed and ordinary communication channels, distributed and local networks of different level and purpose, which gives the possibility to realize wide range of information technologies, provides for operative and reliable cooperation of all levels of management in resolution of interagency level issues, as well as provides wide range of information services to population, state and commercial organizations, foreign users..

With development of the international law the discussions about systemizing always occur, touching the grounds of separation of branches of the law and their precise frames and characteristics.

Within the branch framework the sub-sections and legal institutions are separated. In this respect there is an issue arising about the place of telecommunication international law in the international law system in general.

At present moment it is, perhaps, necessary to describe the telecommunication international law as legal institution, which includes the norms of different branches of the international law: international space law, international sea law,international air law (related to joint use of the resources); international economic law, regulation of scientific-technical progress (related to international cooperation on economic and technical development).

However, in the future, taking into consideration the development of technical progress and cooperation in communication sphere, it is absolutely possible that telecommunication international law will be separated as independent branch of the law.

Considering this problem, it should be mentioned that there are different – traditional and new, revolutionary for us, as well – approaches to this branch abroad. Example of such approach is the work of Darrell Mente, where he considers the result of telecommunication development as new reality, which should influence development of the law system, including international law.

We consider, that such research deserve attention, first of all, because they come beyond practice and take into account new achievements of industrially developed countries technology. The essence of approach described in Darrel Mente's work is the following:as the result of creation of telecommunication network and their active use the unified global information space will be created. Significant problems appear in connection with determination of states' jurisdiction within this information space. In order to overcome these problems the international legal regulation of this telecommunication space is necessary.

Discussing these problems there is made parallel with legal regime of Arctic and Antarctic, which do not belong to any country, with other international resources. Therefore, it is impossible to mention only one general problem, which is reflected by international law.

Considering criminal – legal aspects of using the Internet, related to appearing and expansion of the new types of crimes, it is necessary to note, that their analysis allows to divide them into two groups. First of which is related to participation of the employees of most affected organizations in criminal activity.

The second group includes attempts of unauthorized access to telecommunication systems from outside, using remote attacks and other methods. In these cases, cyber – criminals can attack the system only from generally accessible global networks and use methods which are difficult to combat without their knowledge.

However, neither in domestic nor in foreign literature available for public, the analysis of concrete cases of penetration into computer systems, unfortunately, was not properly described. The reasons of that are: organizations which face the thief of means, damage or disclosure of their data, and cases of blocking their services as the result of cyber – criminal acts, are not interested in disclosing or publication of such reports.

Cyber – crimes that became transnational, force the research of adequate ways of combating. The increase of these negative phenomenon is, on our opinion, conditioned by the following unsettled issues:

- vulnerability and dependence of computer systems within global Internet network. With increased dependence of the society on computer technique and telecommunications systems, the risk of damage of the new technology as the result of criminal acts is significantly increasing. The expansion of computer viruses and program bookmarks once more underlining this danger. However, these cases are just symptoms of serious disease;
- transnational character of cyber - crimes, effective means, directed to endurance the integrity of computer systems became vitally important for economic and social interests of developing countries as well as industrial countries;
- absence of liability. Many aspects cyber – crime in most cases is rather the sequence of week information protection than offenders acts.

Therefore, it is necessary to give more information about vulnerability of computer systems and necessity of effective protection means;

- ineffectiveness of the Civil Code. Criminal laws should be supplemented with appropriate civil sanctions, because court cases on cyber – crime are the most responsible procedure due to difficulty of proving and may not fall within traditional legal frames;
- imperfection of the legislation and absence of international cooperation. Great use of Internet significantly surpass the level of development of the national and international social and legal norms, which regulate the sphere of information protection;
- enforcement of criminal sanctions does not ensure the success in combating the cyber - crime, because the laws currently in force does not have precise classification and difficulty of interpretation and application of articles restrict the law enforcement agencies activity. The necessary mechanism of ensuring activities and cooperation of the law enforcement agencies for proper detection and punishment of cyber – crime is not yet developed.

The absence of certain international agreements affects the normal functioning of the law enforcement agencies, taking into consideration the following:

- criminal cases related to cyber – crime may fall within several jurisdiction. Proving that the crime has been committed stays the most difficult component of investigation, since experienced offenders cover their tracks, going through the justice system, especially in those countries which refuse to cooperate while collecting evidences;
- even if quite reliable elements of crime where detected in separate country, i.e. evidence exists, this country may not have the necessary jurisdiction to prosecute the offender;
- the country having jurisdiction may appear not properly authorized in prosecution of the offender, if s/he lives in the other country, which does not have legislation which provides for extradition of offenders in such cases;
- even there, where prosecution of offenders succeeded, the courts makes nominal sentences.

Complex resolution of the indicated problems is current urgent need, their resolution will allow to overcome most risks, and will condition the prevention, detection and criminal prosecution of virtual offenders.

Notwithstanding the fact that in our country there are many other urgent problems necessary to resolve, the problem of combating the cyber – crime can not be put out of attention.

It is necessary to develop methodological, theoretical and practical basis for information protection within global Internet network.

Almost all relationship between the subjects of the information society will base on consuming and exchange of information. In this case the issue of information protection will became priority. Development of the legal regulation of using Internet in our country must be directed to foreign experience as well as national interests of Ukraine in informational sphere.

Special attention should be attracted to detection and research of defects in order to avoid them further in law-making and law enforcement activity and to prevent negative sequences of informatization. This should be realized by way of scientific approach, involving wide circle of domestic specialists, who possess knowledge of legal theory and practice of Ukraine and foreign countries as well having certain background in the sphere of information technology and information protection.

3

Cyberspace Terrorism

The definition of "terrorism" has been well studied, defined, and documented. There is also a degree of understanding of the meanings of *CyberTerrorism*, either from the popular media, other secondary sources, or personal experience. This paper examines the future of CyberTerrorism - a term the author coined a decade ago, as the indicia of technological dependence and frailty were forming in our New World disOrder. Indeed, that future has come to fruition, today.

The face of terrorism is changing. While the motivations remain the same, we are now facing new and unfamiliar weapons. The intelligence systems, tactics, security procedures and equipment that were once expected to protect people, systems, and nations, are powerless against this new, and very devastating weapon. Moreover, the methods of counter-terrorism that our world's specialists have honed over the years are ineffectual against this enemy. Because, this enemy does not attack us with truckloads of explosives, nor with briefcases of Sarin gas, nor with dynamite strapped to the bodies of fanatics. This enemy attacks us with one's and zero's, at a place we are most vulnerable: the point at which the *physical* and *virtual* worlds converge. Let us first define theses two domains.

The Physical World

The physical world is matter and energy - light, dark, hot and cold, all physical matter - that place in which we live and function.

The Virtual World

The virtual world is symbolic - true, false, binary, metaphoric representations of information - that place in which computer programs function and data moves.

The physical and virtual worlds are inherently disparate worlds. It is now the intersection, the convergence, of these two worlds that forms the vehicle of CyberTerrorism, the new weapon that we face.

Reliance and Dependence

This convergence of the physical and virtual worlds, this lattice, is growing larger and more complex as we venture further into technological dependence. Each day, we move ahead with blinding speed into the computerization of every task and process that we face. We are becoming ever more inextricably reliant and dependent on the convergence of these two worlds.

Points of Convergence

What are some of the more obvious points of convergence?

- A garage door opener.
- A heart pacemaker.
- The computer chip in a late model car.
- A microwave oven.

These are all things taken for granted. Yet, as we progress into a far more technological world, what other points of convergence are taken for granted?

- Food processing plants
- Pharmaceutical processing plants
- Electric and natural gas utilities
- Train crossings and traffic control systems
- Next generation air traffic control systems
- Virtually all modern military equipment
- Military and public safety communications
- Civilian communications

Convergence Drivers

What is driving the convergence of these two worlds? There are three goals:

1. Access: the goal of universal, ubiquitous interface;
2. Control: the goal of remote administration; and
3. Mining: the goal of knowledge acquisition.

Convergence Vehicles

To achieve these goals, there are four vehicles:

- Transmission: longer lines across land and through space;
- Connections: more links to more points;

- Aggregation: more information centralized, and disconnected information linked; and
- Retrieval: more ways of retrieving information, and more importantly, knowledge.

Achieving CyberTerrorist Goals

So how does a CyberTerrorist achieve his mission? Like any terrorist, a CyberTerrorist actively exploits the goals of the target population in areas in which they take for granted. There are three potential acts in CyberTerrorism at the point of convergence:

1.Destruction;

2.Alteration; and

3.Acquisition and retransmission (these are a unit).

As we will see, these three types of acts are most heinous at the point where the physical and virtual worlds converge.

To achieve a true terrorist goal, as we know, we must have *scale* and *publicity*. So how does the CyberTerrorist approach a new age - an age of convergence of the physical and virtual worlds? An age where, thanks to our goals, he can perform his CyberTerrorist acts from his living room, undetected, from 8,000 kilometers away?

Cracker or CyberTerrorist?

A great deal of "cracks" are committed for the purposes of anarchy, humor, or as often stated by the perpetrators, "to be annoying." However, is this the mindset of a CyberTerrorist? Does the CyberTerrorist make a garage door go up and down? Does he change an Internet web site to say a country's government is evil? Does he hack into a major corporation's voice mail system to make long distance calls? No - that is not the domain of the CyberTerrorist - that is the domain of the amateur cracker community that exists worldwide.

A CyberTerrorist's mindset is quite different. A CyberTerrorist would not alter a voice mail, or even abuse credit cards.

Potential CyberTerrorist Acts

Let us examine some example CyberTerrorist acts. Based on the definitions of terrorism, a determination can be made if they in fact constitute terrorism:

- A CyberTerrorist will remotely access the processing control systems of a cereal manufacturer, change the levels of iron supplement, and sicken and kill the children of a nation enjoying their food. That CyberTerrorist will then perform similar remote alterations at a processor of infant formula. The key: the CyberTerrorist does not have to be at the factory to execute these acts.

- A CyberTerrorist will place a number of computerized bombs around a city, all simultaneously transmitting unique numeric patterns, each bomb receiving each other's pattern. If bomb one stops transmitting, all the bombs detonate simultaneously. The keys: 1) the CyberTerrorist does not have to be strapped to any of these bombs; 2) no large truck is required; 3) the number of bombs and urban dispersion are extensive; 4) the encrypted patterns cannot be predicted and matched through alternate transmission; and 5) the number of bombs prevents disarming them all simultaneously. The bombs *will* detonate.
- A CyberTerrorist will disrupt the banks, the international financial transactions, the stock exchanges. The key: the people of a country will lose all confidence in the economic system. Would a CyberTerrorist attempt to gain entry to the Federal Reserve building or equivalent? Unlikely, since arrest would be immediate. Furthermore, a large truck pulling along side the building would be noticed. However, in the case of the CyberTerrorist, the perpetrator is sitting on another continent while a nation's economic systems grind to a halt. Destabilization *will* be achieved.
- A CyberTerrorist will attack the next generation of air traffic control systems, and collide two large civilian aircraft. This is a realistic scenario, since the CyberTerrorist will also crack the aircraft's in-cockpit sensors. Much of the same can be done to the rail lines.
- A CyberTerrorist will remotely alter the formulas of medication at pharmaceutical manufacturers. The potential loss of life is unfathomable.
- The CyberTerrorist may then decide to remotely change the pressure in the gas lines, causing a valve failure, and a block of a sleepy suburb detonates and burns. Likewise, the electrical grid is becoming steadily more vulnerable.

In effect, the CyberTerrorist will make certain that the population of a nation will not be able to eat, to drink, to move, or to live. In addition, the people charged with the protection of their nation will not have warning, and will not be able to shut down the terrorist, since that CyberTerrorist is most likely on the other side of the world. Sadly, these examples are not science fiction. All of these scenarios can be executed today. As you may know, some of these incidents already have occurred in various nations. More of such acts will take place tomorrow. Are you prepared?

CyberTerrorists: Who, Where, and Why?

The purpose of this paper is to help you understand the threats that exist, and hopefully, to help you prevent these types of atrocities. But know this

- there are people out there with very different goals, who are our real threats, and who are, or will be, attacking us. Make no mistake, *the threats are real, today.* Who are the CyberTerrorists? There a great many poor movies and too many works of fiction about the hacker and cracker communities. In the popular media, there recently was the Kevin Mitnick incident, where one cracker broke into another cracker's systems. This spawned endless press and at least two best selling books. While this incident received much attention, the events amounted to meaningless children's games.

By and large, the cracker community, based primarily in the United States, Europe, the Middle East, Asia, and in the nations of the former Soviet Union, is composed of individuals who see the cracking process merely as a challenge, a brain teaser, a puzzle. They view themselves as not only being innocent of any crime, but perhaps even doing something righteous, something to counter the dark monoliths of the corporate and government worlds. They believe they are being persecuted. These individuals believe that what they are doing is not doing any true damage. At its least harmful, these crackers just look at information. However, privacy issues and military secrecy can render such infiltrations acts of terror.

Sometimes crackers make minor changes, just for fun, to be annoying, or to make a statement. The potential for damage here is enormous.

Crackers as Facilitators

Individuals with a background in intelligence are aware that a frequent element of case execution is enlisting the indigenous, sometimes called "facilitators," to assist in a campaign. At the convergence of the physical and virtual worlds, the indigenous are the crackers. There is the incorrect assumption in the cracking community that they, the crackers, are so sophisticated or so knowledgeable as to know when they are being approached for a truly illicit reason (e.g., to be enlisted as a facilitator to commit an act of terrorism). However, despite cracker arrogance, these individuals are easy targets for enlistment.

What about those crackers who actively *wish* to cross the line, or more basically, need money? To a teenager, a $1,000 U.S. can purchase a good many compact disks, a new modem, and a great deal of libation. Beyond youths, there are professionals in this arena as well.

Historically, individuals engaged in the practice of terror tended not to be people working upon a computer 20 hours per day. Terrorists have not been in the business of tracking the latest holes found in UNIX or an obscure government telnet opportunity. There *are* people, however, who are in that business - for illicit as well as good cause. As stated, just as indigenous people may be turned into soldiers, so can crackers be turned into CyberTerrorists. Sometimes such a transition may be motivated by money or prestige. Usually, this transition will occur without the cracker's cognizance. The potential threat from such transitions is mind boggling, considering the damage even one mis-directed cracker can cause.

Further, as young, educated people are brought into the folds of terrorist groups, this new generation will have the talent to execute the acts of CyberTerrorism of which we have spoken.

We are going to see increasing levels of in-house expertise, and concomitant exponential increases CyberTerrorism. Unlike other methods of terrorism, CyberTerrorism is safe and profitable, and difficult to counter without the right expertise and understanding of the CyberTerrorist's mind. Combine our increasing vulnerability, with the explosive increases in the level of violence, and increasing expertise available inside terrorist organizations through new blood and outside through facilitators, and we can see that at the point where the physical and virtual worlds converge, the old models of managing terrorism are obsolete.

Methods of Protection: No Easy Answers

We must consider the following elements when building a counter-CyberTerrorist program:

- We must accept that while the theories of terrorism stand true, the way in which we approach counter-terrorism, in this case, counter-CyberTerrorism, must change.
- We must cooperate and share intelligence in ways we have never have before.
- We must enlist the assistance of those individuals who understand the weapons we are facing and have experienced fighting these wars.
- We must learn the new rules, the new technologies, and the new players.

Unfortunately, one cannot learn how to fight this very unconventional warfare from someone who hasn't been there, nor from someone whose experience is in the old ways and old technologies. The old data processing, auditing, and computer security models in use today are obsolete. On this battlefield, against this weapon, the terrorist is already far ahead. The building of a counter-CyberTerrorist team *must* be real-time and dynamic, as the weapons will continually change, to morph, in an attempt to beat you, your systems, and your people. There is no re-machining, and unlike other terrorists, if the CyberTerrorist loses today, he does not die - he learns what did not work, and will use that information against you tomorrow.

EXAGGERATED OF CYBERTERROR THREAT

Amid all the dire warnings and alarming statistics that the subject of cyberterrorism generates, it is important to remember one simple statistic: so far, there has been no recorded instance of a terrorist cyberattack on U.S. public facilities, transportation systems, nuclear power plants, power grids, or other key components of the national infrastructure. Cyberattacks are common, but they have not been conducted by terrorists and they have not sought to inflict the kind of damage that would qualify them as cyberterrorism.

When U.S. troops recovered al Qaeda laptops in Afghanistan, officials were surprised to find its members more technologically adept than previously believed. They discovered structural and engineering software, electronic models of a dam, and information on computerized water systems, nuclear power plants, and U.S. and European stadiums. But the evidence did *not* suggest that al Qaeda operatives were planning cyberattacks, only that they were using the Internet to communicate and coordinate physical attacks. Neither al Qaeda nor any other terrorist organization appears to have tried to stage a serious cyberattack. For now, the most damaging attacks and intrusions, experts say, are typically carried out either by disgruntled corporate insiders intent on embezzlement or sabotage or by individual hackers—typically young and male—seeking thrills and notoriety. According to a report issued in 2002 by IBM Global Security Analysis Lab, 90 percent of hackers are amateurs with limited technical proficiency, 9 percent are more skilled at gaining unauthorized access but do not damage the files they read, and only 1 percent are highly skilled and intent on copying files or damaging programs and systems. Most hackers, it should be noted, concentrate on writing programs that expose security flaws in computer software, mainly in the operating systems produced by Microsoft. Their efforts in this direction have sometimes embarrassed corporations but have also been responsible for alerting the public and security professionals to major security flaws in software.

Moreover, although there are hackers with the ability to damage systems, disrupt e-commerce, and force websites offline, the vast majority of hackers do not have the necessary skills and knowledge. The ones who do, generally do not seek to wreak havoc. Douglas Thomas, a professor at the University of Southern California, spent seven years studying computer hackers in an effort to understand better who they are and what motivates them. Thomas interviewed hundreds of hackers and explored their "literature." In testimony on July 24, 2002, before the House Subcommittee on Government Efficiency, Financial Management and Intergovernmental Relations, Thomas argued that "with the vast majority of hackers, I would say 99 percent of them, the risk [of cyberterrorism] is negligible for the simple reason that those hackers do not have the skill or ability to organize or execute an attack that would be anything more than a minor inconvenience." His judgment was echoed in *Assessing the Risks of Cyberterrorism, Cyber War, and Other Cyber Threats*, a 2002 report for the Centre for Strategic and International Studies, written by Jim Lewis, a sixteen-year veteran of the State and Commerce Departments. "The idea that hackers are going to bring the nation to its knees is too far-fetched a scenario to be taken seriously," Lewis argued. "Nations are more robust than the early analysts of cyberterrorism and cyberwarfare give them credit for. Infastructure systems [are] more flexible and responsive in restoring service than the early analysts realized, in part because they have to deal with failure on a routine basis."

Many computer security specialists believe it is virtually impossible to use the Internet to inflict death on a large scale and scoff at the notion that terrorists would bother trying. The resilience of computer systems to attack, they point out, is no accident but rather the result of significant investments of time, money, and expertise. Nuclear weapons and other sensitive military systems enjoy the most basic form of Internet security. They are "air-gapped," meaning that they are not physically connected to the Internet and are therefore inaccessible to outside hackers. The Defence Department has been particularly vigilant in protecting key systems by isolating them from the Internet and even from the Pentagon's internal computer network. All new software must be submitted to the National Security Agency for security testing.

The 9/11 hijackings understandably led to an outcry that airliners are particularly susceptible to cyberterrorist attacks. In 2002, for instance, Senator Charles Schumer (D-N.Y.) described "the absolute havoc and devastation that would result if cyberterrorists suddenly shut down our air traffic control system, with thousands of planes in mid-flight." In fact, cybersecurity experts give some of their highest marks to the Federal Aviation Authority, which separates its administrative and air traffic control systems. And there is a reason the 9/11 hijackers used box-cutters instead of keyboards: it is impossible to hijack a plane remotely, which eliminates the possibility of a high-tech 9/11 scenario in which planes are used as weapons. Another source of concern is terrorist infiltration of the intelligence agencies. But here, too, the risk is described by Internet experts as slim. The CIA's classified computers are also air-gapped, as is the FBI's entire computer system.

That leaves less-well-protected secondary targets such as power grids, oil pipelines, and dams that do not present opportunities as nightmarish as do nuclear weapons systems but that nonetheless might be used to inflict other forms of mass destruction. Because most of these systems are in the private sector, they tend to be less secure than government systems. In addition, as noted above, companies increasingly use the Internet to manage SCADA systems that control such processes as regulating the flow of oil in pipelines and the level of water in dams. To illustrate the supposed ease with which terrorists could seize control of a dam, a story in the *Washington Post* in June 2003 on al Qaeda cyberterrorism related an anecdote about a twelve-year-old who hacked into the SCADA system at Arizona's Theodore Roosevelt Dam in 1998 and was, according to the article, within mere keystrokes of unleashing millions of gallons of water upon helpless downstream communities. However, a subsequent investigation by the tech-news site CNet.com revealed the tale to be largely apocryphal; investigators concluded that the hacker could not have gained control of the dam and that no lives or property were ever at risk.

To assess the potential threat of cyberterrorism, experts such as Denning suggest that two questions be asked: Are there targets that are vulnerable to cyberattacks? And are there actors with the capability and motivation to carry out such attacks? The answer to the first question is yes: critical infrastructure systems are complex and therefore bound to contain weaknesses that might be exploited, and even systems that seem "hardened" to outside manipulation might be accessed by insiders, acting alone or in concert with terrorists, to cause considerable harm. But what of the second question?

Few people besides a company's own employees possess the specific technical know-how required to run a specialized SCADA system. The most commonly cited example of SCADA exploitation bears this out. In April 2002, an Australian man used an Internet connection to release a million gallons of raw sewage along Queensland's Sunshine Coast after being turned down for a government job. When police arrested him, they discovered that he had worked for the company that designed the sewage treatment plant's control software.

It is possible, of course, that such disgruntled employees might be recruited by terrorist groups, but even if the terrorists did enlist inside help, the degree of damage they could cause would still be limited. As Joshua Green argues in "The Myth of Cyberterrorism" (which appeared in the *Washington Monthly* in November 2002), the employees of companies that handle power grids, oil and gas utilities, and communications are well rehearsed in dealing with the fallout from hurricanes, floods, tornadoes, and other natural disasters. They are also equally adept at containing and remedying problems that stem from human action.

In August 1999, the Centre for the Study of Terrorism and Irregular Warfare at the Naval Postgraduate School (NPS) in Monterey, California, issued a report titled *Cyber-terror: Prospects and Implications.*

The report concluded that terrorists generally lack the wherewithal and human capital needed to mount attacks that involve more than annoying but relatively harmless hacks. The study examined five types of terrorist groups: religious, New Age, ethnonationalist separatist, revolutionary, and far-right extremists. Of these, only the religious groups were adjudged likely to seek the capacity to inflict massive damage. Hacker groups, the study determined, are psychologically and organizationally ill suited to cyberterrorism, and any massive disruption of the information infrastructure would run counter to their self-interest.

In October 2000, the NPS group issued a second report, this one examining the decision-making process by which substate groups engaged in armed resistance develop new operational methods, including cyberterrorism. The report concluded that while substate groups may find cyberterror attractive as a nonlethal weapon, terrorists have not yet integrated information technology into their strategy and tactics and that significant barriers between hackers and terrorists may prevent their integration into one group.

Another illustration of the limited likelihood of terrorists launching a highly damaging cyberattack comes from a simulation sponsored by the U.S. Naval War College. The college contracted with a research group to simulate a massive cyberattack on the nation's information infrastructure.

Government hackers and security analysts gathered in July 2002 in Newport, R.I., for a war game dubbed "Digital Pearl Harbor." The results were far from devastating: the hackers failed to crash the Internet, although they did cause serious sporadic damage. According to a CNet.com report on the exercise published in August 2002, officials concluded that terrorists hoping to stage such an attack "would require a syndicate with significant resources, including $200 million, country-level intelligence and five years of preparation time."

SECURITY AWARENESS

Especially the results of the last section show that a severe problem lies in the level of protection at the different sites. Unprotected systems – especially if they are responsible for valuable infrastructure, services, or data – pose a just too tempting target for cybercriminals as well as for terrorists. Therefore, a strong initiative should be started to incite the public and the private sector to invest more time, money, and care into security measures.

In the public sector, several instruments have been introduced that were targeted to either test security level of public institutions or to raise their awareness towards security issues. The well known test called "Eligible Receiver" that was conducted in 1997, for example, was able to point out several serious vulnerabilities in the military's computer network. Other tests have led to similar results.

With a view to a raised awareness towards security issues, the U.S. FISMA is a good example. Through this act public institutions are forced to inspect and adjust their measures at regular intervals. Similar initiatives could lead to better results also in the private sector. Currently, many companies might not be aware of their importance for the economy as a whole – or at least they do not act according to this role. According to Richard Clarke a typical company devotes only one quarter of one percent of its information technology budget to cyber security or – as he puts it – "slightly less than they spend on coffee". Today, these figures have changed slightly, but still more than half of the companies that answered to the CSI survey of 2007 stated that they spent 5% or less.

A possible initiative could – as a first step – classify companies according to their endangerment. If – according to this classification – high- and medium-risk businesses would also be audited (comparable to FISMA), this again could have two positive effects: First, it would be known, which companies are responsible for certain critical infrastructures. In the U.S. alone, for example, some 5,700 companies are deemed to be essential to national security. Secondly, it would become known which dependencies between these companies currently exist. Thirdly, due to the auditing, also companies in the private sector would have to increase their security level constantly.

Terrorist Contents

The final recommendation regards the interaction with terrorist contents, e.g. websites and training materials. It might sound provocatively, but the (young) history of the Internet shows that all efforts to censor and control media and communication are doomed to fail. Technically, it is almost impossible to effectively hinder websites or to block communication between terrorists – especially if encryption technology or other methods to obscure their communications are being used. Additionally, all of these efforts threaten civil liberties and the freedom of law-abiding citizens. Finally, it is still unclear how the valuation of crimes and ethics in different countries can safely be combined.

Therefore, countries should refrain from enacting ineffective control methods of a purely symbolic nature that seriously infringes the freedom of information rights and that can lead to the development of uncontrolled surveillance. Instead, advantage should be taken of the situation that terrorists communicate over open channels. This can be used, for instance, to register activities, assess the size and possibly future actions of terrorist groups.

Communication Paths

The second recommendation against digital attacks concerns the communication between different institutions in the case of an attack. Most cybercrime cases involve not only resources in one, but in many different countries or institutions at the same time. Therefore, fast and efficient communication is of the essence to fight digital attacks. Several initiatives have been made so far to strengthen this sharing of information in the event of a digital attack.

Article 35 of the Convention on Cyber Crime by the Council of Europe, for example, asks the member countries to introduce contact points that are available on a 24 hour, 7 day per week basis in order to ensure immediate assistance for the purpose of investigations or proceedings concerning criminal offences related to computer systems and data. This 24/7 network is an important step towards fast communication paths between different countries.

Similar activities, however, are needed not only between countries, but also between the different institutions within each country. In the U.S., for example, the National Infrastructure Protection Centre (NIPC) was created in 1998. Its mission is to provide "a national focal point for gathering information on threats to the infrastructures, and providing the principal means of facilitating and coordinating the federal government's response to an incident, mitigating attacks, investigating threats, and monitoring reconstitution efforts.".

To accomplish this mission, the NIPC believes that it is necessary to build a "coalition of trust amongst all government agencies, between the government and the private sector, amongst the different business interests within the private sector itself, and in concert with the greater international community."

In essence, fixed communication paths have to be established between (1) different countries (e.g. through the 24/7 network of the Council of Europe), (2) between the different institutions and services in the public sector, and (3) between important companies in the private sector and institutions in the public sector. As a guide on what companies have to be considered "important" in this context, the infrastructure definition of the NIPC can be taken into account. It defines infrastructure as "those physical and cyber-based systems essential to the minimum operations of the economy and government, including telecommunications, energy, banking and finance, transportation, water systems, emergency systems, both governmental and private".

CYBERSPACE AT A GLANCE

For the most part, the Internet is built upon national and international telecommunications infrastructures, including the landlines of most public phone systems and wireless, and satellite communications. Beyond the Internet, these telecommunications infrastructures tend to be highly dependent on computing technology. Thus, by our definition, they are part of cyberspace. There are currently about 1.3 billion Internet users worldwide. The Internet now comes to ground in over 200 "countries" (Top-Level Domains, i.e. the letters which follow the dot after the domain name).

This enormous growth has been achieved since the early 90s. The only thing growing faster than the Internet is cellular telephony, with about three billion phones in use, to which 1.6 million users are added every day. The fact that soon cellular telephones will be a platform for the Internet means that at least a billion new users will have access to this resource, and this expansion will mostly be in developing countries.

(In)Security (Internet Security) at a Glance

The architecture, design, and practice of the Internet emphasize *access* (ease of use, low cost, universality). It has almost never considered security as a primary or important factor. It is an unfortunate result of the history of the way the Internet was developed that the protocols used by the Internet today are derived from those that were established in the early days of the ARPANet, where there were only a few wellrespected researchers using the infrastructure, and they were trusted to do no harm. Consequently, security considerations were not built in to the Internet. All cybersecurity measures taken today to protect the Internet are add-on measures that do not remedy the underlying security deficiencies.

The situation we have as a result is that current technology asymmetrically favors the attackers; it provides them great "nonlinear leverage", and attackers get their innovations into practice more quickly and effectively than defenders. If we make a comparison between cyber attacks and modern warfare, we would say that it is an asymmetrical conflict. While the state, because of its capacity, has a huge technological advantage over terrorists, the problem is that the kinds of nonlinearities associated with what terrorists do in cyberspace give leverage to those with relatively little technical capability. What has always been thought of as one of the great advantages of the networks can also threaten them: They give a small number of relatively weak people extensive access to a lot of information, each other, potential recruits and sympathizers, and prospective targets. There is also a negative aspect of tightening access against terrorists or other malicious users more generally because it would compromise access and privacy for many, many more "good" users.

The functionality of the Internet ranges greatly. Of particular concern for those aware of the threat of terrorism is the fact that SCADA (Supervisory

Control and Data Acquisition) systems now more commonly use the Internet to transmit data and control instructions, rather than the dedicated networks that had been used before. Additionally, very few of the "cyber" parts of the critical infrastructures were designed or implemented with security as much of a consideration, if it was considered at all. Most are riddled with vulnerabilities, which are defined as weaknesses that can be exploited through either hostile attacks or accidents. It would be almost impossible to create "patches" to protect programs from malicious people who seek to find and exploit these vulnerabilities. Another problem to recognize is that Internet defense pushes the burden outward to the end user organizations; most of these find it difficult, and often increasingly difficult, to defend themselves.

In particular, most of the over two hundred connected countries have little or no national cybersecurity capabilities.

International Threats Arising from Globalization

One area of concern that extends broadly across all of the stages of defense is that globalization creates new populations of "insiders"—people who have authorized access with the potential for abuse that can cause great harm. Insiders still probably account for a majority of successful penetrations for criminal purposes. The problem is complicated by changes in organizational relations and technical architectures that make "inside" and "outside" more difficult even to define. The possibility that a terrorist or a terrorist sympathizer might gain employment that would enable him or her to conduct a devastating attack or to provide critical information or access to others cannot be discounted or ignored.

The two most general ways of dealing with infiltration are through deep preemployment investigations, something that most non-government entities are neither capable of doing nor permitted to do in many countries, and through stronger forms of containment and compartmentalization of access within an organization. Globalization has meant that the Internet is now less secure, with vulnerabilities resulting from new systems "intimacies". Transfer of information now takes place in unprecedented transnational contexts.

A particular problem for those who want to control or police the Internet is the spread and ownership of, and access to, transnational transportation infrastructures. Much of the day to day running is outsourced, and offshoring (outsourcing to foreign entities) means that any attempts to control the Internet require international cooperation.

Terrorists in Cyberspace

What do we know or anticipate that terrorists want to do in cyberspace? I believe the answers to this question fall into three categories:

1. Terrorists want to support their activities and infrastructure, but not directly through an attack, using the Internet.
2. They may want explicitly to attack parts of the cyber infrastructure.
3. They may use cyberspace as a means of attacking other targets. These might include compromising transportation or other supervisory control systems to cause disasters resulting in extensive consternation and costing many lives.

It is certain that terrorists and their supporters have been engaging in extensive activities under category 1, and that they will continue to do so. This would cover communications, including encrypted communications with each other; recruiting and "advertising" (for example, via Web sites); and financial transactions such as money transfers and laundering. Training manuals for terrorists, including information about bomb-making and avoiding detection, are freely available. Terrorists are also likely to be scouring cyberspace for information on potential targets and on weapons of mass destruction.

As far as we can tell, terrorists have not been responsible for any of the major attacks or accidents that have occurred in recent years under categories 2 or 3. So much has been written about such possibilities—and they have had some prominence in the media—that it is inconceivable that terrorists are not aware of them. So far, for reasons we can only speculate about, they do not seem to have chosen to pursue these possibilities with vigor and effect, or perhaps they have tried and failed.

Systems and Networks at Risk

Should an attack be launched against systems and networks, the following would be at risk:

1. The Internet.
2. Embedded/real-time computing (e.g. avionics systems for air traffic control, SCADA systems used by the amenities, routing for shipping containers, and process control for toxic chemical production, switching of telecommunications, bank teller machines, floodgates).
3. Dedicated computing devices (e.g. desktop computers).

Each has a different role, and may be the subject of different kinds of attack. Terrorists might attack the Internet physically or "through the wires", the latter being potentially more destructive. One type of attack that we see is directed against Internet operations. Such attacks are often based on self-replicating programs (worms and viruses) that are transmitted from system to system, consuming prodigious amounts of router processing time and network channel bandwidth. In recent years, some of these worms and viruses have been transmitted without explicitly destructive payloads and yet have been able to disrupt key Internet backbone subnetworks for several days. Another kind of attack on Internet operations seeks to corrupt the routing tables that determine how a packet should travel through the Internet. In both cases, the intent of the attack is to reduce the normally expected functionality of the Internet for some significant portion of its users—that is, a denial-of-service attack in intent, although not one necessarily based on flooding traffic.

An attacker might also target the Internet's Domain Name System (DNS), which translates domain names (e.g. "example.com") to specific Internet Protocol (IP) addresses (e.g. 123.231.0.67) denoting specific Internet nodes. A relatively small number of "root name servers" underpins the DNS. Although the DNS is designed to provide redundancy in case of accidental failure, it has some vulnerability to an attack that might target all name servers simultaneously. Although Internet operations would not halt instantly, an increasing number of sites would, over a period of time measured in hours to days, become inaccessible without root name servers to provide authoritative translation information. Physical replacement of damaged servers would be achievable in a matter of days, but changing the IP addresses of the root name servers would be more complicated.

Recommendations: Focus on Terrorists

It is only a matter of time before cyber terror attacks, at present largely a threat, become a reality. Both government and private sector need to focus on preparations. There are a number of measures that must be taken. Build Much Stronger Defenses, More Integrated Emergency Preparedness and Response Systems, and Improve the Processes for Their Use.

The first order of business is to provide indications and warnings that an attack is taking place. This is a difficult area, and intrusion detection has become a particularly active area in research and development. Not surprisingly, detection and notification are more difficult and prone to false positives during the early stages of an attack, before significant damage has been done.

To prevent penetration of the system at risk from the outside, we try to erect barriers and otherwise harden it. Both cyber and physical approaches are necessary. Passwords are the oldest, and still most widely used, cybertechnique. More recent and somewhat widely used techniques are firewalls and proxy servers. Like all forms of cyberdefense, these can be defeated, although it is possible to make them real barriers against many attempted attacks. Physical protection needs to consider several forms of penetration or attempts to isolate the system. These include attacks on electronics using electromagnetic pulses, and attempts to cut cable endings. A wide variety of forms of physical protection are possible, ranging from fences to biometrics.In the event of an attack there needs to be a system for incident management, mitigating an attack, and damage limitation. A next line of defense is internal compartmentalization and containment. In this instance, the goals are to limit penetration and damage, protect surviving assets, and protect and gather information to help with recovery and response after the attack. Approaches include creating internal physical barriers and cyberbarriers through compartmentalization and need-to-know access controls, intrusion tolerance schemes, setting up decoys, maintaining protected redundancies, and hiding assets. All have both static (pre-positioned and unchanging during the attack) and dynamic variants.

Another approach is automatic or partial shutdown and reallocation. A system that senses it is under attack would start erecting internal barriers that would not be tolerable during normal operations, in an attempt to isolate those parts of the system that had been compromised. It would also involve load-shedding strategies to reallocate surviving capabilities to the most important functions required by the organization. All of this amounts to various forms of real-time reassignment and reconfiguration under rapid degradation. Particular attention needs to be given to preserving and collecting information during an attack. This is done most easily if the attack has a clear and precise starting time and backups are made regularly, or if the organization maintains a redundant "shadow" system. More insidious attacks that build up slowly present a much more difficult problem in identifying a state where the system is free from inserted malicious code. It is also important to have strong audit functions to identify when an attack starts and to collect information that might assist in the identification and apprehension of the attacker and help the organization better defend itself against similar attacks in the future.

Organizations should establish security policies and plans for defending against attacks. Special attention should be given to preventing and dealing with insider attacks. Staff should know who to call for help. It might be a good idea to test the plan through the use of exercises. However, most organizations avoid live "fire drills" because they can be expensive, disruptive, and risky in their own right. Many information systems are delicate and their owners are afraid something will go wrong, resulting in the selfinflicted equivalent of a serious attack.

Improve the security of systems that control physical processes (e.g., SCADA). From the standpoint of counter terrorism, we would imagine that attacking physical targets via control and management systems would result in the kind of mass casualties, damage, fear, and loss of confidence that terrorists favor. Many of these systems are vulnerable to tampering with control signals, especially by insiders.

Increasing the security for DC/SCADA systems poses particularly difficult problems. These systems are often small and self-contained, and have constrained power needs (including backup). Security may not readily fit with the space, real-time, or power requirements. Security measures could also reduce performance or be problematic in the synchronization of other more extensive processes. Additionally, most of these systems are in the private or mixed sectors (for example, airports). Their owners and operators may not have sufficient resources to secure them more effectively. National governments that are in positions to do so should give priority to protecting the small percentage of cyberspace users who are private owners and operators of digital control and management systems. This would include providing them with various forms of assistance and technology. Particular attention should be given to transportation systems because for decades they have been highly favored by terrorists both as targets and as the means of delivering an attack.

This kind of defensive work is essentially "target hardening". This can be defined as the use of various technologies and products and procedures (for example, those governing outside dial-in or reconstitution and recovery) to protect the information technology (IT) assets owned or operated by an individual or organization.

It is important to notice that many of these recommendations would have more general value than just vs. terrorists (e.g., they would help against accidents, natural disasters, serious crime, and non-terrorist forms of conflict). However, as defense does not involve serious risk or impose a penalty on the attacker, there is also the need to develop deterrents. For this we need laws:

Design and Implement a Stronger "System of Justice", Especially Its International Dimensions

International cooperation should concentrate on effective intelligence operations. This is an area where a considerable amount of success could be expected, which would create the atmosphere for a long-term international legal framework.

The problems of jurisdiction are greatly compounded by the easy transnational access provided by many components of cyberspace, most notably the Internet. What may be perceived as serious in one country whose cyberinfrastructure may be used as part of a terrorist action may not even make the legal radar screen of others that are part of an attack that crosses multiple sovereign physical jurisdictions. Most countries have given little or no thought to making serious crimes of the various forms of cyberattack, and "without law there is no sin". Seeking widely adopted national laws at least criminalizing attacks against or using the networks is an important objective. Legislating against the support functions to which terrorists put the Internet would be a more distant prospect. The enforcement and prosecution of these laws are also critical elements of cybersecurity.

Given the many technical and evidentiary problems of identifying cybercriminals and prosecuting them, nobody has any delusion that such laws would end criminal or terrorist activities in cyberspace. Nonetheless, they might reduce the enormous amount of malicious "noise" in cyberspace, and this would help make it easier to more readily identify more serious activities. They would also provide a necessary basis for encouraging people to report malicious cyberactivities, and for international cooperation in dealing with several kinds of problem.

Recommendations: CIIP at Every Stage

Security must become a criterion for any system used for CII from the design stage onwards. The priorities in design have been access and throughput. Added security is not just costly; it may also result in reduced efficiency and functionality. Furthermore, so far there does not seem to be much incentive for people to design or redesign systems to be much more secure. There has been much speculation that the design or redesign of systems will occur only in the aftermath of a "digital Pearl Harbor" or in response to the forces of legal liability or insurance necessities and standards. Even better, security should be a factor to be considered over the entire life cycle of such systems. Organizations should build cadres of capable defenders, and contingency plans (including internationally) for crisis and emergency conditions need to be in place. There could be national-level CERTs or CSIRTs (Cybersecurity Incident Response Teams).

A postdesign and implementation variant is to try to prevent attacks by finding and fixing vulnerabilities before an attacker can try to exploit them. Red teams, test beds, or simulations may be used to do this. Another approach, at least to the often-serious threat of possible insider attacks, is to more thoroughly screen employees with potentially sensitive access. It is clear that for a number of these measures operational contingencies among owners and operators and their governments need to be established.

TERRORISTS IN CYBERSPACE

Terrorists have moved into cyberspace to facilitate traditional forms of terrorism such as bombings. They use the Internet to communicate, coordinate events, and advance their agenda. While such activity does not constitute cyberterrorism in the strict sense, it does show that terrorists have some competency using the new information technologies.

By 1996, the headquarters of terrorist financier Osama bin Laden in Afghanistan was equipped with computers and communications equipment.

Egyptian "Afghan" computer experts were said to have helped devise a communication network that used the Web, e-mail, and electronic bulletin boards. Hamas activists have been said to use chat rooms and e-mail to plan operations and coordinate activities, making it difficult for Israeli security officials to trace their messages and decode their contents. The Revolutionary Armed Forces of Columbia (FARC) uses e-mail to field inquiries from the press.

The Web is especially popular as a medium for reaching a global audience. For example, after the Peruvian terrorist group Tupac Amaru stormed the Japanese Ambassador's residence in Lima on December 17, 1996 and took 400 diplomatic, political, and military officials as hostage, sympathizers in the United States and Canada put up solidarity Web sites. One site included detailed drawings of the residence and planned assault.

In February 1998, Hizbullah was operating three Web sites: one for the central press office (www.hizbollah.org), another to describe its attacks on Israeli targets, and the third for news and information. That month, Clark Staten, executive director of the Emergency Response & Research Institute (ERRI) in Chicago, testified before a U.S. Senate subcommittee that "even small terrorist groups are now using the Internet to broadcast their message and misdirect/misinform the general population in multiple nations simultaneously." He gave the subcommittee copies of both domestic and international messages containing anti-American and anti-Israeli propaganda and threats, including a widely distributed extremist call for "jihad" (holy war) against America and Great Britain.

In June 1998, *U.S. News & World Report* noted that 12 of the 30 groups on the U.S. State Department=s list of terrorist organizations are on the Web. Now, it appears that virtually every terrorist group is on the Web. Forcing them off the Web is impossible, because they can set up their sites in countries with free-speech laws. The government of Sri Lanka, for example, banned the separatist Liberation Tigers of Tamil Eelam, but they have not even attempted to take down their London-based Web site. Even in democracies, however, there are limits to what terrorists can post on the Net. After a group of anti-abortionists put up a Web site terrorizing doctors who performed abortions, a federal jury ordered the pages be taken down and damages of more than $100 million paid. The Nuremberg Files site had listed the names of about 200 abortion providers under the heading of "baby butchers." Readers were invited to send in such personal details as the doctors' home addresses, license plate numbers, and the names of their children. Three doctors whose names appeared on the list were killed, and after each, the doctor's name was promptly crossed out. Doctors named on the site testified that they lived in constant fear and used disguises, bodyguards, and bulletproof vests. In ordering the site down, the federal jury said the site and "wanted" posters amounted to death threats against the doctors.

Many terrorists are using encryption to conceal their communications and stored files, compounding the difficulties of providing effective counter-terrorism. Hamas, for example, reportedly has used encrypted Internet communications to transmit maps, pictures, and other details pertaining to terrorist attacks. Ramsey Yousef, a member of the international terrorist group responsible for bombing the World Trade Centre in 1994 and a Manila Air airliner in late 1995, encrypted files on his laptop computer. The files, which U.S. government officials decrypted, contained information pertaining to further plans to blow up eleven U.S.-owned commercial airliners in the Far East. The Aum Shinrikyo cult, which gassed the Tokyo subway in March 1995, killing 12 people and injuring 6,000 more, also used encryption to protect their computerized records, which included plans and intentions to deploy weapons of mass destruction in Japan and the United States.

CYBERSPACE ATTACKS

Cyberspace is constantly under assault. Cyber spies, thieves, saboteurs, and thrill seekers break into computer systems, steal personal data and trade secrets, vandalize Web sites, disrupt service, sabotage data and systems, launch computer viruses and worms, conduct fraudulent transactions, and harass individuals and companies. These attacks are facilitated with increasingly powerful and easy-to-use software tools, which are readily available for free from thousands of Web sites on the Internet.

Many of the attacks are serious and costly. The ILOVEYOU virus and variants, for example, was estimated to have hit tens of millions of users worldwide and cost billions of dollars in damage. Denial-of-service attacks against Yahoo, CNN, eBay, and other e-commerce Web sites were estimated to have caused over a billion in losses. They also shook the confidence of business and individuals in e-commerce. Governments are particularly concerned with terrorist and state-sponsored attacks against the critical infrastructures that constitute their national life support systems. The Clinton Administration defined eight: telecommunications, banking and finance, electrical power, oil and gas distribution and storage, water supply, transportation, emergency services, and government services.

There have been numerous attacks against these infrastructures. Hackers have invaded the public phone networks, compromising nearly every category of activity, including switching and operations, administration, maintenance, and provisioning (OAM&P). They have crashed or disrupted signal transfer points, traffic switches, OAM&P systems, and other network elements. They have planted "time bomb" programs designed to shut down major switching hubs, disrupted emergency 911 services throughout the eastern seaboard, and boasted that they have the capability to bring down all switches in Manhattan. They have installed wiretaps, rerouted phone calls, changed the greetings on voice mail systems, taken over voice mailboxes, and made free long-distance calls at their victims= expense — sticking some victims with phone bills in the hundreds of thousands of dollars. When they can=t crack the technology, they use "social engineering" to con employees into giving them access.

In March 1997, one teenage hacker penetrated and disabled a telephone company computer that serviced the Worcester Airport in Massachusetts. As a result, telephone service to the Federal Aviation Administration control tower, the airport fire department, airport security, the weather service, and various private airfreight companies was cut off for six hours. Later in the day, the juvenile disabled another telephone company computer, this time causing an outage in the Rutland area. The lost service caused financial damages and threatened public health and public safety. On a separate occasion, the hacker allegedly broke into a pharmacist=s computer and accessed files containing prescriptions.

Banks and financial systems are a popular target of cyber criminals. The usual motive is money, and perpetrators have stolen or attempted to steal tens of millions of dollars. In one case of sabotage, a computer operator at Reuters in Hong Kong tampered with the dealing room systems of five of the company=s bank clients. In November 1996, he programmed the systems to delete key operating system files after a delay long enough to allow him to leave the building. When the "time bombs" exploded, the systems crashed. They were partially restored by the next morning, but it took another day before they were fully operational. However, the banks said the tampering did not significantly affect trading and that neither they nor their clients experienced losses. In another act of sabotage against a critical infrastructure, a fired employee of Chevron's emergency alert network disabled the firm=s alert system by hacking into computers in New York and San Jose, California, and reconfiguring them so they=d crash. The vandalism was not discovered until an emergency arose at the Chevron refinery in Richmond, California, and the system could not be used to notify the adjacent community of a noxious release. During the 10-hour period in 1992 when the system was down, thousands of people in 22 states and 6 unspecified areas of Canada were put at risk.

An overflow of raw sewage on the Sunshine Coast of Australia in June was linked to a 49-year-old Brisbane man, who allegedly penetrated the

Maroochy Shire Council's computer system and used radio transmissions to create the overflows. The man faced 370 charges that included stealing, computer hacking, and use radio communications equipment without authority.

Government computers, particularly Department of Defence computers, are a regular target of attack. Detected attacks against unclassified DoD computers rose from 780 in 1997 to 5,844 in 1998 and 22,144 in 1999.

The most damaging and costly attacks have been conducted for reasons other than the pursuit of terrorism. As the above cases illustrate, they have been motivated by greed, thrills, ego, revenge, and a variety of other non-ideological factors. They are properly classifified as cybercrimes, but not cyberterrorism

Politically and Socially Motivated Cyberattacks

Terrorism is normally associated with attacks conducted in furtherance of political and social objectives. Numerous cyberattacks have been so motivated. For example, in 1998, ethnic Tamil guerrillas swamped Sri Lankan embassies with 800 e-mails a day over a two-week period. The messages read "We are the Internet Black Tigers and were doing this to disrupt your communications." Intelligence authorities characterized it as the first known attack by terrorists against a country's computer systems.

Also in 1998, Spanish protestors bombarded the Institute for Global Communications (IGC) with thousands of bogus e-mail messages. E-mail was tied up and undeliverable to the San Francisco based ISP's users, and support lines were tied up with people who couldn't get their mail. The protestors also spammed IGC staff and member accounts, clogged their Web page with bogus credit card orders, and threatened to employ the same tactics against organizations using IGC services.

They demanded that IGC stop hosting the Webs site for the *Euskal Herria Journal*, a New York-based publication supporting Basque independence. Protestors said IGC supported terrorism because a section on the Web pages contained materials on the terrorist group Fatherland and Liberty, or ETA, which claimed responsibility for assassinations of Spanish political and security officials, and attacks on military installations. IGC finally relented and pulled the site because of the "mail bombings." During the Kosovo conflict in 1999, NATO computers were blasted with e-mail bombs and hit with denial-of-service attacks by hacktivists protesting the NATO bombings. In addition, businesses, public organizations, and academic institutes received highly politicized virus-laden e-mails from a range of Eastern European countries, according to reports. Web defacements were also common. After the Chinese

Embassy was accidentally bombed in Belgrade, Chinese hacktivists posted messages such as "We won't stop attacking until the war stops!" on U.S. government Web sites.

Since December 1997, the Electronic Disturbance Theater (EDT), a New York City based activist group, has been conducting Web sit-ins against various sites in support of the Mexican Zapatistas. At a designated time, thousands of protestors point their browsers to a target site using software that floods the target with rapid and repeated download requests. EDTs software has also been used by animal rights groups against organizations said to abuse animals. Electrohippies, another group of hacktivists, conducted Web sit-ins against the WTO when they met in Seattle in late 1999. These sit-ins all require mass participation to have much effect, and thus are more suited to use by activists than by relatively small groups of terrorists operating in secrecy.

While the above incidents were motivated by political and social reasons, whether they were sufficiently harmful or frightening to be classified as cyberterrorism is a judgement call. To the best of my knowledge, no attack so far has led to violence or injury to persons, although some may have intimidated their victims. Both EDT and the Electrohippies view their operations as acts of civil disobedience, analogous to street protests and physical sit-ins, not as acts of violence or terrorism. This is an important distinction. Most activists, whether participating in a street march or Web sit-in, are not terrorists.

However, there are a few indications that some terrorist groups are pursuing cyberterrorism, either alone or in conjunction with acts of physical violence. In February 1998, Clark Staten told the Senate Judiciary Committee Subcommittee on Technology, Terrorism, and Government Information that it was believed that "members of some Islamic extremist organizations have been attempting to develop a 'hacker network' to support their computer activities and even engage in offensive information warfare attacks in the future."

In November 1998, the *Detroit News* reported that Khalid Ibrahim, who claimed to be a member of the militant Indian separatist group Harkat-ul-Ansar, had tried to buy military software from hackers who had stolen it from Department of Defence computers they had penetrated. The attempted purchase was discovered when an 18-year-old hacker calling himself Chameleon attempted to cash a $1,000 check from Ibrahim. Chameleon said he did not have the software and did not give it to Ibrahim, but Ibrahim may have obtained it or other sensitive information from one of the many other hackers he approached. Harkat-ul-Ansar declared war on the United States following the August cruise-missile attack on a suspected terrorist training camp in Afghanistan run by bin Laden, which allegedly killed nine of their members.

The Provisional Irish Republican Army employed the services of contract hackers to penetrate computers in order to acquire home addresses of law enforcement and intelligence officers, but the data was used to draw up plans to kill the officers in a single "night of the long knives" if the British government did not meet terms for a new cease-fire. As this case illustrates, terrorists may use hacking as a way of acquiring intelligence in support of physical violence, even if they do not use it to wreak havoc in cyberspace.

Terrorists might also engage in computer network attacks as a way of financing physical operations. For example, they could penetrate an e-commerce Web site and steal credit card numbers, conduct fraudulent transactions against an Internet bank, or extort money from victims by threatening electronic sabotage.

Potential Threat

To understand the potential threat of cyberterrorism, two factors must be considered: first, whether there are targets that are vulnerable to attack that could lead to violence or severe harm, and second, whether there are actors with the capability and motivation to carry them out.

Looking first at vulnerabilities, several studies have shown that critical infrastructures are potentially vulnerable to cyberterrorist attack. Eligible Receiver, a Ano notice@ exercise conducted by the Department of Defence in 1997 with support from National Security Agency penetration testing teams, found the power grid and emergency 911 systems had weaknesses that could be exploited by an adversary using only publicly available tools on the Internet. Although neither of these systems were actually attacked, study members concluded that service on these systems could be disrupted. Also in 1997, the President=s Commission on Critical Infrastructure Protection issued its report warning that through mutual dependencies and interconnectedness, critical infrastructures could be vulnerable in new ways, and that vulnerabilities were steadily increasing, while the costs of attack were decreasing.

Although many of the weaknesses in computerized systems can be corrected, it is effectively impossible to eliminate all of them. Even if the technology itself offers good security, it is frequently configured or used in ways that make it open to attack. In addition, there is always the possibility of insiders, acting alone or in concert with other terrorists, misusing their access capabilities. According to Russia's Interior Ministry Col. Konstantin Machabeli, the state-run gas monopoly, Gazprom, was hit by hackers in 1999 who collaborated with a Gazprom insider. The hackers were said to have used a Trojan horse to gain control of the central switchboard which controls gas flows in pipelines, although Gazprom, the worlds largest natural gas producer and the largest gas supplier to Western Europe, refuted the report.

Consultants and contractors are frequently in a position where they could cause grave harm. This past March, Japan's Metropolitan Police Department reported that a software system they had procured to track 150 police vehicles, including unmarked cars, had been developed by the Aum Shinryko cult. At the time of the discovery, the cult had received classified tracking data on 115 vehicles. Further, the cult had developed software for at least 80 Japanese firms and 10 government agencies. They had worked as subcontractors to other firms, making it almost impossible for the organizations to know who was developing the software. As subcontractors, the cult could have installed Trojan horses to launch or facilitate cyberterrorist attacks at a later date. Fearing a Trojan horse of their own, last February, the U.S. State Department sent an urgent cable to about 170 embassies asking them to remove software, which they belatedly realized had been written by citizens of the former Soviet Union. If we take as given that critical infrastructures are vulnerable to a cyberterrorist attack, then the question becomes whether there are actors with the capability and motivation to carry out such an operation. While many hackers have the knowledge, skills, and tools to attack computer systems, they generally lack the motivation to cause violence or severe economic or social harm. Conversely, terrorists who are motivated to cause violence seem to lack the capability or motivation to cause that degree of damage in cyberspace.

TYPES OF CYBERTERROR CAPABILITY

The following three levels of cyberterror capability is defined by Monterey group:

- Simple-Unstructured: The capability to conduct basic hacks against individual systems using tools created by someone else. The organization possesses little target analysis, command and control, or learning capability.
- Advanced-Structured: The capability to conduct more sophisticated attacks against multiple systems or networks and possibly, to modify or create basic hacking tools. The organization possesses an elementary target analysis, command and control, and learning capability.
- Complex-Coordinated: The capability for a coordinated attack capable of causing mass-disruption against integrated, heterogeneous defenses (including cryptography). Ability to create sophisticated hacking tools. Highly capable target analysis, command and control, and organization learning capability.

Concerns

As the Internet becomes more pervasive in all areas of human endeavor, individuals or groups can use the anonymity afforded by cyberspace to threaten citizens, specific groups (i.e. with membership based on ethnicity or belief), communities and entire countries, without the inherent threat of capture, injury, or death to the attacker that being physically present would bring.

Many groups such as Anonymous, use tools such as Denial-of-service attack to attack and censor groups who oppose them, creating many concerns for freedom and respect for differences of thought.

Many believe that cyberterrorism is an extreme threat to our economy, and fear an attack could potentially lead to another Great Depression. Several leaders agree that cyberterrorism has the highest percentage of threat over other possible attacks on U.S. territory.

Although natural disasters are considered a top threat and have proven to be devastating to people and land, there is ultimately little that can be done to prevent such events from happening. Thus, the expectation is to focus more on preventative measures that will make Internet attacks impossible for execution.

As the Internet continues to expand, and computer systems continue to be assigned increased responsibility while becoming more complex and interdependent, sabotage or terrorism via the Internet may become a more serious threat and is possibly one of the top 10 events to "end the human race."

Dependence on the internet is rapidly increasing on a worldwide scale, creating a platform for international cyber terror plots to be formulated and executed as a direct threat to national security. For terrorists, cyber-based attacks have distinct advantages over physical attacks. They can be conducted remotely, anonymously, and relatively cheaply, and they do not require significant investment in weapons, explosive and personnel. The effects can be widespread and profound. Incidents of cyberterrorism are likely to increase. They will be conducted through denial of service attacks, malware, and other methods that are difficult to envision today.

In an article about cyber attacks by Iran and North Korea, the New York Times observes, "The appeal of digital weapons is similar to that of nuclear capability: it is a way for an outgunned, outfinanced nation to even the playing field. 'These countries are pursuing cyberweapons the same way they are pursuing nuclear weapons,' said James A. Lewis, a computer security expert at the Center for Strategic and International Studies in Washington. 'It's primitive; it's not top of the line, but it's good enough and they are committed to getting it.'"

History

Public interest in cyberterrorism began in the late 1980s. As 2000 approached, the fear and uncertainty about the millennium bug heightened, as did the potential for attacks by cyber terrorists.

Although the millennium bug was by no means a terrorist attack or plot against the world or the United States, it did act as a catalyst in sparking the fears of a possibly large-scale devastating cyber-attack. Commentators noted that many of the facts of such incidents seemed to change, often with exaggerated media reports.

The high profile terrorist attacks in the United States on September 11, 2001 and the ensuing War on Terror by the US led to further media coverage of the potential threats of cyberterrorism in the years following. Mainstream media coverage often discusses the possibility of a large attack making use of computer networks to sabotage critical infrastructures with the aim of putting human lives in jeopardy or causing disruption on a national scale either directly or by disruption of the national economy.

Authors such as Winn Schwartau and John Arquilla are reported to have had considerable financial success selling books which described what were purported to be plausible scenarios of mayhem caused by cyberterrorism. Many critics claim that these books were unrealistic in their assessments of whether the attacks described (such as nuclear meltdowns and chemical plant explosions) were possible. A common thread throughout what critics perceive as cyberterror-hype is that of non-falsifiability; that is, when the predicted disasters fail to occur, it only goes to show how lucky we've been so far, rather than impugning the theory.

U.S. military

The US Department of Defense (DoD) charged the United States Strategic Command with the duty of combating cyberterrorism. This is accomplished through the Joint Task Force-Global Network Operations, which is the operational component supporting USSTRATCOM in defense of the DoD's Global Information Grid. This is done by integratingGNO capabilities into the operations of all DoD computers, networks, and systems used by DoD combatant commands, services and agencies.

On November 2, 2006, the Secretary of the Air Force announced the creation of the Air Force's newest MAJCOM, the Air Force Cyber Command, which would be tasked to monitor and defend American interest in cyberspace. The plan was however replaced by the creation of Twenty-Fourth Air Force which became active in August 2009 and would be a component of the planned United States Cyber Command.

On December 22, 2009, the White House named its head of Computer security as Howard Schmidt to coordinate U.S Government, military and intelligence efforts to repel hackers. He left the position in May, 2012. Michael Daniel was appointed to the position of White House Coordinator of Cyber Security the same week and continues in the position during the second term of the Obama administration.

Estonia and NATO

The Baltic state of Estonia was target to a massive denial-of-service attack that ultimately rendered the country offline and shut out from services dependent on Internet connectivity for three weeks in the spring of 2007. The infrastructure of Estonia including everything from online banking and mobile phone networks to government services and access to health care information was disabled for a time. The tech-dependent state was in severe problem and there was a great deal of concern over the nature and intent of the attack. The cyber attack corresponded to an Estonian-Russian dispute over the removal of a bronze statue depicting a World War II-era Soviet soldier from the center of the capital, Tallinn. In the midst of the armed conflict with Russia, Georgia likewise was subject to sustanined and coordinated attacks on its electronic infrastructure in August 2008. In both of these cases, circumstantial evidence point to coordinated Russian attacks, but attribution of the attacks is difficult; though both the countries point the finger at Moscow, proof establishing legal culpability is lacking.

Estonia joined NATO in 2004, therefore NATO carefully monitored its member state's response to the attack and worried both about escalation and the possibility of cascading effects beyond Estonia's border to other NATO members. In 2008, directly as a result of the attacks, NATO opened a new center of excellence on cyberdefense to conduct research and training on cyber warfare in Tallinn.

China

The Chinese Defense Ministry confirmed the existence of an online defense unit in May 2011. Composed of about thirty elite internet specialists, the so-called "Cyber Blue Team," or "Blue Army," is officially claimed to be engaged in cyber-defense operations, though there are fears the unit has been used to penetrate secure online systems of foreign governments.

Israel

May 2011 Israeli Prime Minister Benjamin Netanyahu announced the establishment of the National Internet Defense Taskforce, charged with developing tools to secure vital Israeli online infrastructure. "The main responsibility of the taskforce will be to expand the state's ability to defend vital infrastructure networks against cybernetic terrorist attacks perpetrated by foreign countries and terrorist elements."

Examples

An operation can be done by anyone anywhere in the world, for it can be performed thousands of miles away from a target. An attack can cause serious damage to a critical infrastructure which may result in casualties. Attacking an infrastructure can be power grids, monetary systems, dams, media, and personal information. Some attacks are conducted in furtherance of political and social objectives, as the following examples illustrate:

- In 1996, a computer hacker allegedly associated with the White Supremacist movement temporarily disabled a Massachusetts ISP and damaged part of the ISP's record keeping system. The ISP had attempted to stop the hacker from sending out worldwide racist messages under the ISP's name. The hacker signed off with the threat, "you have yet to see true electronic terrorism. This is a promise."
- In 1998, Spanish protesters bombarded the Institute for Global Communications (IGC) with thousands of bogus e-mail messages. E-mail was tied up and undeliverable to the ISP's users, and support lines were tied up with people who couldn't get their mail. The protestors also spammed IGC staff and member accounts, clogged their Web page with bogus credit card orders, and threatened to employ the same tactics against organizations using IGC services. They demanded that IGC stop hosting the Web site for the Euskal Herria Journal, a New York-based publication supporting Basque independence. Protestors said IGC supported terrorism because a section on the Web pages contained materials on the terrorist group ETA, which claimed responsibility for assassinations of Spanish political and security officials, and attacks on military installations. IGC finally relented and pulled the site because of the "mail bombings."
- In 1998, ethnic Tamil guerrillas attempted to disrupt Sri Lankan embassies by sending large volumes of e-mail. The embassies received 800 e-mails a day over a two-week period. The messages read "We are the Internet Black Tigers and we're doing this to disrupt your communications." Intelligence authorities characterized it as the first known attack by terrorists against a country's computer systems.
- During the Kosovo conflict in 1999, NATO computers were blasted with e-mail bombs and hit with denial-of-service attacks by hacktivists protesting the NATO bombings. In addition, businesses, public organizations, and academic institutes received highly politicized virus-laden e-mails from a range of Eastern European countries, according

to reports. Web defacements were also common. After the Chinese Embassy was accidentally bombed in Belgrade, Chinese hacktivists posted messages such as "We won't stop attacking until the war stops!" on U.S. government Web sites.

- Since December 1997, the Electronic Disturbance Theater (EDT) has been conducting Web sit-ins against various sites in support of the Mexican Zapatistas. At a designated time, thousands of protestors point their browsers to a target site using software that floods the target with rapid and repeated download requests. EDT's software has also been used by animal rights groups against organizations said to abuse animals. Electrohippies, another group of hacktivists, conducted Web sit-ins against the WTO when they met in Seattle in late 1999. These sit-ins all require mass participation to have much effect, and thus are more suited to use by activists than by terrorists.
- In 2000, a Japanese Investigation revealed that the government was using software developed by computer companies affiliated with Aum Shirinkyo, the doomsday sect responsible for the sarin gas attack on the Tokyo subway system in 1995. "The government found 100 types of software programs used by at least 10 Japanese government agencies, including the Defense Ministry, and more than 80 major Japanese companies, including Nippon Telegraph and Telephone." Following the discovery, the Japanese government suspended use of Aum-developed programs out of concern that Aum-related companies may have compromised security by breaching firewalls. gaining access to sensitive systems or information, allowing invasion by outsiders, planting viruses that could be set off later, or planting malicious code that could cripple computer systems and key data system.
- In March 2013, the New York Times reported on a pattern of cyber attacks against U.S. financial institutions believed to be instigated by Iran as well as incidents affecting South Korean financial institutions that originate with the North Korean government.
- In August 2013, media companies including the New York Times, Twitter and the Huffington Post lost control of some of their websites Tuesday after hackers supporting the Syrian government breached the Australian Internet company that manages many major site addresses. The Syrian Electronic Army, a hacker group that has previously attacked media organisations that it considers hostile to the regime of Syrian president Bashar al-Assad, claimed credit for the Twitter and Huffington Post hacks in a series of Twitter messages. Electronic records showed that NYTimes.com, the only site with an hours-long outage, redirected visitors to a server controlled by the Syrian group before it went dark.

Sabotage

Non-political acts of sabotage have caused financial and other damage, as in a case where a disgruntled employee, Vitek Boden (aka Peter Markan) caused the release of 800,000 litres of untreated sewage into waterways in Maroochy Shire, Australia.

More recently, in May 2007 Estonia was subjected to a mass cyber-attack in the wake of the removal of a Russian World War II war memorial from downtown Tallinn. The attack was a distributed denial-of-service attack in which selected sites were bombarded with traffic to force them offline; nearly all Estonian government ministry networks as well as two major Estonian bank networks were knocked offline; in addition, the political party website of Estonia's current Prime Minister Andrus Ansip featured a counterfeit letter of apology from Ansip for removing the memorial statue.

Despite speculation that the attack had been coordinated by the Russian government, Estonia's defense minister admitted he had no conclusive evidence linking cyber attacks to Russian authorities. Russia called accusations of its involvement "unfounded," and neither NATO nor European Commission experts were able to find any conclusive proof of official Russian government participation. In January 2008 a man from Estonia was convicted for launching the attacks against the Estonian Reform Party website and fined.

During the Russia-Georgia War, on 5 August 2008, three days before Georgia launched its invasion of South Ossetia, the websites for OSInform News Agency and OSRadiowere hacked. The OSinform website at osinform.ru kept its header and logo, but its content was replaced by a feed to the Alania TV website content.

Alania TV, a Georgian government supported television station aimed at audiences in South Ossetia, denied any involvement in the hacking of the websites. Dmitry Medoyev, at the time the South Ossetian envoy to Moscow, claimed that Georgia was attempting to cover up information on events which occurred in the lead up to the war.

One such cyber attack caused the Parliament of Georgia and Georgian Ministry of Foreign Affairs websites to be replaced by images comparing Georgian president Mikheil Saakashvili to Adolf Hitler. Other attacks involved denials of service to numerous Georgian and Azerbaijani websites, such as when Russian hackers allegedly disabled the servers of the Azerbaijani Day.Az news agency.

Website Defacement and Denial of Service

Even more recently, in October 2007, the website of Ukrainian president Viktor Yushchenko was attacked by hackers. A radical Russian nationalist youth group, the Eurasian Youth Movement, claimed responsibility. In 1999 hackers attacked NATO computers. The computers flooded them with email and hit them with a denial of service (DoS). The hackers were protesting against the NATO bombings of the Chinese embassy in Belgrade. Businesses, public organizations and academic institutions were bombarded with highly politicized emails containing viruses from other European countries.

In fiction

- The Japanese cyberpunk manga, *Ghost in the Shell* (as well as its popular movie and TV adaptations) centers around an anti-cyberterrorism and cybercrime unit. In its mid-21st century Japan setting such attacks are made all the more threatening by an even more widespread use of technology including cybernetic enhancements to the human body allowing people themselves to be direct targets of cyberterrorist attacks.
- Dan Brown's *Digital Fortress.*
- Amy Eastlake's *Private Lies.*
- In the movie *Live Free or Die Hard,* John McClane (Bruce Willis) takes on a group of cyberterrorists intent on shutting down the entire computer network of the United States.
- The movie *Eagle Eye* involves a super computer controlling everything electrical and networked to accomplish the goal.
- The plots of *24* Day 4 and Day 7 include plans to breach the nation's nuclear plant grid and then to seize control of the entire critical infrastructure protocol.
- The Tom Clancy created series Netforce was about a FBI/Military team dedicated to combating cyberterrorists.
- Much of the plot of *Mega Man Battle Network* is centered around cyberterrorism.
- In the 2009 Japanese animated film *Summer Wars,* an artificial intelligence cyber-terrorist attempts to take control over the world's missiles in order to "win" against the main characters that attempted to keep it from manipulating the world's electronic devices.
- In the 2012 film Skyfall, part of the James Bond franchise, main villain Raoul Silva (Javier Bardem) is an expert cyberterrorist who is responsible for various cyberterrorist incidents in the past.
- Cyberterrorism plays a role in the 2012 video game Call of Duty: Black Ops II, first when main antagonist Raul Menendez cripples the Chinese economy with a cyberattack and frames the United States for it, starting

a new Cold War between the two powers. Later, another cyberattack with a computer worm leads to Menendez seizing control of the entire U.S drone fleet. Finally, one of the game's endings leads to another attack similar to the latter, this time crippling the U.S' electrical and water distribution grids. An alternate ending depicts the cyberattack failing after it is stopped by one of the game's characters pivotal to the storyline.

- The plot of the 2013 video game Watch Dogs is heavily influenced by cyber-terrorism. In which players take control of the game's protagonist, Aiden Pierce, an accused murder suspect, who hacks into a ctOS (Central Operating System), giving him complete control of Chicago's mainframe in order to hunt down his accusers.
- The video game *Metal Slug 4* focuses on Marco and Fio, joined by newcomers Nadia and Trevor, to battle a terrorist organization known as Amadeus that is threatening the world with a computer virus.
- The visual novel *Baldr Force* has the main character Tooru Souma joining a military organization to fight cyberterrorism to avenge the death of his friend.
- The Japanese Manga and Live Action *Bloody Monday* is Highly influenced with Hacking and Cracking, the main character Takagi Fujimaru is a Super Elite hacker which use his hacking knowledge to fight against his enemies.

UNDERSTANDING CYBERTERRORISM

Without a doubt, cyberterrorism poses a real threat to governments, organizations and individuals around the globe. In today's high-tech world, all types of computer networks are logical targets for all sorts of adversaries. In fact, according to a figure from U.S. officials, an astounding 60,000 new malicious computer programs are identified every day.

But how does one exactly define cyberterrorism? In a 2000 testimony before the Armed Services Committee of the U.S. Representatives, Dorothy Denning of Georgetown University coined a still-popular definition of cyberterrorism: "the convergence of terrorism and cyberspace...generally understood to mean unlawful attack and threats of attack against computers, networks and the information stored therein when done to intimidate or coerce a government or its people in furtherance of political or social objectives."

While that may be a mouthful, it does seem to sum it up. Depending on who you ask, however, cyberterrorism can have a somewhat surprising variety of meanings. Why this ambiguity? Well, since cyberterrorism is a relatively new term and is a product of the technological age in which we currently live, its definition is naturally still evolving. And as the technology surrounding cyberterrorism itself changes, the definition of the term will continue to change as well.

"It's hard to define something that's so intangible, so shifty, so below the radar of an otherwise law-abiding society," said Carmi Levy, an independent technology analyst and journalist. "It's also hard to define something most of us would rather shunt out of sight. This is typical behavior, and nothing we haven't seen with earlier forms of anomalous technology-related threats, such as viruses and malware."

The other hurdle he sees is our collective unfamiliarity with the threat. "It's hard to define something until the majority of society agrees it's a problem and has seen enough of it to merit actual recognition," said Levy. "Unfortunately, we're not there yet. Until it touches more of us in a more direct manner, expect it to remain difficult to pin down." Perhaps the thorniest issue is that the term's root word is something society still struggles to define. "The simpler term 'terrorism' itself can have a variety of definitions, and 'cyber' just adds layers of complexity and misunderstanding to the issue," said Kurt Baumgartner, a senior security researcher at Kaspersky Lab, a Moscow-based computer security company.

As the terms "terrorist" and "freedom fighter" have been debated in the past, when it comes to cyberattacks, there can be a fine line between activism and terrorism. And which side of that line an event falls on often varies depending on your perspective. In today's digital world, some see the progression from activist to "hacktivist" as a natural one.

"It's pretty easy to imagine past activist heroes might well have engaged in some type of hacktivism depending if they'd had access to the technology," said John Kindervag, a security expert and principal analyst at Forrester, a research company in Cambridge, Massachusetts.

Kindervag also wonders if defacing a website or bringing down an ecommerce portal, like the 2011 disruption of Sony's Play Station Network, an online video game platform, is actually terrifying or merely inconvenient. "For me, the issue is if individual lives are in jeopardy at the moment of the action," said Kindervag. "Disrupting the air-traffic control system to make planes crash would definitely be cyberterrorism. The Sony Play Station Network attack would not be."

What Kind of Damage Can Cyberterrorism Do?

Since cyberterrorism is such a new brand of crime, we as a society do tend to be somewhat complacent when it comes to cybersecurity. However, in the near future, we can only expect to hear more about both cyberterrorism threats and actual incidents.

"The threat will only grow with the passage of time," said Levy. "And it's up to everyone to begin treating it as it deserves to be treated: with respect." Currently, the most frightening potential attacks are those that come from all angles. Baumgartner envisions a scenario in which cyberterrorists simultaneously disrupt communications systems, infrastructure controls and financial markets. Such a wide-net strike would be difficult to pull off, but the resources may exist—for the right price.

"It somewhat depends on the attackers' goals and capabilities," he said, "but capabilities are for sale."

In terms of actually inciting terror, most rightfully fear bombings and explosions more than anything else. But the damage caused by cyberterrorism attacks can induce a different brand of fear since they are orchestrated by a faceless evildoer.

"Tangibly, we can all relate: a power plant could be taken offline, a company's finances could be wrecked and a region's ability to communicate wiped out," said Levy. "Intangibly, the psychological impact could be even greater and longer-lasting, as cyberterrorism strikes at the very heart of what makes us feel safe in a supposedly safe society."

This can lead to a feeling of helplessness. "It allows enemies to easily bypass the traditional barriers of military and geography, and it allows them to get at the soft underbelly of day-to-day society," said Levy. "Fear of these types of attacks, in many respects, is just as debilitating as the overt effects might be."

While definitive, public accounts of large-scale acts of cyberterrorism can be difficult to come by, there have been some comparatively smaller-scale examples of cyberattacks in the recent past. The hacker group Anonymous, for example, has launched multiple attacks against authorities. Founded in 2003, this group of loosely associated hackers is extremely opposed to any type of internet surveillance and censorship.

"These attacks illustrate the broadly disruptive impact of a distributed, focused campaign to take down resources controlled by forces they deem the enemy," said Levy. "Chicago's police department, for example, was taken down earlier this year, and law enforcement agencies in Ontario had usernames and passwords published by hackers claiming to be affiliated with Anonymous."

While groups with agendas similar to Anonymous will likely continue to carry out attacks regardless of the day's political climate, social factors have driven other hacktivists to action. "The Occupy movement as well as the Arab Spring spawned an upsurge in this type of activity," said Levy. With respect to governmental organizations, Stuxnet, a malicious computer "worm" designed to interfere with the nuclear program in Iran, was accidentally discovered in 2010 when the virus left the digital perimeter of Iran's Natanz plant and reached the wider internet.

According to the *New York Times,* this malicious code was developed by both the United States and Israel. Since then, two new versions of this worm have been discovered.

In May 2012, another piece of malware, a virus called Flame, was uncovered. This virus infiltrated the computers of high-ranking officials in Iran with the goal of collecting information. Flame appeared to be approximately five years old when it is was found, and the *Washington Post* has reported that it was designed by the United States; publicly, U.S. officials have not stated that they were responsible for creating this particular virus.

During April and May of 2007, Estonia was the victim of violence, riots and cyberattacks after officials moved a memorial commemorating the Soviet liberation of Estonia from the Nazis during World War II. Hackers shut down government ministry websites, two important banking websites and political party websites.

They even disabled the email server for the Estonian parliament. Officials in Estonia accused the Russian government of orchestrating the denial-of-service attacks, but NATO and the European Commission were unable to find concrete evidence to prove these allegations.

In 2011, researchers from various high-tech companies uncovered a Trojan horse called Sykipot. This cyberweapon attempted to obtain documents from high-ranking executives, mainly those in the defense field at companies that developed unmanned drone planes. Officials believe that these attacks are coming from an established group located in China.

While we all like to hope that our government infrastructure is infallible, such attacks show that 100% protection is likely impossible. "Every system has areas of vulnerability, and there is no such thing as an inviolable or impenetrable solution," said Levy. "Like conventional crime, military and quasi-military threats, it's foolish to think we'll ever be 100% safe. The world has simply never worked that way, and it isn't about to start now."

How Do We Stop Cyberterrorists?

While no amount of improvement will ever ensure society is cyberattack-free, experts say that governments and organizations should be proactive when it comes to investing in preventative measures. As technology continues to move forward at an alarming rate, so too must the laws regarding cyberactivities. Because currently, neither civilian nor government officials are truly able to combat this new and ever-changing threat. "Traditional law enforcement tools and processes need to be updated or replaced entirely," said Levy. Baumgartner feels similarly. "It is important to get past the short-term political gimmicks and silliness that we have seen and get down to business," he said. "Addressing the problem effectively is a complex and difficult task, and overburdening defenders with ineffective tasks that waste time instead of necessary solutions is a difficult balance."

To reach the proper balance, Levy recommends that law enforcement officials and business leaders strive for improved task forces, specialized training, and a re-prioritization of resources toward this class of crime. This, he believes, will greatly reduce the risk of attack and lower the severity and impact if an attack does occur.

"They can raise the vulnerability bar sufficiently high to discourage the lesser-skilled and motivated attackers, and make life sufficiently difficult on the true pros," said Levy.

Unfortunately, in his view, those who built the last-generation standards of policing the digital world may not be up to the task without extensive and expensive retraining. And even then, they may not be able to adapt their capabilities to this new reality.

"The existing culture within law enforcement may be inadequate," said Levy. "No one project or initiative will be enough to adapt. Nothing short of a wholesale rebuild of government and law enforcement best practices will do."

4

Military Information Technology

Arabian sands had no safe haven for U.S. troops during Operation Iraqi Freedom. Dotting the barren Kuwaiti and Iraqi frontier, soldiers and airmen routinely found themselves targets of enemy rocket attacks and frontline probing actions.

Seasoned combat troops might expect such dangers, but not reservists in the 335th Theater Signal Command, who built, secured and maintained the American and coalition forces' IT networks. Firewalls and IDSes kept enemy hackers off their systems, but they relied on nearby Patriot batteries to keep Saddam Hussein's Ababil-100 missiles at bay.

It has been a year since U.S. troops pushed across the Kuwaiti border in their drive toward Baghdad. In the weeks leading up to the war and those tumultuous two months of heavy fighting, the network and security specialists supporting the combat divisions found that there are worse things than a bad day at the office.

"Everything is relative," says Tom Lantzy, a major in the U.S. Army Reserve who recently returned to his job as an infrastructure project manager for CocaCola. "If you've never been in a situation where someone is shooting at you, it may be that the server crash is the biggest problem you've ever dealt with."

Modern armed forces depend on high technology. Military intelligence, battle plans, troop movements and the availability of supplies are just some of the information that's converted into digital form and transmitted over cables, radio and satellites. Leave even a single crack and an enemy with access to computers and trained experts (hardly in short supply these days) could tap your entire command and control infrastructure. In other words, a breach could cost lives.

"Computer network defense issues and challenges in the commercial world and the military world are similar," says Lt. Col. Thomas Michelli, a Virginia National Guardsman deployed in Kuwait, where he oversees the Southwestern Asia CERT. "Except that the risks – mission-critical systems equal human lives – are much higher in the military world."

Marching Orders

The hurdles faced by the 335th dwarfed those of the civilian world, where mortar fire and missiles don't rain down. Creating and managing network systems – which link all U.S. units with those of 30 nations contributing troops or logistical support – was equivalent to integrating the complete IT systems for eight to 10 medium-sized corporations. The 335th rolled out the systems in just two months, an operation Lantzy estimates would have taken a full year in the corporate world.

"We moved more than 250,000 soldiers, Marines and coalition forces into a very small country about the size of Massachusetts," says Maj. Gen. Rip Dettamore, commander of the 335th and head of communications for all land forces in the Middle East.

Military units had to be plugged into the infrastructure that would connect them to their lifeblood – supplies, intelligence and instructions. Although there was a secure backbone for units already stationed in Kuwait, the 335th had to scale the infrastructure from 10 routers to approximately 600. Network bandwidth had to jump from 16 Mbps to nearly 200. Every unit needed a satellite link, IDS, router and other hardware and software.

The mission was immeasurably difficult because different services used different systems and standards. Even the various parts of the U.S. Armed Forces using the same equipment would configure them differently. Then, there was the need to integrate different databases and OSes to provide unified views of theater operations.

Another aggravating factor was that responsibility for critical IT jobs was split among different organizations because the total task was larger than the Army, the Air Force or the Marines could handle individually. For instance, the Army would install IDSes, but the Air Force would run them.

"I'm going to send this airman out, who is going to put in this new intrusion detection sensor, and you're going to have to reengineer the data package, maybe change the IP subnetting, which influences the way the routers work," Lantzy says.

While much of the equipment is off the shelf, important elements of the infrastructure are specific to the military and make securing the network easier. The Army uses one unsecured network that's connected to the Internet, and two closed satellite- and microwave-based networks for all critical information, as well as voice communications and video teleconferencing. Frequency-hopping and NSA Type-1 encryption are standard issue. All traffic and networks are protected with layers of firewalls, IDSes, proxy servers and tightly configured routers.

Hostile Environment

The climate was as hazardous and unwelcoming to the equipment as it was to the IT soldiers. In the first days of the war, the worst sandstorms in decades kicked up, leaving foot-deep drifts overnight and driving sand everywhere. Soldiers venturing into the open had to completely cover themselves to avoid getting burned by the blasting particles. The weather became a concern for the 335th, which had to keep shifting and blowing sand from tearing apart the infrastructure.

"Opening up a server over there at a garrison base where it had been running a couple of months, the dust was an eighth of an inch thick, at least," says Lantzy. "It looked like somebody took the cover off and just poured it in there." Soldiers had to constantly clear out equipment with brushes and fans. In some cases, they improvised makeshift telecom facilities and data centers to protect equipment from the elements.

At first, in mid-March and early April 2003, the heat wasn't too bad in Kuwait, hovering in the 70s. Later, temperatures crept up to summer highs of 130 degrees. "You could be standing outside, and you felt that you had 2,000-watt hair dryers blowing in your face," says Dettamore. The 335th deployed air conditioning units to keep buildings, tents and shelters cool.

"You'd much rather be in the air conditioning taking care of the equipment than trying to sleep in a tent when it's 130 degrees," he laughs. "Given the two choices, it's no wonder that the equipment was clean."

Combat Conditions

Even with the occasional relief of cool air, the 335th had to keep systems up and secure under difficult conditions. Under the threat of chemical attack, Lantzy and his unit lived in their heavy protective suits for nearly two weeks. A rising and falling wail announced incoming missiles, and everyone at the base had to don a gas mask, boots and gloves. The sirens would give way to the whoosh of intercepting Patriots.

The threat of chemical-tipped missiles didn't stop the mission. IT specialists often had to work through the air raids, which presented their own challenges.

"It's hard to type," Lantzy says. "Most people use a pencil to type one letter at a time, because the gloves are so [thick] that you mash several keys at the same time. It's a very frustrating exercise." No matter the threat, the basic tasks facing corporate information security personnel were the same. IDSes and firewalls needed configuring, servers needed patching and AV needed updating. Soldiers of the 335th had to monitor attempts to breach the network. Their mission was complicated by the massive scale of their operation and the possibility that the next moment might be their last.

In one case, a server in one of the forward units hadn't installed a critical patch. When the command centre called, the unit said it would take a while to install the fix — its sysadmin had been wounded in a mortar attack.

All the work paid off, with uptimes on all equipment and systems exceeding 99 percent. Dettamore reports that not a single critical video teleconference or data link was lost during the war.

Coming Home

Things are quieter on the home front, and many of the veterans have a greater clarity of mind knowing that safety will always be more important than the latest Internet worm.

But their minds wander back to the desert. Some miss the adrenaline boost of near death and total commitment to a job. Newscasts also bring reality to their doorsteps.

"One of the guys we did some planning with was killed in November," says a subdued Lantzy. "They're your friends, your coworkers, and they're still over there, and there's still a threat."

MILITARY USE OF HIGH TECHNOLOGY

While superior technology has been a decisive factor in wars in all of history, it was only in the last century that the armed forces incorporated science into their organisation in a systematic way. In particular after World War 2, rich/large/leading nations built up big centers for military research and development (R&D) and funded innovation in military industry on a large scale. Much of this was connected to nuclear weapons and their carriers, but increasingly was carried over to all other areas of warfare. Armed conflict is about breaking the will of an opponent by violent force.

The law and rules of civilian society – that exclude pursuing one's will by force – no longer apply. Only the law of warfare poses some limits on how force is used; in peace time, agreed arms limitations can reduce the likelihood of war and restrict the number and quality of its tools. Success in armed conflict depends on many factors, among them technology, strategy, morale and surprise. Since highest national values may be at stake, there is an immanent tendency to circumvent the rules in order to prevail. In peace time, there is a motive to covertly compile more armaments than what arms-control agreements stipulate. This emphasises the importance of verification of compliance. In actual conduct of war, on the other hand, compliance with the international law of warfare depends on the spirit of a force; public scrutiny, experience with rule-keeping by the opponent, but also the fear of reprisal play a role. When armed conflict is raging, there is no reliance on the law of warfare; the necessity of prosecuting war criminals by international courts is only too obvious. Since technology increasingly provides advantages in battle, all potential opponents have strong motives to stay in the lead, or at least to keep the lag small.

New fields of technology make possible new ways of destruction. Military exploitation of new technology means putting the new possibilities into practice: researching the potential, developing and testing devices. Sometimes international law or arms-control treaties impose limits– e.g. the Biological and Toxin Weapons Convention of 1972 prohibits all non-peaceful uses of biological agents and toxins, including development and testing.

Offensive biological weapons are prohibited thus, whereas defensive protection (such as gas masks, vaccination) is allowed. However, in principle an opponent might break the rules covertly and achieve victory in this way. Thus, there is a strong motive to understand what such an opponent could bring to bear in order to be prepared to counter such development.

As a consequence, even a defensive-minded state can feel a need for some R&D of the forbidden offensive weapons. In such a way, scientific-technical advance has a tendency to undermine agreed limitation treaties.

The only ways to contain this danger between potential opponents are 1) reliable verification of compliance with existing agreements, and 2) early conclusion of treaties for new technologies, that is preventive arms control.

A central means of securing effectiveness in combat is secrecy. Knowledge of technical details, strategies, plans, even the motivation of an opponent's armed forces makes attacking them easier, thus there is a strong motive to keep such information secret on the own side– and to gain it by espionage on the others.

There can be many additional motives for secrecy, and states differ widely how they handle it. The more secretive an armed force is, the higher is the possibility of a covert breakout: massing of weapons or personnel, introduction of qualitatively new weapons so that one side would suddenly dominate militarily.

This problem becomes more urgent if new technology promises revolutionary change, as is the case with NT. Again it points at the necessity of supporting agreed limits by reliable verification, but it also emphasises the need to balance the required transparency with the (perceived) need for secrecy.

When potential military opponents prepare for the possibility of war by using new technology, small differences in technology can lead to high differences in the outcome. It is relative differences that count mostly. Shooting somewhat faster, at somewhat longer range, looking somewhat farther etc. can all mean that one's systems survive whereas the other's are destroyed.

This explains the race for the "leading edge" and the high price that the military are prepared to pay for new technology. It makes agreement on limitations more difficult. However, there are additional factors; e.g. a more defensive orientation can give more tolerance.

Mainly because of their very task – prevailing in armed conflict by selective or massive destruction – the armed forces want to prepare many of the bad and ugly uses of new technologies that civilian society will try hard to preclude. Criminal development of such prohibited uses – new poisons, eavesdropping equipment etc. – within society is severely restricted. Access to laboratories, expertise, testing grounds etc. is very difficult if one has to work clandestinely, under permanent threat of prosecution. On the other hand, in military R&D such activities are carried out in an organised manner under the protection and with the resources of the states. This sets a conceptually different framework for technology assessment and subsequent regulation.

Within societies, there is a higher authority with the monopoly of legitimate force that protects sub-state actors from attacks by others and prosecutes perpetrators. The international system, on the other hand, can still be characterised by the security dilemma. There is no overarching authority with a monopoly of force – states try to make themselves secure by their individual armed forces. Usually, strengthening the latter increases the mutual threats, leading to motives for further strengthening. If unchecked, the net outcome is decreased security of all.

There are several ways out of this security dilemma– they are mutually reinforcing. One is voluntary agreement limiting the mutual armed forces (arms control). Since the armed forces keep their task of prevailing in war, should it occur, there is an obvious friction between the motives for limitation and the motives for combat effectiveness. Nevertheless, an enlightened view of national security should lead to the preference of mutual limitations. A second alternative is restructuring of the armed forces so that combat efficiency is high in static defence of the own territory, but is low in attacking others. A third way out of the security dilemma is political détente, economic co-operation etc. so that one could not gain from an attack and it would become politically/culturally unthinkable. Finally, states could develop the United Nations to the international authority with monopoly of legitimate force similarly to the one that governments represent within states.

NEW MILITARY TECHNOLOGIES

The purpose of armed forces is to break the will of an organized opponent by violent force. Who will prevail depends to some extent on comparative recklessness. Thus, war and the preparations for it do not only go beyond civilized behaviour, but carry an inherent tendency to transcend all other rules, including the ones applying to armed conflict. Innovation in military technology can become an extension of warfare itself. Being ahead in technology provides an important advantage in armed conflict, and if the lead position is not attainable, then one should at least stay as close as possible behind.

Thus, all potential opponents have constant strong motives for military research and development and for incorporating their results into the armed forces. Secrecy and worst-case assumptions – both to some extent necessary elements of military preparation – increase these motives. Military applications of new technologies take place in a framework that is quite different from civilian ones: the bad and ugly uses are not results of accidents or criminal actions – they are prepared in an organized way on a large scale by and with the resources of the state. A special problem arises here: states have to reckon with an opponent using any means at hand. If technology allows new, more effective weapons, they might be used– even if they violate the law of warfare. In order to protect oneself, one needs to know the characteristics of the new weapon; this creates a motive to research and develop the new weapon oneself – which, in turn, creates mistrust and fear between potential opponents.

An example of this mechanism can be seen in the debate regarding biological-weapons – what constitutes legitimate defensive research, and where does forbidden development of biological-warfare agents begin? Of course, the economic capacity of the state limits its pursuit of weapons, and limitation is also possible by political decision. Self-restraint may be exercised in respect of national or international public opinion. Limits are also implied by the international law of warfare. Finally, potential opponents may agree on mutual limitations (arms control). In general, for these to be effective, there need to be reliable ways of verifying compliance.

General Aspects of War and Peace

Throughout history, improved technology has provided advantages in battle. In the 20th century, science and technology became tightly integrated with the system for waging and preparing war. Following the Second World War, military research and development (R&D) continued to expand, in particular in the USA and USSR.

The 1950s to 1970s, roughly, marked the era of "big science" – big in budget and in physical scale, while often in pursuit of control over the very small. Nuclear bombs, nuclear-driven submarines, long-range ballistic missiles, and orbiting satellites mark some of the important milestones in the qualitative and quantitative arms race of the Cold War – achieved at extremely high cost and effort. Even though the Cold War is over, military threats are still at work as instruments of geopolitical will as well as the basic mechanisms of national and international security. Nuclear deterrence is a doctrine still in effect, and thus nuclear war could still start at any time, although this may be improbable. Despite massive reductions (from a high of 65,000 in 1986), there remain about 20,000 nuclear warheads on Earth. The experience of the World Wars has led to a fundamental change in international law.

Through the centuries, states assumed a natural right to go to war – for whatever reason or purpose. With the founding of the UN and the acceptance of its Charter in 1945, maintaining international peace and security became the central imperative (Art. 1). The use of force and threat to use force in international relations were forbidden (Art. 2), with few exceptions: one is force legitimized by the UN Security Council to restore peace and security, and the other is in self-defense until the Security Council has taken its measures (Art. 51). The security mechanisms foreseen in the UN Charter were hardly implemented, and nuclear war after 1945 was not prevented by adherence to its articles, but rather by the threat of mutual annihilation.

Yet the norm established in the UN Charter has had strong effects on the international community. Wars waged since 1945 have usually been claimed to be defensive, and when such claims have been rejected the offending power has often come under collective pressure to cease or restrain its aggression. Of course, the principle of refraining from the use of force except in self-defense is severely endangered if preventive wars are being waged based on perceptions of threats, not on actual aggression.

Thus, we believe the 2003 US war against Iraq has weakened the UN and the international mechanisms of maintaining and restoring peace and security. When armed conflict occurs, regardless of whether it constitutes legitimate or illegitimate use of force according to the UN Charter, the warring parties are limited in their choice of means and methods of warfare by international humanitarian law, which consists of basic as well as specific rules, often written down in international agreements, which evolve over time. Many rules have become customary international law and are binding for all parties to a conflict; this holds, *e.g.*, for the principle of attacking only military targets or of humane treatment of combatants *hors de combat*. Some rules are only obligatory for the respective signatory parties, *e.g.*, the Additional Protocol 2 to the Geneva Conventions of 1949 on non-international armed conflict. Before introducing a new weapon, means or method of warfare, the states are obliged to check whether its employment would be prohibited by international law.

Arms Control and Disarmament

Despite the nuclear threat that loomed throughout the 1950s, limitation talks between the Cold War antagonists were unsuccessful until the experience of the Cuban missile crisis (1962) when nuclear war seemed imminent. Real progress in arms control started with the Partial Test Ban Treaty in 1963.

Important multilateral treaties that followed included the Outer Space Treaty (1967) and the Nuclear Non-Proliferation Treaty (1968). Political relations between the USA and the USSR improved enough to permit the bilateral Anti-Ballistic Missile (ABM) Treaty and SALT I (1972), later SALT II (1979). Another tense period of confrontation and impasse in bilateral arms control followed, until the Soviet approach changed under Gorbachev, leading to the INF and START I Treaties (1987/1991). Full disarmament, that is reduction to zero, was agreed for biological weapons (1972, multilateral), and chemical weapons (1993, multilateral). Nuclear test explosions (1996), and anti-personnel land mines (1997) have also been banned. These agreements have been mostly successful, despite the lack of full participation by all relevant powers, and despite some serious violations which have been detected and exposed – most notably with respect to the Biological Weapons Convention which was implemented without provisions for verification, inviting contempt. General and complete disarmament (all countries, all armaments and armed forces) has been the declared goal of the UN and was mentioned in several arms-control treaties, but this goal has not been seriously pursued in actual policy.

Arms control must be considered an unfinished project, and important gaps remain: there is no ban on nuclear weapons, there is no prohibition on space weapons (except for weapons of mass destruction deployed in space), and limitations on conventional arms and forces exist only in Europe. Recently, arms control and humanitarian law have become endangered by actions of the USA. Even before Sept. 11, 2001 the US refused to ratify the Comprehensive Test Ban Treaty and blocked the negotiations on a Verification Protocol to the Biological Weapons Convention. Recently there have been moves towards easier re-sumption of nuclear tests. In 2002, the USA abrogated the ABM Treaty. The US has also systematically sought to undermine the International Criminal Court that was instituted by the international community.

MILITARY NANOTECHNOLOGY

Nanotechnology will change many aspects of our lives. Powerful computers will be ubiquitous. With the advance of artificial intelligence, the replacement of human labor by artificial systems will accelerate. New materials will lead to higher energy efficiency. Therapeutic drugs will be designed for the individual. Along with opportunities, there are also potential risks, be it to health, the environment, social justice or privacy. Convergence of nano-scale, biomedical, information, and cognitive science and technology (NBIC) can lead to applications with profound impacts on the human condition. The 2001/2 U.S. workshop on NBIC convergence mentioned, *e.g.*, nano-implant devices, slowing down or reversing aging, direct brain-machine interfaces, human-like artificial intelligence.

These and other far-reaching concepts of manipulating the human body and mind imply risks and dangers, as well as ethical challenges, on an unprecedented scale. Containing abuse and unintended consequences will be difficult even in the civilian realm. Military NT applications pose special risks – first, because of the reparations for destructive uses and second because of secrecy. Tackling this problem calls for special efforts. In order to provide reliable information, one can look at actual military NT research and development in the USA, which is both the leader in military NT and also much more transparent about its military research and development than any other country. In addition, one can extrapolate scientific-technical advances and assess what military applications will become possible in principle.

Military NT R&D in the USA: In the USA, military research and development in nanotechnology (NT) has surged. Of the funds for the National Nanotechnology Initiative, one quarter to one third goes to the Department of Defense – in 2003, $ 243 million of $ 774 million. This is far more than any other country – the UK expenditures, for example, were stated as about $ 2.6 million in 2001. Assuming total West European funding five times as high, with similar levels respectively for Russia, China and the remaining countries that are active in military NT R&D, the US expenditure would be five times the sum of all the rest of the world. (In military R&D at large, the USA accounts for two thirds of the global total.)

U.S. work spans a wide range in the spectrum from basic research to advanced technology development – development of actual systems for deployment is still several to many years off. University research grants fund nanoscale machines, carbon nanotubes, quantum computing and magnetic nanoparticles. The Defense Advanced Projects Agency funds projects in magnetic memory, bio-computing, bio-molecular motors, sensors for chemical and biological warfare agents, and micro robots, among many others. The research laboratories of the armed services work on self-assembly of nanostructures, organic light-emitting diodes, carbon nanotubes and composites, nanomaterials for explosives and propellants as well as for armor and projectiles, and many similar topics.

In 2002, the Army selected the Massachusetts Institute of Technology to house an Institute for Soldier Nanotechnologies, with up to 150 staff to work in seven multidisciplinary research teams. Their goals include a battle suit that protects against bullets, chemical and biological agents, and stiffens on demand to act as compress or splint. Sensors are to monitor the body status. For carrying heavy loads, an exoskeleton with "muscles" from artificial molecules is envisaged.

Potential Military Applications of NT: In general, NT can lead to improvements in traditional military systems and to qualitatively new ones. Very small but highly capable computers will be used in weapons, uniforms, logistics, and communication systems. Increasingly sophisticated and discriminating sensors may become very small, and cheap enough that they can be scattered in high numbers to saturate an area, ostensibly yielding "total awareness". Guns will shoot farther, projectiles and missiles with cheap guidance systems will become smaller and more accurate. Vehicles will become lighter and more agile, with more powerful engines and greater range. Energy storage is a key problem for many military systems, and NT is often considered a key to solving it.

Autonomous vehicles (robots) for reconnaissance and communication, but also for fighting, will arrive; some of them may be very small. NT ultimately raises the prospect of even microscopic mobile robots, although macroscopic vehicles are needed for high speed or long distance travel. Sophisticated fighting robots, the successor to today's killer drones and prototype robot combat planes (UCAVs), will be enabled by advanced computers, smart materials, advanced energy and propulsion systems, and other NT-based refinements.

Similarly, NT will contribute to lowering the cost and increasing the capability of space systems, including possibly very small antisatellite weapons. Robotics will be used in logistics, production and automation of complex weapons systems. A key enabler of robotics applications will be advanced computers capable of situation assessment and action planning, for example the motion planning needed to coordinate dextrous manipulators, or to maneuver through "battlespace".

New chemical or biological warfare (CBW) agents may become possible that act selectively only against the intended targets. Nanobiotechnology is ambitious enough to propose robotized artificial microbes, which could become tools of assassination or mass murder. At the same time, nanomaterials for filtration and neutralization, and NT-based sensors and nanomedicine in general may provide new approaches to CBW defense. Advances in biocompatible materials and portable biomedical systems may allow the creation of body implants to monitor health status, release drugs or interface to the nerves and brains of fighters. Their portable computers may evolve into wearable information appliances producing an "augmented reality" which simultaneously gives the fighter access to information from the net and also gives command access to the soldier, placing her under some degree of "remote control".

The tendency toward cyborgization follows directly from such military goals and culminates in the vision of direct brain-technology interfaces, but the possibility of improving in this way on the performance of well-trained human senses and bodies, whether for fighting or for piloting or for thinking interactively, seems remote. NT can be used in enhanced versions of existing nuclear weapons incorporating improvements to safety, reliability, etc., or possibly new types of conventional explosive in the fission primary. More speculative concepts include qualitatively new weapon types such as pure-fusion explosives of arbitrarily small yield. It is hard to predict how NT advances may impact nuclear weapons production and barriers to proliferation, but we have seen substantial advances in these technologies since 1945 and further improvement seems possible.

Scenarios along these lines, of more or less visionary character, are being discussed within the military and national security establishments of the world, particularly the USA, but many of these concepts will not prove militarily effective, as has been the case through-out history. Countermeasures to NT weapons will exploit NT as well, giving rise to complicated correlations of forces and complex arsenals within which unexpected interactions can arise.

Preventive Arms Control

Preventive arms control is qualitative arms control applied to the future; it is about stopping or at least limiting dangerous military developments before they become actual, in particular weapons exploiting or based on new technologies. Limitations can be designed to intervene at the stages of development or testing, or sometimes research. Precedents include:

i) the ABM Treaty, which prohibited not only deployment, but also development of anti-ballistic missile systems that are sea-based, air-based, space-based or mobile land-based;

ii) the nuclear testing treaties, which preclude certain experiments with actual nuclear explosions; and iii), the Protocol on Blinding Laser Weapons (1995), which explicitly bans only the use of blinding lasers but led to halting their development.

Preventive arms control assesses a potential new military technology using several criteria. One group of criteria concerns dangers to arms control and the international law of warfare: will the new technology undermine existing controls, law and norms? Another set of criteria concerns stability: will the new technology destabilize the military situation, *e.g.*, by reducing reaction times? Will it lead to a technological arms race? How about proliferation, in particular to regions with high probability of conflict? Finally, one needs to consider unintended hazards to humans, society or the environment. If there are good arguments for restricting a particular technology, then one needs to take into account any positive uses – in particular in the civilian realm – and if possible devise rules that exclude the negative applications without overly restricting the positive ones. Methods for verifying compliance also have to be thought out – they must provide assurance that illegal activity would be detected, but must not be too intrusive or too burdensome.

Preliminary Assessment

When considering the various potential military NT applications under criteria of preventive arms control, one finds several that will be close to civil uses, such as small, fast, distributed computers or strong, light-weight structural materials. A few uses could help to protect against terrorism or would act mostly defensively. Examples are sensors and decontamination agents for biological weapons or improved injury care. Preventive limitation would be unrealistic or counterproductive in such areas. However, there are several potential military applications of NT and/or NBIC at large that raise serious concerns under criteria of preventive arms control. In the medium term, the most dangerous ones involve:

- New selective chemical or biological warfare agents: These would violate the existing conventions, while posing new challenges to verification; they could be used either as weapons of mass destruction or for targeted assassinations, not only by armed forces but also by terrorists.
- Autonomous fighting systems – robots and robotic vehicles on land, in water or air: They would violate the international law of warfare if they would produce superfluous injury or could not recognize non-combatants or combatants *hors de combat*. Autonomous tanks or combat aircraft considered outside of the definitions of the Treaty on Conventional Armed Forces in Europe could undermine and endanger that treaty. Small satellites capable or attacking other satellites by direct hit or by manipulation after docking would destabilize the situation in outer space – not without consequences on Earth.
- Mini-/micro-sensors and-robots, including biological/artificial hybrids: They could be pre-deployed covertly in an opponent's territory to

strike at an appointed time or on command, or to guide other weapons. If such devices are produced at low cost in large numbers, diffusion to other countries and to criminals is probable, creating the possibility of their use in asymmetric warfare or terrorist attacks.

- Body manipulation including implants: Under the imperative of combat efficiency, armed forces may more readily explore new possibilities for body manipulation than civilian society. Soldiers might voluntarily, or maybe under some pressure, accept risky or ethically questionable technologies that modify body chemistry, rewire brain, nerve and muscle, or otherwise radically alter the human organism. This could create "facts" and circumvent barriers in civilian society, preempting a thorough debate on benefits, risks, ethical aspects and needs for regulation.

MOLECULAR NANOTECHNOLOGY

Molecular nanotechnology, sometimes called molecular manufacturing, is a term given to the concept of engineered nanosystems (nanoscale machines) operating on the molecular scale. It is especially associated with the concept of a molecular assembler, a machine that can produce a desired structure or device atom-by-atom using the principles of mechanosynthesis. Manufacturing in the context of productive nanosystems is not related to, and should be clearly distinguished from, the conventional technologies used to manufacture nanomaterials such as carbon nanotubes and nanoparticles. When the term "nanotechnology" was independently coined and popularized by Eric Drexler it referred to a future manufacturing technology based on molecular machine systems. The premise was that molecular scale biological analogies of traditional machine components demonstrated molecular machines were possible: by the countless examples found in biology, it is known that sophisticated, stochastically optimised biological machines can be produced.

It is hoped that developments in nanotechnology will make possible their construction by some other means, perhaps using biomimetic principles. However, Drexler and other researchers have proposed that advanced nanotechnology, although perhaps initially implemented by biomimetic means, ultimately could be based on mechanical engineering principles, namely, a manufacturing technology based on the mechanical functionality of these components (such as gears, bearings, motors, and structural members) that would enable programmable, positional assembly to atomic specification. The physics and engineering performance of exemplar designs were analysed in Drexler's book *Nanosystems*. In general it is very difficult to assemble devices on the atomic scale, as all one has to position atoms are other atoms of comparable size and stickyness.

Chemistry and Environment

Chemical catalysis and filtration techniques are two prominent examples where nanotechnology already plays a role. The synthesis provides novel materials with tailored features and chemical properties: for example, nanoparticles with a distinct chemical surrounding (ligands), or specific optical properties. In this sense, chemistry is indeed a basic nanoscience. In a short-term perspective, chemistry will provide novel "nanomaterials" and in the long run, superior processes such as "self-assembly" will enable energy and time preserving strategies.

In a sense, all chemical synthesis can be understood in terms of nanotechnology, because of its ability to manufacture certain molecules. Thus, chemistry forms a base for nanotechnology providing tailor-made molecules, polymers, etcetera, as well as clusters and nanoparticles. Chemical catalysis benefits especially from nanoparticles, due to the extremely large surface to volume ratio. The application potential of nanoparticles in catalysis ranges from fuel cell to catalytic converters and photocatalytic devices. Catalysis is also important for the production of chemicals.

Platinum nanoparticles are now being considered in the next generation of automotive catalytic converters because the very high surface area of nanoparticles could reduce the amount of platinum required. However, some concerns have been raised due to experiments demonstrating that they will spontaneously combust if methane is mixed with the ambient air. Ongoing research at the Centre National de la Recherche Scientifique (CNRS) in France may resolve their true usefulness for catalytic applications. Nanofiltration may come to be an important application, although future research must be careful to investigate possible toxicity.

A strong influence of nanochemistry on waste-water treatment, air purification and energy storage devices is to be expected. Mechanical or chemical methods can be used for effective filtration techniques.

One class of filtration techniques is based on the use of membranes with suitable hole sizes, whereby the liquid is pressed through the membrane. Nanoporous membranes are suitable for a mechanical filtration with extremely small pores smaller than 10 nm ("nanofiltration") and may be composed of nanotubes. Nanofiltration is mainly used for the removal of ions or the separation of different fluids. On a larger scale, the membrane filtration technique is named ultrafiltration, which works down to between 10 and 100 nm.

One important field of application for ultrafiltration is medical purposes as can be found in renal dialysis. Magnetic nanoparticles offer an effective and reliable method to remove heavy metal contaminants from waste water by making use of magnetic separation techniques. Using nanoscale particles increases the efficiency to absorb the contaminants and is comparatively inexpensive compared to traditional precipitation and filtration methods. Some water-treatment devices incorporating nanotechnology are already on the market, with more in development. Low-cost nanostructured separation membranes methods have been shown to be effective in producing potable water in a recent study.

Molecular Mechanics

More complex analyses, particularly analyses that involve searching through large configuration spaces, can limit the size of system that can be effectively handled. The need to search through large configuration spaces (as when determining the native folded structure of an arbitrary protein) can be avoided by the use of relatively rigid structures (which differ from relatively floppy proteins and have few possible configurations).

The modeling of machine components in vacuum reduces the need to model solvation effects, which can also involve significant computational effort. In molecular mechanics the individual nuclei are usually treated as point masses. While quantum mechanics dictates that there must be a certain degree of positional uncertainty associated with each nucleus, this positional uncertainty is normally significantly smaller than the typical internuclear distance. Bowen and Allinger provide a good recent overview of the subject.

While the nuclei can reasonably be approximated as point masses, the electron cloud must be dealt with in quantum mechanical terms. However, if we are content to know only the positions of the nuclei and are willing to forego a detailed understanding of the electronic structure, then we can effectively eliminate the quantum mechanics.

For example, the H_2 molecule involves two nuclei. While it would be possible to solve Schrodinger's equation to determine the wave function for the electrons, if we are content simply to know the potential energy contributed by the electrons (and do not enquire about the electron distribution) then we need only know the electronic energy as a function of the distance between the nuclei.

That is, in many systems the only significant impact that the electrons have on nuclear position is to make a contribution to the potential energy E of the system. In the case of H_2, E is a simple function of the internuclear distance r. The function E(r) summarizes and replaces the more complex and more difficult to determine wave function for the electrons, as well as taking into account the inter-nuclear repulsion and the interactions between the electrons and the nuclei. The two hydrogen nuclei will adopt a position that minimizes E(r). As r becomes larger, the potential energy of the system increases and the nuclei experience a restoring force that returns them to their original distance. Similarly, as r becomes smaller and the two nuclei are pushed closer together, we also find that a restoring force pushes them farther apart, again restoring them to an equilibrium distance.

More generally, if we know the positions r_1, r_2.... r_N of N nuclei, then E(r_1, r_2.... r_N) gives the potential energy of the system. Knowing the potential energy as a function of the nuclear positions, we can readily determine the forces acting on the individual nuclei and therefore can compute the evolution of their position over time. The function E is a newtonian potential energy function (not quantum mechanical), despite the fact that the particular value of E at a particular point could be computed from Schrodinger's equation. That is, the potential energy E is a newtonian concept, but the particular values of E at particular points are determined by Schrodinger's equation.

While it would in principle be possible to determine E by solving Schrodinger's equation, in practice it is usual to use available experimental data and to infer the nature and shape of E by interpolation. This approach, in which empirically derived potential energy functions are created by interpolation from experimental data, has spawned a wide range of potential energy functions, many of which are sold commercially. Because the gradient of the potential energy function E defines a conservative force field F, molecular mechanics methods are also called "force field" methods.

While it is common to refer to "empirical force field" methods, the more recent use of ab initio methods to provide data points to aid in the design of the force fields makes this term somewhat inaccurate, though still widely used. The utility of molecular mechanics depends crucially on the development of accurate force fields. Good quality force fields have been developed for a fairly broad range of compounds including many compounds of interest in biochemistry.

While we will not attempt to survey the wide range of force fields that are available, one particular subset of compounds for which good quality force fields are available involve H, C, N, O, F, Si, P, S, Cl when they are restricted to form chemically uncomplicated structures (*e.g.*, bond strain is not too great, dangling bonds are few or absent, etc.). Many atomically precise structures which should be useful in nanotechnology fall in this class and can be modeled with an accuracy adequate to determine the behaviour of molecular machines. The, given essentially arbitrary coordinates of the carbon and hydrogen atoms in a system, Brenner's potential will return the energy of the system. This permits molecular dynamical modeling of arbitrary hydrocarbon systems, including systems which use synthetic reactions involved in the synthesis of diamond.

Brenner has commented on the utility of this potential for modelling proposed molecular machine systems. Of course, the "accuracy" of the force fields depends on the application. A force field which was accurate to (say) 10 kcal/mole would be unable to correctly predict many properties of interest in biochemistry.

For example, such a force field would lead to serious errors in predicting the correct three-dimensional structure of a protein. Given the linear sequence of amino acids in a protein, the protein folding problem is to determine how it will fold in three dimensions when put in solution.

Often, the correct configuration will have an energy that differs from other (incorrect) configurations by a relatively modest amount, and so a force field of high accuracy is required. Unlike the protein folding problem, where an astronomical range of configurations of similar energy are feasible, the bearing basically has only one configuration: A bearing. While the protein has many unconstrained torsions, there are no unconstrained torsions in the bearing. To significantly change any torsion angle in the bearing would involve ripping apart bonds. Thus, the same force field which is of marginal utility in dealing with strands of floppy protein is quite adequate for solid blocks of stiff diamondoid material. Not only will small errors in the force field still result in an accurate prediction of the global minima, (which in this case will be a single large basin in the potential energy surface) but also the range of possible structures is so sharply limited that little or no computational effort need be spent comparing the energies of different configurations. Long computational runs to evaluate the statistical properties of ensembles of configurations are thus eliminated.

This style of design has been called, only half in jest, "molecular bridge building" because bridges are also designed with large safety margins. This observation, that the same force field that is inadequate for one class of structures is quite adequate for the design and modelling of a different class of structures, leads to a more general principle.

Computational experiments generally provide an answer with some error distribution. If the errors produced by the model are of a similar size to the errors that would result in incorrect device function, then the model is unreliable. On the other hand, if the errors in the model are small compared with the errors that will produce incorrect device function, then the results of the model are likely to be reliable. If a device design falls in the former category, *i.e.*, small errors in the model will produce conflicting forecasts about device function, then the conservative course of action is to reject the proposed design and keep looking. An even stronger (although somewhat more subtle) statement is possible.

The bearing illustrated in figures is simply a single bearing from a very large class of bearings. The strain in the axle and the sleeve is proportional to the diameter of the bearing. By increasing the diameter, we can reduce the strain. Thus, we can design bearings in this broad class in which the strain can be reduced to whatever level we desire. Because we are dealing with what amounts to a strained block of diamond, the fact that we can reduce strain arbitrarily means that we can design a bearing whose local structure bears as close a resemblance to an unstrained block of diamond as might be wished.

We can therefore be very confident indeed that some member of this class will perform the desired function (that of a bearing) and will work in accordance with our expectations. Given that we have developed software tools that are capable of creating and modelling most of the members of a broad class of devices, then we can investigate many individual class members. This investigation then lets us make rather confident statements about the functionality that members of this class can provide, even if there might be residual doubts about individual class members. A moments reflection will show that the class of objects which are chemically reasonably inert, relatively stiff (no free torsions), and which interact via simple repulsive forces that occur on contact; can describe a truly vast class of machines. Indeed, it is possible to design computers, robotic arms and a wide range of other devices using molecular parts drawn from this class.

AN IMPLEMENTATION STRATEGY FOR NANOTECHNOLOGY

Because nanotechnology represents a new and dramatically different approach to manufacturing and utilization, it would behoove the Army to enlist public support from the earliest possible time. To the maximum extent possible, an effort should be made to involve stakeholders to avoid issues similar to the lingering and unsubstantiated concerns surrounding genetically modified foods. Thus, the Army should encourage citizen participation in the development of nanotechnology for military applications. Army acquisition strategy, through the Acquisition, Logistics and Technology infrastructure can be used to shape the development of nanotechnology in a manner both protective of the worker and soldier as well as protective of the environment. The Army Environmental Policy Institute (AEPI) can provide guidance and oversight of the safety and environmental aspects of the acquisition requirements and process. The Army, and specifically AEPI, can influence the progress of nanotechnology through a carefully crafted acquisition strategy. For example, the Army can demand high standards for testing new materials. Developmental shortcuts may be tempting, but the goal must be the safe advancement of the technology without the lingering environmental disasters that were experienced with the manufacture of nuclear weapons. Similarly, the Army must insist that contractors must comply with the recognized best practices in the nanotechnology industry.

What's Nanotechnology?

The prefix "nano" means a billionth or 10^{-9}. Nanotechnology and nanosciences are therefore concerned with devices and phenomena talking place on the nanometre scale (it is often considered that anything under 100 nm qualifies as nano). As a comparison a carbon atom has a radius of roughly 0.1 nanometres. It can be argued that the synthesis of objects in this dimension is hardly new. In fact, the chemistry of small molecules always produces nanoscale entities. Similarly, the wood fires (or car engines) release nano particles. So what is different now? Why are we talking of nanotechnology as the next industrial revolution?

It was early on realised that if one could design a material with atomic resolution, the properties such material would exhibit could be entirely new. This is due to the fact that under a certain size, matter stops behaving according to the rules of classical physics and begins to act according to the ones of quantum physics. By engineering material carefully, one can arrange the atoms so that we can use this different set of rules in a useful way. To achieve such a feat, two distinct areas have to be developed in parallel: the understanding of the physical laws governing matter at this scale and the instrument enabling the manipulation and characterisation of matter at this scale. These two fields "feed" one another, advancement in one enabling further progress in the other.

A crucial step was made in 1981 with the development of the Scanning Tunnelling Microscope or STM. Relying on a quantum mechanical effect, this instrument enables for the first time researchers to image individual atoms resting on a surface. Soon after it was discovered that, using the same apparatus, one could probe the physical properties of an atom or group of atoms. Lastly, it was noticed that you could also use an STM to move individual atoms. This produced the well known STM picture in which the letter "I", "B" and "M" were written with xenon atoms.

The ability to design, synthesise and study objects with at least one of their dimension in the nanometre scale is what can be called nano-technology. The level of control we can attain now gives us the opportunity to create a whole new range of devices: from self cleaning glass, to new catalysts, better batteries, stronger materials or bio-compatible bone substitute. As one can see, it is a very vast field of science and technology where many different techniques come into play. A very interesting corollary that comes with working at this scale is that to a large extent the boundaries between what we know as physics, chemistry and biology are abolished. Indeed one can use semiconductor production techniques to create a series of trench on a material, coat them with hydrophilic functional groups to make them suitable to transport water, add "nano-engine" constituted by ATP converting bio molecules (taken from animal cells) to move the water around and finally insert molecular sensors: you obtain what is called a "lab on a chip." Nanotechnology will impact fairly fast nearly every domain of the manufacturing and electronics industries. It will then slowly diffuse to the health related industries. It will also most probably yield in its progress a number of important scientific discoveries. There is one trait that might make nanotechnology different from previous scientific and industrial revolutions (at least for a while): its apparent absolute character. Indeed, as there are few prospects to go for the sub-atomic level in common appliances due to the energies that it would involve, nanotechnology is seen by some as a kind of "ultimate frontier" for the control of matter.

Funding and why is the Military Interested?

Funding for nanotechnology and nanosciences has increased tremendously in the past years across the globe. The scale of the discoveries to be made in this field as well as the potential for commercially viable applications are two of the many reasons behind this increase. It is believed that the bulk of today's effort comes from states with private companies providing much less. This is however hard to check as detailed information on research investment of companies is understandably not easily available.

The EU (member states and European Commission), for example, spends roughly 800 millions euros each year on nano-related research and this figure is planned to increase in the subsequent years. In the USA, the National Nanotechnology Initiative (NNI) was launched in 2000 to provide an integrated framework for nanotechnology research, the 2004 fiscal year request for this initiative is of 849 millions dollars. The sum is shared between several federal agencies such as the NSF, the NIH or the DoE. In 2003 however, none of these agencies were the main recipient of NNI funds.

The department of defense (DoD), with 243 millions dollars out of a total of 774 millions, received 31.3% of total allocated resources. In Europe as well, the military is one of the key investors in this new area even if getting the information is harder. Sweden will spend 11 millions euros in the next 5 years on military nanotechnology research programs through the FOI (Swedish defence research agency). In the UK, the Ministry of Defence (MoD) spends roughly 1.5 million pounds/year on nano R&D. This will mostly go toward research on new structural materials and electronic devices. It was decided that the MoD would mostly rely in the short-term on civilian nanotechnology but would establish a technology watch on the subject. It is worrying to see that such a disproportionately important part of the research effort in this field is funded by the military. What aims is the defence sector pursuing in funding research in this area? What are the associated risks?

The Strategic Vision and Examples of Programs

The vision that drives military research is not one filled with nano-robots. It is not today envisioned that nanotechnology itself will provide new types of weapons. The changes brought by nanotechnology will be of a more pervasive nature. In the words a Clifford Lau, the Pentagon senior science adviser: *"Nanotechnology is a 'force multiplier'. It will make us faster and stronger on the battlefield."* In the short term, nanotechnology will be used in continuity with previous programs developed by relying on "traditional" material science, microelectronics and chemistry.

The improvements in materials, using nanostructured materials, will provide stronger and lighter armour, reduce maintenance costs and marginally improve the performance of kinetic weapons (better penetration of shells, etc). The shrinking of electronic circuits will enable sophisticated communication devices and sensors to be deployed on a near permanent basis (using better energy sources). The survivability of troops will also be improved by the insertion of sensors in their uniforms providing real time medical monitoring and deployment of chemical and biological agents' sensors. In the medium term, the army will be seeking to improve human performance on the battlefield by means of an exo-skeleton. All these technical advances will combine to produce an increase in the soldiers' "lethality." The US army anticipates that the deployment of troops with capabilities so far beyond that of their enemies would provoke awe and thus ensure victory. The nanosciences and nanotechnology advances will also affect weapons development in the field of bio, chemical and nuclear weapons in several ways.

For example, it is believed that the nano-structuring of nuclear material pellets is essential to provoke chain reactions in laser driven nuclear research facilities such as the National Ignition Facility or the mégajoule laser. This in turn has the potential to enable new nuclear weapons to be developed. The potential effect on global security will be discussed later. In the assessment of risks associated with military research programs one must distinguish the different types of programs currently carried out. I will adopt a classification with regards to the aims pursued.

Three broad classes can be identified:

1. Programs with civilian research objectives i.e. that could be looked after by civilian entities.

Example: Department of Defence-ID: 04-00861 Next-Generation antibiotics.

Extracts: "There is a growing national crisis in the treatment of infectious disease driven by the dramatic rise in pathogen multi-drug resistance (MDR)."

Aim: Identify resistance gene in mobile genetic elements.

2. Programs with "classical" military research objectives i.e. seeking to develop military technologies in continuity with previous ones and that do not rely exclusively on nanotechnology.

   Example: Department of Defence – ID: 04-00040, Enhanced Alternative Kinetic Energy Penetrators.

   Aim: "To enhance the penetration capability and behind armour effects of tungsten alloy projectiles via chemistry, mechanical properties and geometry variations, as well as processing innovations or other novel means."

3. "Nano-military" programs contingent on nano effects or properties.

   Example: Central Intelligence Agency – ID: 04-00398 Bio-Nano electronic circuitry

"The combination of biological science with nanotechnology offers the potential to produce a new class of electronic circuitry that rival the complexity and capacity of a human neuro-system"

As expected few risks are associated to the first category of programs, whereas the programs in the third one rise obvious concerns.

MILESTONES IN NANOTECHNOLOGY

The nano-level world is an entirely different place where materials with familiar properties take on new and unfamiliar properties. At this level of scale, often referred to as the mesoscale, physical properties are subject to a combination of rules of quantum and classical physics.

Basic Definitions and Concepts

Nanotechnology is still an emerging technology and the nomenclature and classification of the materials is yet to be developed. The American National Standards Institute (ANSI) is in the process of establishing a standardized nomenclature for nanomaterials and has formed a Nanotechnology Standards Panel which first assembled in late September 2004. For now, the basic concepts in nanotechnology may be known by multiple names.

Nanoparticle

Typically, a nanoparticle is formed from a single element or a simple compound and has at least one dimension less than 100 nanometers. At this magnitude, the laws of classical physics become blurred and at sizes less than 50 nanometers, the rules of quantum physics take precedence. As opposed to classical physics, quantum physics is the special set of physical rules applicable to matter on the molecular or atomic scale. The transition from classical physics to quantum mechanics begins at approximately 50 nanometers; at this very small scale familiar materials take on new properties. For example, materials have different colors and their magnetic qualities are altered.

What is more interesting is that as the size of the particle shrinks, the ratio between mass and surface area changes and the surface area becomes proportionally much greater. It is possible for one gram of a nanomaterial to have a surface area of 1000 square meters. Because chemical reactions take place at the surface interfaces, nanoparticles are much more reactive than their bulky macro relatives. There are particular subtypes of nanoparticles.

Nanotubes

A nanotube is a cylindrical and hollow structure usually less than 100 nanometers in length, but may be much longer. Carbon nanotubes were discovered by the NEC Corporation in 1991. Nanotubes may consist of materials in addition to carbon, but the prototype for the nanotech building block remains the carbon nanotube (CNT), a hugely versatile object. The CNT is a tubular form of carbon with diameter of 1 nm and a variable length ranging from nanometers to microns. The cylindrical CNT is basically a layer of carbon atoms arranged as a sheet rolled into a tube. The CNT has special properties; it has extraordinary strength, nearly 100 times stronger than steel and is as stiff as a diamond with a tensile strength to 200 GPa. In addition, the CNT has a maximum strain that is 10% more than any other known material and a strength to weight ratio 500x more than aluminum.

The electrical properties of nanotubes make them particularly interesting; the CNT can be metallic or semiconducting depending on chirality. (Chirality is a term reflecting variation in the number of layers and the direction in which they spiral.) The nanotube has a tunable bandgap and electrical properties which may be altered by application of a magnetic field or mechanical deformation. The conductivity of a CNT is 6 orders of magnitude higher than that of copper and with a very high current carrying capacity. Interestingly, the thermal conduction of a CNT is directional; it is much greater in the axial direction versus the radial direction and it far exceeds copper's ability to retain heat with almost no thermal leakage. The tubes can carry electrical charges at twice the speed of silicon circuits. Carbon nanotubes may allow the construction of three dimensional integrated circuits, something not possible with contemporary silicon technology. All these unique properties make CNT especially valuable to the microelectronics and computer industries.

Buckyball

A buckyball, or fullerene, is named after Buckminster Fuller, a futurist and global thinker best known for the invention of the geodesic dome. The structure consists of 60 carbon atoms arranged in a sphere with a pattern of hexagons and pentagons similar to a soccer ball. The buckyball is hollow, but can be used to carry another material; the outside surface of the buckyball can also be coated. A buckyball is also a semiconductor and small enough to penetrate biomembranes ordinarily thought relatively impenetrable such as cell walls or the blood brain barrier. Given these unique properties, it is not surprising that buckyballs are source of great interest to engineers and pharmaceutical researchers. The discovery of the fullerene was important enough to earn Richard Smalley, Robert Curl and Sir Harold Kroto the 1985 Nobel Prize for chemistry.

Quantum Dot

Quantum dots are nanoscale crystals made of a few hundred atoms. Their small size allows them to be inserted into cell and they can be used to trace biological changes in the cell. Quantum dots can be made from a variety of substances and can be designed to fluoresce in almost any colour.

Although humans have always been exposed to nanoscale particles from forest fires or volcanic eruptions, the recent history of nanotechnology dates to 1959. In a December 1959 speech to the American Physical Society at the California Institute of Technology, Physicist Richard Feynman reports that the laws of physics, as he understood them, did not prohibit man from designing devices intended to move individual molecules.

The term nanotechnology was introduced by Norio Taniguchi in 1974 and taken to mean the very precise, indeed, the ultra precise, machining of materials on a molecular scale. Implied in this notion are the concepts of nanomeasurement and nanomanipulation, namely, the notion of manufacture on a molecular level. The goal of nanotechnology is described as the ability "to produce complex products on demand using simple raw materials".

The next milestone in the evolution of nanotechnology came in 1981: Binnig and Rohrer of the IBM Zurich Research Laboratory invented the scanning tunneling microscope (STM) for which they received the 1986 Nobel Prize in Physics. The STM allowed researchers to "see" materials on the atomic scale and led to the development of the atomic force microscope which allows the manipulation of nanoparticles on surfaces, i.e., nanoparticles could now be arranged to form structures.

The STM does not function like a conventional microscope. Visible light waves are too large to illuminate the details on a nanocoated surface; the STM employs a probe to feel the surface under examination and provide an image of the contours.

Five years later, in 1986 K. Eric Drexler published *Engines of Creation: The Coming Era of Nanotechnology* in which he discusses a coming change in manufacturing methods and he visualizes molecular assemblers. The molecular assembler, as proposed, is a nanoscale device, basically a machine that would assemble other machines. In theory, given the raw materials, time and the proper instructions, the assembler could manufacture a vacuum cleaner or similar object in a few hours and with a minimum of energy and virtually no waste or pollution. Contrast this method of production with the current system of top down production in which requires an enormous source of raw materials, including a source of copper and iron ore, a coal mine, etc. and then to refine and process the raw materials to derive the components of the vacuum cleaner all the while using substantial amounts of energy which produce excess heat and waste greenhouse gases.

Drexler believed that the assemblers will build with molecular precision, using only the precise amounts of resources and energy required and avoiding virtually all pollution and with no adverse environmental impacts. This technique of manufacture was described as "bottom up" manufacture as opposed to the conventional methods which are described as "top down" manufacture. He suggested that nanotechnology may even enable man to colonize solar system and approach immortality. However, Drexler saw some potential danger with uncontrolled self replication of robots. There was some fear that self replicating nanorobots might escape and embark on a rampage of self replication with widespread and uncontrolled consumption of raw materials.

This would lead to swarming waves of nanorobots forming a sort of "grey goo". This fear was found unjustified based on considerations of energy requirements for the nanorobots.

In 2000 the Clinton administration announced the National Nanotechnology Initiative (NNI) dramatically increasing the funding to the fledging industry in the United States. The initial budget for the NNI was $500 million. The developmental path of nanotechnology was not entirely smooth.

Also in 2002, Roco and Bainbridge published a report *Converging Technologies for Improving Human Performance* in which they saw the convergence of four areas of research (science, bioscience and medicine, information technology and cognitive science); the resulting new discipline will become the body of knowledge for nanotechnology. They predicted that the new technology will lead to major improvements in social outcomes, human abilities, productivity, quality of life and overall environmental improvements over the next 20 years. In early 2004, Drexler and Chris Phoenix withdrew their earlier concerns about self replicating robots, the so-called "grey goo", and instead warned that nanotechnology lends itself to the development of new weapons systems that may lead to undesirable shifts in economic and political power, even beyond the shifts occurring with globalization. Nevertheless, Drexler favored aggressive development in nanotechnology.

A 1995 study by RAND (Max Nelson and Calvin Shipbaugh) suggested that nanotechnology may not have a certain future and hinted that nanotechnology may go the way of controlled nuclear fusion, i.e. a good idea on paper but either not capable of being harnessed or simply more difficult than anticipated. The authors proposed a number of hurdles that nanotechnology must overcome in the years after 1995 to demonstrate the technology's viability: first, materials would have to be produced at the nanoscale and then processed into components. Second, the components would have to be connected and made to interface with the macroenvironment. Third, there must be the ability to control a massive number of nanodevices in a coordinated fashion. Finally, these devices would subsequently have to be powered. All but the last of these hurdles has been surpassed thus suggesting that the technology will demonstrate its viability as a discipline.

NANOTECHNOLOGICAL IMPROVEMENT OF EXISTING TYPES OF NUCLEAR WEAPONS

Nuclear weapon technology is characterised by two sharply contrasting demands. On the one hand, the nuclear package containing the fission and fusion materials is relatively simple and forgiving, i.e. rather more sophisticated than complicated. On the other hand, the many ancillary components required for arming the weapon, triggering the high-explosives, and initiating the neutron chain-reaction, are much more complicated. Moreover, the problems related to maintaining political control over the use of nuclear weapons, i.e. the operation of permissive action links (PALs), necessitated the development of protection systems that are meant to remain active all the way to the target, meaning that all these ancillary components and systems are submitted to very stringent requirements for security, safety, and reliable performance under severe conditions. The general solution to these problems is to favour the use of hybrid combinations of mechanical and electronic systems, which have the advantage of dramatically reducing the probability of common mode failures and decreasing sensitivity to external factors. It is this search for the maximisation of reliability and ruggedness which is driving the development and application of nanotechnology and MEMS engineering in nuclear weapons science.

To give an important example: modern nuclear weapons use insensitive high-explosives (IHE) which can only be detonated by means of a small charge of sensitive high-explosive that is held out of alignment from the main charge of IHE. Only once the warhead is armed does a MEMS bring the detonator into position with the main charge. Since the insensitive high-explosive in a nuclear weapon is usually broken down into many separate parts that are triggered by individual detonators, the use of MEMS-based detonators incorporating individual locking mechanisms are an important ingredient ensuring the use-control and one-point safety of such weapons.

Further improvements on existing nuclear weapons are stemming from the application of nanotechnology to materials engineering. New capacitors, new radiation-resistant integrated circuits, new composite materials capable to withstand high temperatures and accelerations, etc., will enable a further level of miniaturisation and a corresponding enhancement of safety and usability of nuclear weapons. Consequently, the military utility and the possibility of forward deployment, as well as the potentiality for new missions, will be increased.

Consider the concept of a "low-yield" earth penetrating warhead. The military appeal of such a weapon derives from the inherent difficulty of destroying underground targets. Only about 15 % of the energy from a surface explosion is coupled (transferred) into the ground, while shock waves are quickly attenuated when travelling through the ground. Even a few megatons surface burst will not be able to destroy a buried target at a depth or distance more than 100-200 meters away from ground zero. A radical alternative, therefore, is to design a warhead which would detonate after penetrating the ground by a few tens of meters or more. Since a free-falling or rocket-driven missile will not penetrate the surface by more than about ten meters, some kind of active penetration mechanism is required. This implies that the nuclear package and its ancillary components will have to survive extreme conditions of stress until the warhead is detonated.

Fourth-Generation Nuclear Weapons

First-and second-generation nuclear weapons are atomic and hydrogen bombs developed during the 1940s and 1950s, while third-generation weapons comprise a number of concepts developed between the 1960s and 1980s, e.g. the neutron bomb, which never found a permanent place in the military arsenals. Fourth-generation nuclear weapons are new types of nuclear explosives that can be developed in full compliance with the Comprehensive Test Ban Treaty (CTBT) using inertial confinement fusion (ICF) facilities such as the NIF in the US, and other advanced technologies which are under active development in all the major nuclear-weapon states-and in major industrial powers such as Germany and Japan. In a nutshell, the defining technical characteristic of fourth-generation nuclear weapons is the triggering-by some advanced technology such as a superlaser, magnetic compression, antimatter, etc.-of a relatively small thermonuclear explosion in which a deuterium-tritium mixture is burnt in a device whose weight and size are not much larger than a few kilograms and litres. Since the yield of these warheads could go from a fraction of a ton to many tens of tons of high-explosive equivalent, their delivery by precision-guided munitions or other means will dramatically increase the fire-power of those who possess them-without crossing the threshold of using kiloton-to-megaton nuclear weapons, and therefore without breaking the taboo against the first-use of weapons of mass destruction. Moreover, since these new weapons will use no (or very little) fissionable materials, they will produce virtually no radioactive fallout. Their proponents will define them as "clean" nuclear weapons-and possibly draw a parallel between their battlefield use and the consequences of the expenditure of depleted uranium ammunition.

In practice, since the controlled release of thermonuclear energy in the form of laboratory scale explosions (i.e., equivalent to a few kilograms of high-explosives) at ICF facilities like NIF is likely to succeed in the next 10 to 15 years, the main arms control question is how to prevent this know-how being used to manufacture fourth-generation nuclear weapons. As we have already seen, nanotechnology and micromechanical engineering are integral parts of ICF pellet construction. But this is also the case with ICF drivers and diagnostic devices, and even more so with all the hardware that will have to be miniaturised and 'ruggedised' to the extreme in order to produce a compact, robust, and cost-effective weapon.

The potential of nanotechnology and microelectromechanical engineering in relation to the emergence of fourth-generation nuclear weapons is therefore of the utmost importance. It is likely that this discussion will be difficult, not just because of secrecy and other restrictions, but mainly because the military usefulness and usability of these weapons is likely to remain very high as long as precision-guided delivery systems dominate the battlefield. It is therefore important to realise that the technological hurdles that have to be overcome in order for laboratory scale thermonuclear explosions to be turned into weapons may be the only remaining significant barrier against the introduction and proliferation of fourth-generation nuclear weapons. For this reason alone-and there are many others, beyond the scope of this paper-very serious consideration should be given to the possibility of promoting an 'Inner Space Treaty' to prohibit the military development and application of nanotechnological devices and techniques.

Near and Long-Term Applications and Implications of Nanotechnology

Considering that nanotechnology is already an integral part of the development of modern weapons, it is important to realise that its immediate potential to improve existing weapons (either conventional or nuclear), and its short-term potential to create new weapons (either conventional or nuclear), are more than sufficient to require the immediate attention of diplomats and arms controllers. In this perspective, the potential long-term applications of nanotechnology (and their foreseeable social and political implications) should neither be downplayed nor overemphasised. Indeed, there are potential applications such as self-replicating nano-robots ('nanobots') which may never prove to be feasible because of fundamental physical or technical obstacles. But this impossibility would not mean that the somewhat larger micro-robots of the type that are seriously considered in military laboratories could never become a reality.

In light of these extant and potential dangers and risks, every effort should be made not to repeat the error of the arms-control community with regard to missile defence. For over thirty years, that community acted on the premise that a ballistic missile defense system will never be built because it will never be sufficiently effective-only to be faced with a concerted attempt to construct such a system! If some treaty is contemplated in order to control or prohibit the development of nanotechnology, it should be drafted in such a way that all reasonable long-term applications are covered.

Moreover, it should not be forgotten that while nanotechnology mostly emphasises the *spatial* extension of matter at the scale of the nanometer (the size of a few atoms), the *time* dimension of mechanical engineering has recently reached its ultimate limit at the scale of the femtosecond (the time taken by an electron to circle an atom). It has thus become possible to generate bursts of energy in suitably packaged pulses in space and time that have critical applications in nanotechnology, and to focus pulses of particle or laser beams with extremely short durations on a few micrometer down to a few nanometer sized targets. The invention of the 'superlaser', which enabled such a feat and provided a factor of one million increase in the instantaneous power of tabletop lasers, is possibly the most significant recent advance in military technology. This increase is of the same magnitude as the factor of one million difference in energy density between chemical and nuclear energy.

MILITARY PONDERS FUTURE OF NANOTECH

While nano-sciences offer an array of potentially useful technology for the Defense Department, not all military researchers have jumped on this bandwagon. The disparity of viewpoints was on clear display at a recent lightweight materials conference, where researchers gave differing assessments of its impact.

"If you think biotech has been moving these last few years, just wait," said James Murday, chief scientist for the laboratories at the Office of Naval Research. "The electronics industry will be all nano by the end of the decade."

Other researchers contend the impact will be far less than the predictions of true believers such as Murday. "I'd be shocked if [nanotechnology] will be the thing in 10 years," noted David Stepp, chief of the materials science division of the Army Research Office. "There's always something after."

The federal government is certainly concentrating on nanotechnology. The Clinton administration's 2001 budget raised an informal "nano-scale science and technology working group" to the level of a federal initiative. The National Nanotechnology Initiative (NNI) was born, an effort that has received steady increased in research and development funding.

Federal funding for nanotechnology research and development has increased from $116 million in 1997 to an estimated $961 million in 2004. President Bush's 2005 budget request calls for an additional 2 percent increase, boosting the NNI budget to $982 million. The Defense Department is one key player in NNI, with a firm interest in developing new materials and manufacturing processes that could determine the shape of a 22nd century fighting force. The Pentagon recognizes 10 broad applications of nano-science, including ultra-small computers, low-power communications systems, bio-chemical defense suites, new targeting lasers and countermeasures and innovative materials for armor systems.

Future plans, Murday said, could include further advances, such as directed self-assembly and repair, nano-porous materials that could screen the passage of particles through a membrane and transparent ceramics and composites that could shame current efforts.

Some long-standing engineering problems may find solutions in nanotech. For example, an artificial sapphire used on the nose cones of infrared-guided missiles could be enhanced using advances in nano-science, said Larry Kabacoff, program manager for nano-structured materials for the Office of Naval Research.

If a new material can be formed, it could be an answer to a problem vexing researchers who are searching for a material tough enough to survive insect and weather damage in flight and transparent enough to allow infrared waves through without refracting them. The current systems rely on sapphires which often are damaged while in flight, Kabacoff told National Defense, and using damage-resistant diamonds is cost prohibitive.

Kabacoff's group found that a single-phase material with a structure 20 times smaller than the infrared wavelengths would allow the light to pass unaffected. The program was cut in 2003, "just as progress was being made." A small project with Raytheon still exists, which is generating data that could be used to mount an argument to resume ONR funding. Other nations also are turning their eyes towards nanotechnology, Murday noted. He called China "a major player" who is investing steadily in the emerging technology, and added that Japan is matching the United States' investment dollar-for-dollar.

"We'd just as soon be on the front end of that curve," Murday told the conference attendees.

Social, Military and Ethical Issues in Nanotechnology

Nanotechnology has become a major area of intensive research funding worldwide. The FP6 of the European Commission has set aside 1.3 billion Euro for research within this field in the period 2003-2006. Many countries-with the USA in a leading position-are strengthening their research in nanotechnology similarly. Norway has followed this international trend in science policy through a strategic cooperation between UiO, IFE, SINTEF and NTNU called FUNMAT. An annual budget of 150 million NOK is set aside for ten years in order to increase national expertise in nanotechnology. However, some critical voices like e.g. the etc.-group claim that our current knowledge is too limited to handle the risks that one may have to face.

But not only the risks are debated, also the ethics of some possible applications that may be generated are discussed. Nanotechnology travels in miniscule dimensions: one nanometer is one billionth of a meter, while e.g. a human hair is about 80,000 nanometer. Within such a scale one is in effect already below the levels of life and touching the very elements of nature. While many scientists recognise the benefits that the nanotechnology revolution could bring, some have serious concerns. This apprehension is not restricted to one field, but covers human health, environmental impacts, effects on international trade and developing countries, and the possible proliferation in armaments.

A major concern is however that we just do not know what the impacts of nanotechnology will be. It is this lack of knowledge that leads some scientists to call for a moratorium on certain aspects of nanotechnology use and research. The question one needs to confront is whether there is an urgent need for a strict and harmonized regulation of research in this field and how ethical issues related to possible applications could be explored before facts are created that may be difficult to contain or control.

The organizers have invited three international experts that shall address some of the problematic issues in their presentations. The experts are:

Dr. Jürgen Altmann, Experimental Physics III at the University of Dortmund, Germany, chair of the group "Physics and disarmament", and chair of the "Bochum Verfication-project". Dr Altmann is author of the book Military Uses of Microsystem Technologies: Dangers and Preventive Arms Control, Münster 2001. He has spoken extensively on the possible military uses of nanotechnology in various fora, among others for the Royal Society, London, working group on nanotechnology and nanoscience. He has just finished a 15-months project on preventive arms control for NT (funded by the new German Foundation for Peace Research DSF), however the book will only appear in 2-3 months. An overview can be gained from an article co-authored with Mark Gubrud. Dr Altmann has made specific proposals for precautionary action in nanotechnology development.

Prof. Vivian Weil is Director of the Center for the Study of Ethics in the Professions at the Illinois Instiute of Technology, Chicago. Dr. Weil is a Fellow of the American Association for the Advancement of Science, a member of the Governing Board of the National Institute for Engineering Ethics, and Chair of the Executive Committee of the Association for Practical and Professional Ethics. She serves on the editorial boards of various journals, including Science and Engineering Ethics and Science Communication.

She received her A.B. and M.A. from the University of Chicago and her Ph.D. in philosophy from the University of Illinois, Chicago. In 1990-1991, she directed the Ethics and Values Studies program of the National Science Foundation (NSF). Recently, she has been involved in NSF conferences to integrate ethics and societal implications in nano science and technology, as a speaker on ethics and as a member of the organizing committee of its most recent conference in December, 2003. Dr. Christoph Baumgartner, from the Interdepartmental Center for Ethics in the Sciences and Humanities (IZEW) of the University of Tübingen, Germany. Dr. Baumgartner, born 1969, studied Chemistry and Theology in Tübingen (Germany) and acts as Academic Coordinator of the IZEW. His doctoral Thesis was about "Problems of Motivation in the context of environmental behaviour as a challenge for environmental ethics." His main areas of research are: Environmental Ethics, Problems of Motivation to Morally Responsible Behaviour, Ethical Aspects of Biopatenting, Ethical Aspects of New Technologies, especially Nanotechnology. He has especially worked with the ethical challenges in medical nanotechnology.

5

Cyberwarfare

Cyberwarfare refers to politically motivated hacking to conduct sabotage and espionage. It is a form of information warfare sometimes seen as analogous to conventional warfare although this analogy is controversial for both its accuracy and its political motivation. Government security expert Richard A. Clarke, in his book *Cyber War* (May 2010), defines "cyberwarfare" as "actions by a nation-state to penetrate another nation's computers or networks for the purposes of causing damage or disruption." The *Economist* describes *cyberwarfare* as "the fifth domain of warfare," and William J. Lynn, U.S. Deputy Secretary of Defense, states that "as a doctrinal matter, the Pentagon has formally recognized cyberspace as a new domain in warfare... [which] has become just as critical to military operations as land, sea, air, and space."

In 2009, President Barack Obama declared America's digital infrastructure to be a "strategic national asset," and in May 2010 the Pentagon set up its new U.S. Cyber Command (USCYBERCOM), headed by General Keith B. Alexander, director of the National Security Agency (NSA), to defend American military networks and attack other countries' systems. The United Kingdom has also set up a cyber-security and "operations centre" based in Government Communications Headquarters (GCHQ), the British equivalent of the NSA. In the U.S. however, Cyber Command is only set up to protect the military, whereas the government and corporate infrastructures are primarily the responsibility respectively of the Department of Homeland Security and private companies.

In February 2010, top American lawmakers warned that the "threat of a crippling attack on telecommunications and computer networks was sharply on the rise." According to The Lipman Report, numerous key sectors of the U.S. economy along with that of other nations, are currently at risk, including cyber threats to public and private facilities, banking and finance, transportation, manufacturing, medical, education and government, all of which are now dependent on computers for daily operations. In 2009, President Obama stated that "cyber intruders have probed our electrical grids."

The Economist writes that China has plans of "winning informationised wars by the mid-21st century". They note that other countries are likewise organizing for cyberwar, among them Russia, Israel and North Korea. Iran boasts of having the world's second-largest cyber-army. James Gosler, a government cybersecurity specialist, worries that the U.S. has a severe shortage of computer security specialists, estimating that there are only about 1,000 qualified people in the country today, but needs a force of 20,000 to 30,000 skilled experts. At the July 2010 Black Hat computer security conference, Michael Hayden, former deputy director of national intelligence, challenged thousands of attendees to help devise ways to "reshape the Internet's security architecture", explaining, "You guys made the cyberworld look like the north German plain."

METHODS OF ATTACK

Cyberwarfare consists of many different threats:

Espionage and National Security Breaches

Cyber espionage is the act or practice of obtaining secrets (sensitive, proprietary or classified information) from individuals, competitors, rivals, groups, governments and enemies also for military, political, or economic advantage using illegal exploitation methods on internet, networks, software and or computers. Classified information that is not handled securely can be intercepted and even modified, making espionage possible from the other side of the world. Specific attacks on the United States have been given codenames like Titan Rain and Moonlight Maze. General Alexander notes that the recently established Cyber Command is currently trying to determine whether such activities as commercial espionage or theft of intellectual property are criminal activities or actual "breaches of national security."

Sabotage

Military activities that use computers and satellites for coordination are at risk of equipment disruption. Orders and communications can be intercepted or replaced. Power, water, fuel, communications, and transportation infrastructure all may be vulnerable to disruption. According to Clarke, the civilian realm is also at risk, noting that the security breaches have already gone beyond stolen credit card numbers, and that potential targets can also include the electric power grid, trains, or the stock market. In mid July 2010, security experts discovered a malicious software program called Stuxnet that had infiltrated factory computers and had spread to plants around the world. It is considered "the first attack on critical industrial infrastructure that sits at the foundation of modern economies," notes *The New York Times.*

Electrical Power Grid

The federal government of the United States admits that the electric power transmission is susceptible to cyberwarfare. The United States Department of Homeland Security works with industry to identify vulnerabilities and to help industry enhance the security of control system networks, the federal government is also working to ensure that security is built in as the next generation of "smart grid" networks are developed. In April 2009, reports surfaced that China and Russia had infiltrated the U.S. electrical grid and left behind software programs that could be used to disrupt the system, according to current and former national security officials. The North American Electric Reliability Corporation (NERC) has issued a public notice that warns that the electrical grid is not adequately protected from cyber attack. China denies intruding into the U.S. electrical grid. One countermeasure would be to disconnect the power grid from the Internet and run the net with droop speed control only. Massive power outages caused by a cyber attack, could disrupt the economy, distract from a simultaneous military attack, or create a national trauma.

Howard Schmidt, Cyber-Security Coordinator of the US, commented on those possibilities: It's possible that hackers have gotten into administrative computer systems of utility companies, but says those aren't linked to the equipment controlling the grid, at least not in developed countries. [Schmidt] has never heard that the grid itself has been hacked.

Motivations—Military

In the U.S., General Keith B. Alexander, first head of the recently formed USCYBERCOM, told the Senate Armed Services Committee that computer network warfare is evolving so rapidly that there is a "mismatch between our technical capabilities to conduct operations and the governing laws and policies. Cyber Command is the newest global combatant and its sole mission is cyberspace, outside the traditional battlefields of land, sea, air and space." It will attempt to find and, when necessary, neutralize cyberattacks and to defend military computer networks.

Alexander sketched out the broad battlefield envisioned for the computer warfare command, listing the kind of targets that his new headquarters could be ordered to attack, including "traditional battlefield prizes – command-and-control systems at military headquarters, air defense networks and weapons systems that require computers to operate." One cyber warfare scenario, Cyber ShockWave, which was wargamed on the cabinet level by former administration officials, raised issues ranging from the National Guard to the power grid to the limits of statutory authority.

The distributed nature of internet based attacks means that it is difficult to determine motivation and attacking party, meaning that it is unclear when a specific act should be considered an act of war.

Civil

Potential targets in internet sabotage include all aspects of the Internet from the backbones of the web, to the Internet Service Providers, to the varying types of data communication mediums and network equipment. This would include: web servers, enterprise information systems, client server systems, communication links, network equipment, and the desktops and laptops in businesses and homes. Electrical grids and telecommunication systems are also deemed vulnerable, especially due to current trends in automation.

Private Sector

Computer hacking represents a modern threat in ongoing industrial espionage and as such is presumed to widely occur. It is typical that this type of crime is underreported. According to McAfee's George Kurtz, corporations around the world face millions of cyberattacks a day. "Most of these attacks don't gain any media attention or lead to strong political statements by victims." This type of crime is usually financially motivated.

CASUALTIES OF CYBER WARFARE

That the United States and China have engaged in skirmishes in the cyber domain is no secret. Since the beginning of the 21st century, targeted cyberattacks, often with signs of Chinese origin, have attempted to penetrate the computer networks of U.S. corporations and government agencies in search of potentially valuable information.

In response to this new strategic threat, the U.S. Military's Strategic Command commissioned the creation of a sub-unified Cyber Command in 2009, with one of its stated objectives being the "defense of specified Department of Defense information networks."

U.S. President Barack Obama very clearly defined the threat that cyberattacks pose to the economy, in both the public and private sectors, when he said that the "cyber threat is one of the most serious economic and national security challenges we face as a nation." Indeed, conflict in the cyber domain is still having some serious repercussions for the business world.

Civilian Involvement in Cyber Warfare

The characteristic of cyber warfare that makes it so uniquely dangerous to the corporate sector is that military power in the cyber domain must be extended through computer networks provided and maintained by non-governmental bodies. The use of these networks for cyberattacks or defense requires the conscription or cooperation of civilian resources. This creates extreme liabilities for the corporations that provide these networks, as they will quickly become the targets of suspicion and possible retaliation from the enemy state. In recent years, both Chinese and American companies have been caught in just this situation.

On October 8, 2012, the U.S. House of Representatives' intelligence committee released a report that warned of potential national security threats posed by Chinese telecommunication giants Huawei and ZTE. After conducting a year-long investigation of the suspect companies, the intelligence committee found serious vulnerabilities caused by hidden "backdoors" worked into the companies' technologies that would allow access to U.S. government and business networks.

The report advised against the purchase of products manufactured by Huawei or ZTE, and suggested that policymakers block any mergers between either of the two companies and U.S. telecommunication corporations.

These accusations have seriously hurt consumer confidence in the two companies, to the extent that in December of 2013, Huawei's executive vice president dramatically declared"we are not interested in the U.S. market anymore." While Huawei has managed to hold on to a small market share in America, the company's association with Chinese state-sponsored cyberattacks has devastated its ability to operate in the United States.

It became clear last year, though, that the United States was a perpetrator of cyberattacks as well as a victim. In June 2013, former U.S. National Security Agency contractor Edward Snowden provided the world with a look into the intelligence apparatus of the NSA, releasing thousands of classified documents to the media. The released documents revealed that the U.S., like China, was using domestic tech firms (in many cases without their knowledge or consent) as conduits for intelligence gathering cyberattacks. In May 2014, the Chinese government announced that it would no longer purchase or use two of Microsoft's main products, the Windows 8 operating system and the Microsoft Office 365 Suite. Then, in late July and early August, Chinese officials from the State Administration for Industry and Commerce (SAIC) raided multiple offices owned by Microsoft and its contractors in China. While vague statements about an anti-monopoly probe were made, the company's decision to end support for the Windows XP operating system – a move that would expose the many Chinese computers that use the operating system to security risks – was also cited as a factor in the raids.

While it is likely that the ban and subsequent raids were also intended to pave the way for new operating system technologies created in China, the Snowden revelations allowed potential U.S. espionage activities to be cited as a justification. Just as Huawei and ZTE suffered for their association with espionage activities of the Chinese government, Microsoft took a major hit because of the provocative actions of its government.

An Undefined Battlefield

On both sides of the Pacific, it is clear that both U.S. and Chinese tech firms are being caught in the crossfire of these cyber skirmishes between the two countries. Any escalation in tensions in the cyber domain could be disastrous to the private sector. Unfortunately, despite the risks that future cyberwars hold for multinational corporations, there is a marked absence of legislation, precedent, and international norms that could govern the relationships between private companies and the governments looking to use them as avenues through which cyberwar could be conducted.

For as long as these ambiguities exist, corporations that deal in the communication technology industry will exist in the gray area of an unregulated cyber battlefield devoid of any policies meant to protect the assets and infrastructures of civilian actors. It is in the interests of both countries to more clearly define, through domestic cooperation with corporate partners and with bilateral international discussion and agreement, the boundaries between civilians and the military in cyber warfare. Failure to do so could severely hamper the economic interaction that has been so lucrative for both countries and further destabilize an already fragile Sino-American relationship.

Government's Role in Domestic Cyber Security

While organizations have taken extensive measures to provide security against cybercrime, the challenges of a larger cyberwar against a capable and persistent foe require greater national organization and civilian-government cooperation. Unfortunately, in the United States, government responses to engagements in the cyber domain have been slow at best, but more often nonexistent. The cause of this is commonly the difficulty in identifying attackers and the lack of procedures in place for how a national response can and should be mobilized to address an attack on a civilian target. This lack of definition creates additional liability for the civilian counterpart because the opposing state (in this case China) does not know to what extent the civilian is involved with the defense and possible subsequent counterattacks. The lack of clarity directly increases the probability that the civilian will be the target of general suspicion and will suffer financial damage, as was seen with Huawei, ZTE and Microsoft. In broad terms, foreign attacks on domestic civilian targets can be placed in one of two categories: those that pose a national security threat and those that cause potential financial harm to the recipient of the attack. These two types of attacks require specific responses that have not yet been clearly defined by the U.S. government and the business community.

A cyberattack that directly threatens the national security of the United States might require the temporary direct use, or even the partial or complete conscription, of a civilian network. Disruptions of public utilities, theft of sensitive information from a security contractor, or the sabotage of civilian networks necessary for the operation of the military are examples of intrusions that might necessitate such a response. However, the documents released by Edward Snowden revealed that civilian networks were commonly conscripted for foreign surveillance activities, often without the knowledge of their owners. One of the largest barriers that conscription faces to becoming a transparent counter-cyberattack strategy is the ambiguity surrounding the cyber domain in warfare. Because no legislation exists that explicitly defines cyberattacks as acts of war and because the Supreme Court has never ruled on the constitutionality of conscription in any form during peacetime, no precedent has ever been set that would instruct the government on how to publicly organize a defense in the case of a cyberattack against a civilian target that threatened national security. While this does not excuse the NSA of its secrecy, it does indicate the need for legal clarification on the matter of cyber warfare. A decisive answer to the question of the legality of government conscription of civilian network assets in the interests of national security would allow a transparent strategy that involved input from both civilian and government representatives to be formed.

If a cyberattack is not a national security threat, but only threatens the financial health of the victim, the procedures for a government response are even more unclear. With traditional cybercrime, civilians are responsible for their own cyber security and the liability of unsuccessfully defending against an attempted network penetration falls on the civilian's security provider or the civilian's own security measures. However, it seems unreasonable to assume that a civilian would be able to successfully defend against the cyberattacks of a foreign state, which presumably would have greater access to technology, talent and funding.

Say, for example, a cyberattack of Chinese origin manages to steal sensitive information relating to a patented product of an American company. What response could that company expect to receive from the government? The answer to that question has yet to be explicitly defined through any official legislation or successful precedent. However, the Cybersecurity Act of 2013, which was recommended for further consideration in July 2013, might be a step in the right direction.

The bill directs the Secretary of Commerce and the Director of National Institute of Standards and Technology to work toward the, "development of a voluntary, industry-led set of standards and procedures to reduce cyber risks to critical infrastructure." While the bill does not specifically say what measures can be taken to address the problem, a dialogue between the government and the civilian sector is a necessary first step toward assuring that the government will take an active role in preventing damaging cyberattacks on civilian targets.

A Line in the Cyber Sand

The lack of adequate procedural preparation for cyber warfare and ambiguity about the government's role in protecting its civilians from cyberattacks represents a real strategic threat to the United States as well as a financial liability for civilians. Before the release of the NSA documents last year, the U.S. government was acting unilaterally to address the problems presented by aggression from the Chinese in the cyber domain.

The nature of cyber warfare, however, necessitates civilian cooperation. Now there is an opening to create a partnership to more clearly define the lines between state actions that might be internationally provocative and civilian resources that, while necessary to the state's actions, do not represent the civilian's participation as an aggressor. Not only will this protect civilian assets that are not directly involved in cyber warfare efforts, it will also create procedures that will allow for a more effective and efficient strategy for the conduct of cyber warfare.

Given the very real risk that conflict between China and the U.S. in the cyber domain could escalate in the future, we need to find ways to isolate it from the vibrant economic exchange that have benefited both countries. The worst-case scenario would be the disintegration of the line between warfighting assets and civilian assets, such that the intentional targeting of noncombatants becomes a viable strategy. Both China and the U.S. need to act to ensure that their civilians do not become casualties of cyber warfare.

CYBERWARFARE BY COUNTRY

The Internet security company McAfee stated in their 2007 annual report that approximately 120 countries have been developing ways to use the Internet as a weapon and target financial markets, government computer systems and utilities.

CYBERWARFARE IN THE UNITED STATES

Cyberwarfare in the United States is the United States military strategy of proactive cyber defence and the use of cyberwarfare as a platform for attack. The new United States military strategy, makes explicit that a cyberattack is *casus belli* for a traditional act of war. In August 2010, the U.S. for the first time is publicly warning about the Chinese military's use of civilian computer experts in clandestine cyber attacks aimed at American companies and government agencies. The Pentagon also pointed to an alleged China-based computer spying network dubbed GhostNet that was revealed in a research report last year. The Pentagon stated:

"The People's Liberation Army is using "information warfare units" to develop viruses to attack enemy computer systems and networks, and those units include civilian computer professionals. Commander Bob Mehal, will monitor the PLA's buildup of its cyberwarfare capabilities and will continue to develop capabilities to counter any potential threat." The United States Department of Defense sees the use of computers and the Internet to conduct warfare in cyberspace as a threat to national security. The United States Joint Forces Command describes some of its attributes:

Cyberspace technology is emerging as an "instrument of power" in societies, and is becoming more available to a country's opponents, who may use it to attack, degrade, and disrupt communications and the flow of information. With low barriers to entry, coupled with the anonymous nature of activities in cyberspace, the list of potential adversaries is broad. Furthermore, the globe-spanning range of cyberspace and its disregard for national borders will challenge legal systems and complicate a nation's ability to deter threats and respond to contingencies. In February 2010, the United States Joint Forces Command released a study which included a summary of the threats posed by the internet:

With very little investment, and cloaked in a veil of anonymity, our adversaries will inevitably attempt to harm our national interests. Cyberspace will become a main front in both irregular and traditional conflicts. Enemies in cyberspace will include both states and non-states and will range from the unsophisticated amateur to highly trained professional hackers. Through cyberspace, enemies will target industry, academia, government, as well as the military in the air, land, maritime, and space domains. In much the same way that airpower transformed the battlefield of World War II, cyberspace has fractured the physical barriers that shield a nation from attacks on its commerce and communication. Indeed, adversaries have already taken advantage of computer networks and the power of information technology not only to plan and execute savage acts of terrorism, but also to influence directly the perceptions and will of the U.S. Government and the American population.

American "Kill Switch Bill"

On June 19, 2010, United States Senator Joe Lieberman (I-CT) introduced a bill called "Protecting Cyberspace as a National Asset Act of 2010", which he co-wrote with Senator Susan Collins (R-ME) and Senator Thomas Carper (D-DE). If signed into law, this controversial bill, which the American media dubbed the "*Kill switch bill*", would grant the President emergency powers over parts of the Internet. However, all three co-authors of the bill issued a statement that instead, the bill "[narrowed] existing broad Presidential authority to take over telecommunications networks".

CYBERWARFARE IN CHINA

Diplomatic cables highlight US concerns that China is using access to Microsoft source code and 'harvesting the talents of its private sector' to boost its offensive and defensive capabilities.

Cyber Counterintelligence

Cyber counter-intelligence are measures to identify, penetrate, or neutralize foreign operations that use cyber means as the primary tradecraft methodology, as well as foreign intelligence service collection efforts that use traditional methods to gauge cyber capabilities and intentions.

- On April 7, 2009, The Pentagon announced they spent more than $100 million in the last six months responding to and repairing damage from cyber attacks and other computer network problems.
- On April 1, 2009, U.S. lawmakers pushed for the appointment of a White House cyber security "czar" to dramatically escalate U.S. defenses against cyber attacks, crafting proposals that would empower the government to set and enforce security standards for private industry for the first time.
- On February 9, 2009, the White House announced that it will conduct a review of the nation's cyber security to ensure that the Federal government of the United States cyber security initiatives are appropriately integrated, resourced and coordinated with the United States Congress and the private sector.
- In the wake of the cyberwar of 2007 waged against Estonia, NATO established the Cooperative Cyber Defence Centre of Excellence (CCD CoE) in Tallinn, Estonia, in order to enhance the organization's cyber defence capability. The centre was formally established on the 14th of May, 2008, and it received full accreditation by NATO and attained the

status of International Military Organization on the 28th of October, 2008. Since Estonia has led international efforts to fight cybercrime, the United States Federal Bureau of Investigation says it will permanently base a computer crime expert in Estonia in 2009 to help fight international threats against computer systems.

Controversy over Terms

There is debate on whether the term "cyberwarfare" is accurate; for instance, Howard Schmidt, the cybersecurity leader of the United States, said in March 2010 that "there is no cyberwar... I think that is a terrible metaphor and I think that is a terrible concept. There are no winners in that environment." Other experts, however, believe that this type of activity already constitutes a war. The warfare analogy is often seen intended to motivate a militaristic response when that is not necessarily appropriate.

Incidents

- On October 6, 2011, it was announced that Creech AFB's drone and predator fleet's command and control data stream has been keylogged, resisting all attempts to reverse the exploit, for the past two weeks. The Air Force issued a statement that the virus had "posed no threat to our operational mission".
- In July 2011, the South Korean company SK Communications was hacked, resulting in the theft of the personal details (including names, phone numbers, home and email addresses and resident registration numbers) of up to 35 million people. A trojaned software update was used to gain access to the SK Communications network. Links exist between this hack and other malicious activity and it is believed to be part of a broader, concerted hacking effort.
- Operation Shady RAT is an ongoing series of cyber attacks starting mid-2006, reported by Internet security company McAfee in August 2011. The attacks have hit at least 72 organizations including governments and defense contractors.
- On December 4 2010, a group calling itself the Pakistan Cyber Army hacked the website of India's top investigating agency, the Central Bureau of Investigation (CBI). The National Informatics Centre (NIC) has begun an inquiry.
- On November 26 2010, a group calling itself the Indian Cyber Army hacked the websites belonging to the Pakistan Army and the others belong to different ministries, including the Ministry of Foreign Affairs, Ministry of Education, Ministry of Finance, Pakistan Computer Bureau, Council of Islamic Ideology, etc. The attack was done as a revenge of

the Mumbai terrorist attack which had confirmed the involvement of Pakistani terrorists.

- In October 2010, Iain Lobban, the director of the Government Communications Headquarters (GCHQ), said Britain faces a "real and credible" threat from cyber attacks by hostile states and criminals and government systems are targeted 1,000 times each month, such attacks threatened Britain's economic future, and some countries were already using cyber assaults to put pressure on other nations.
- In September 2010, Iran was attacked by the Stuxnet worm, thought to specifically target its Natanz nuclear enrichment facility. The worm is said to be the most advanced piece of malware ever discovered and significantly increases the profile of cyberwarfare.
- In May 2010, In response to Indian Cyber Army defacing Pakistani websites, 1000+ Indian websites were defaced by PakHaxors, TeaMp0isoN, UrduHack & ZCompany Hacking Crew, among those were the Indian CID website, local government of Kerala, Box Office of Indian, Brahmos missile website, Indian HP helpdesk, Indian Institute of Science, and The Indian Directorate General of Shipping.
- In July 2009, there were a series of coordinated denial of service attacks against major government, news media, and financial websites in South Korea and the United States. While many thought the attack was directed by North Korea, one researcher traced the attacks to the United Kingdom.
- Russian, South Ossetian, Georgian and Azerbaijani sites were attacked by hackers during the 2008 South Ossetia War.
- In 2007 the website of the Kyrgyz Central Election Commission was defaced during its election. The message left on the website read "This site has been hacked by Dream of Estonian organization". During the election campaigns and riots preceding the election, there were cases of Denial-of-service attacks against the Kyrgyz ISPs.
- In September 2007, Israel carried out an airstrike on Syria dubbed Operation Orchard. U.S. industry and military sources speculated that the Israelis may have used technology similar to that used by the United States Suter airborne network attack system to allow their planes to pass undetected by radar into Syria. Suter is a computer program designed to interfere with the computers of integrated air defense systems
- In April 2007, Estonia came under cyber attack in the wake of relocation of the Bronze Soldier of Tallinn. The largest part of the attacks were coming from Russia and from official servers of the

authorities of Russia. In the attack, ministries, banks, and media were targeted.

- In the 2006 war against Hezbollah, Israel alleges that cyber-warfare was part of the conflict, where the Israel Defense Force (IDF) intelligence estimates several countries in the Middle East used Russian hackers and scientists to operate on their behalf. As a result, Israel attached growing importance to cyber-tactics, and became, along with the U.S., France and a couple of other nations, involved in cyber-war planning. Many international high-tech companies are now locating research and development operations in Israel, where local hires are often veterans of the IDF's elite computer units. Richard A. Clarke adds that "our Israeli friends have learned a thing or two from the programs we have been working on for more than two decades."

CYBER-WARFARE TACTICS

Other cyber tactics are less sophisticated. The attack that temporarily brought down Estonian networks began with a flood of bogus messages targeting government servers, called a "denial of service" attack. The approach harnesses "botnets"—massive networks of interconnected computers—to bombard targeted networks with information requests while masking the location of the primary attacker. James Lewis, a security expert with the Center for Strategic and International Studies (CSIS), says hackers in the Estonia example likely took control of tens of thousands of computers around the world without the knowledge of their owners and directed them at the government's servers. The result, he says, was a relatively minor attack that was nearly impossible to trace.

Another technique is the use of "malware," "spyware," and other malicious programs imbedded into computer systems to steal information without user knowledge. The software is designed to hide undetected and siphon information from its host—everything from secrets stored on personal computers to Pentagon military mainframes. A December 2007 analysis of U.S. Air Force cyber vulnerabilities notes much of the Pentagon's operating systems are off-the-shelf components manufactured overseas, due to cheaper costs. But pinching pennies has potentially opened U.S. military networks to intrusion. "Foreign countries could place hidden components inside the computers, making the computers vulnerable for attack and/or spying," the analysis concludes.

"Our ability to penetrate into enemy computer networks, our ability to exploit communication networks, to manipulate digital information, is real."
–Defense Analyst William M. Arkin

Less common but far more worrisome are cyber attacks aimed at critical infrastructure—like nuclear-power-plant control systems, banks, or subways. In March 2007 the Department of Energy's Idaho Lab conducted an experiment to determine whether a power plant could be compromised by hacking alone.

The result—a smoking, self-combusting diesel generator incapacitated by nothing more than keystrokes—sent shivers (CNN) through the private sector. The worries were apparently well-founded.

In January 2008 a CIA analyst told U.S. utilities that hackers had succeeded in infiltrating electric companies in undisclosed locations outside the United States and, it at least one instance, shut off power to multiple cities. The hackers then demanded money (AP). "The [U.S.] government is scrambling to try and protect its own systems, to try and check the Chinese from reading government email," says economist Scott Borg, director of the U.S. Cyber Consequences Unit, a nonprofit research institute that studies cyber threats. "But the focus probably needs to be critical infrastructure. That's what we need to defend."

Patching the Holes

On paper the U.S. government appears to agree. For over a decade government-sanctioned studies have delved into the subject; the Pentagon published a report on "Information Warfare-Defense" (PDF) in 1996, when public use of the Internet was still in its infancy. Saydjari says all of these studies reached the same conclusion: "The threat and vulnerabilities to our national infrastructure is serious, it's getting worse, and it's getting worse at an increasingly fast rate."

But only recently has the concern been a constant focus of attention for the security and intelligence communities. Part of the attention deficit lies with the difficulty in defining the cyber threat. A 2006 Air Force task force termed cyberspace "a warfighting domain bounded by the electromagnetic spectrum," but air force officials acknowledge "a full understanding of the domain is years away."

What is understood is how potentially devastating the loss of cyberspace dominance could be to U.S. interests. In his annual threat assessment to Congress delivered in February 2008, Director of National Intelligence Michael McConnell discussed "cyber threats" before talking about the war in Afghanistan.

"Our information infrastructure ...increasingly is being targeted for exploitation and potentially for disruption or destruction by a growing array of state and non-state adversaries," McConnell said. "We assess that nations, including Russia and China, have the technical capabilities to target and disrupt" the United States' information infrastructure.

"Chinese [cyber warfare] capabilities have evolved from defending networks from attack to offensive operations against adversary networks." –U.S. Deputy Under Secretary for Defense Richard P. Lawless

The Pentagon, too, has acknowledged the threat to its infrastructure. The Defense Department is considering banning nonofficial traffic (Federal Computer Week) from its servers, and the U.S. Air Force is creating a Cyber Command to defend Pentagon networks. "When we talk about the speed range and flexibility of air power, the thing that enables this for us is the fact of our cyber-dominance," Air Force Gen. Robert Elder told United Press International.

The recent flurry of high-level pronouncements also comes amid a renewed funding commitment from Washington. In November 2007 the Bush administration called on the National Security Agency to coordinate with the Department of Homeland Security to protect government and civilian communication networks from hackers.

The $144 million plan, unveiled quietly in White House budget documents (PDF), aims to enhance "civilian agency cybersecurity and strengthen defenses to combat terrorism."

In January 2008 President George W. Bush signed two presidential directives calling for the creation of a comprehensive national cybersecurity initiative. According to an article by the Wall Street Journal, the White House's 2009 budget request takes the program exponentially further, with an estimated $6 billion request to build a secretive system to protect U.S. communications networks. Details of the proposed program remain classified, angering some civil libertarians who fear monitoring of civilian networks could infringe on privacy rights. Rep. Bennie G. Thompson (D-MS), chairman of the House Homeland Security Committee, has called for the program to be put on hold (PDF) until Congress can adequately review it.

Measuring the Threat

Cyber experts don't dispute that electronic espionage is a vexing problem, or that the United States is a prime target. But they do disagree on how pervasive such attacks are, who is behind them, and how disruptive they may prove to be.

According to a tally by the Heritage Foundation, a conservative Washington think tank, the hackers may already be winning: In 2007 the Department of Homeland Security logged an estimated 37,000 attempted breaches of private and government computer systems, and over 80,000 attacks on Pentagon systems. Some hacks "reduced the U.S. military's operational capabilities," the report says. Economist Borg says the biggest threat from cyber attacks may be economic. He estimates a shutdown of electric power to any sizable region for more than ten days would stop over 70 percent of all economic activity in that region.

"If you can do that with a pure cyber attack on only one critical infrastructure, why would you bother with any traditional military attack?" CSIS' Lewis takes a less alarmist view.

"The U.S. is a very big set of targets, and some of our important networks are very secure. So you could inflict damage on the U.S. but it wouldn't be crippling or decisive," he says. "I've seen people who say a cyber attack could turn the United States into a third-world nation in a matter of minutes. That's silly. We have to be realistic about this."

6

Cyberterrorists to Target Critical Infrastructure

A cyberterror attack on vital national infrastructure such as power facilities, transport networks and the financial sector could be imminent—and international governments are ill-prepared, cybersecurity experts have warned. "It's not easy to predict what will happen, but the worst terrorist attacks are not expected," Eugene Kaspersky, the co-founder and chief executive of global IT security firm Kaspersky Labs, told CNBC. So I am afraid that if we face this cyberterrorism, it will be very unpredictable in a very unpredictable place, but with very visible damage. Unfortunately, there are many possible victims."

In recent months, the business world and political establishment has seen an uptick in the use of debilitating digital attacks. As well as the Sony attacks, allegedly by North Korea, and the widespread hacking of international news agencies by the "Syrian Electronic Army," On Monday, Malaysian Airlines refuted that its website had been hacked by a group calling itself the "Cyber Caliphate" and claiming affiliation with the Islamic State (ISIS).

'Critical Infrastructure'

Now, there are concerns that the next big attack will be against national critical infrastructure and could cripple a country's ability to function. Kaspersky told CNBC that each country needed to make a "very serious audit" of the critical infrastructure within its borders. In order of importance, he noted that the infrastructure most vulnerable was the power network, "because if the power plants and power grid don't work, then nothing else works," followed by telecommunications, financial services and transportation.

"A security strategy needs to be made for all of these components," Kaspersky said.

He warned that governments needed to allocate a good part of their budgets over the next decade to making critical infrastructure systems more secure.

"Technically it's possible to make them immune from attacks, but it's complicated, it's expensive and it will take time and budgets," Kaspersky said.

'War Games'

Budget cuts in the U.K. and Europe have undoubtedly challenged government attempts to counter cyberterrorism, but a spokesperson for the U.K. Cabinet Office told CNBC that cybersecurity was a priority. "Cybersecurity is already a tier-one national security priority and our investment of £860 million ($1.3 billion) over five years in the National Cyber Security Programme (NCSP) supports a wide range of projects to develop the U.K.'s cyber security capabilities. This is a clear signal of just how seriously the Government is treating the threat," the spokesperson said.

Kaspersky noted that there needed to be far stronger international cooperation against cyberterrorism, including in the sharing of information, in order to relay early warnings ahead of potential attacks.

The U.K. and U.S. have already pledged to work together in a bid to remain one step ahead of terrorism groups like Islamic State that are increasingly using computers as means of attack.

In particular, there are the so-called war games involve "cybercells" of U.S. and U.K. intelligence agents staging attacks against each another, in order to test the resilience of certain sectors to cyberattacks. The first exercise will test the financial sector, with simulated attacks on the City of London, including the Bank of England, and Wall Street.

Fighting the Attacks

E.J. Hilbert, the heads Kroll's cyber unit for Europe, the Middle East and Africa, told CNBC that hundred, if not thousands attacks were already taking place—and that more attacks were coming.

"There are hundreds of attacks taking place against the U.K. and U.S. nuclear industry and financial system every day. There is this non-stop badgering of the system by hackers who are hoping that one day the system will crack," said Hilbert, a former FBI agent in the cybercrime and counterterrorism field.

He was emphatic that national governments were unprepared for a cyberattack on critical infrastructure. He said that the proposed "war games" would have limited effect in acting as a pre-warning to governments on the weaknesses of critical systems.

"These tests don't do what the bad guys are going to do, they don't go far enough. If the bad guys want to shut a system down, they'll shut it down and unless you've tested for that, you don't actually know if there's a way of bringing a system back," Hilbert said.

If an attack is so bad that all else has failed, governments can always choose to shut down their own infrastructure systems. But taking such steps can have alarming consequences, such as lack of power if power plants are shut down, lack of water if water facilities are closed, and permanent system failure.

With that in mind, Hilbert said "it might be better to fight the attack then shut down the system."

CYBER SECURITY AND CRITICAL INFRASTRUCTURE PROTECTION IN INDIA

Cyber Security of India is an essential part of National ICT Policy and Strategy of India. Despite some very good suggestions and critical evaluations, the Government of India (GOI) has not considered it necessary to take some action in this regard. There has been repetitive wake up calls given to the GOI but it seems the GOI is in indefinite sleep.

On the other hand, the International Community is stressing really hard to make cyber security an essential part of their day to day lives. Dartmouth's Institute for Information Infrastructure Protection (I3P) has recently provided its cyber security research recommendations.

They are in the form of a set of recommendations for advancing research in cyber security that can be implemented in the next five to 10 years. The report recognises four areas of need that emerged during the forum:

(1) A coordinated and collaborative approach is needed.

(2) Metrics and assessment tools must be developed.

(3) An effective legal and policy framework for security must be created.

(4) The human dimension of security must be addressed.

It may be a coincidence that similar suggestions were provided by Mr. Praveen Dalal, Managing Partner of Perry4Law to the Government of India. He has also provided the Indian Policies and Strategies for Critical ICT Infrastructure Protection and Management in India. The stress upon Legal Enablement of ICT Systems in India is very important to make Cyber Law of India strong and effective.

There are lot of Problems through which the present Cyber Law of India is passing through. A good account of the same can be found at this nice piece of work. The problem still remains the same. In India we don't have a dedicated resource that is taking care of Techno-Legal Laws of India in a holistic manner. Of course, we have a Cyber Law Database of India.

We also have a Techno-Legal ICT Regulations Database in India. These two resources are tracing back the history of cyber law in India. However, we need a resource that can trace both history of cyber law in India as well as its current position and the prospective future of the same.

The task is very difficult but it has been successfully achieved by Mr. Praveen Dalal, Managing Partner of Perry4Law. He has successfully come out with a "Dedicated Resource" on cyber law in India. The same is titled "Legal Enablement Of ICT Systems in India" and is the exclusive, most comprehensive and holistic web resource in India dealing with Techno-Legal ICT Laws and Regulations in India. All the cyber law observers can now access information about cyber law in India and the changes that are proposed or actually made from time to time. The resource is very futuristic and promising in nature and it would be good idea if the Government of India (GOI) consults the same while making, amending or reformulating techno-legal laws in India. One of the important aspects of this resource is that it is the exclusive resource that is providing a "Constitutional Analysis" of the present as well as proposed techno-legal laws in India. Therefore all of the "Civil Liberty Crusaders" keep a close eye upon this resource for issues like Privacy Rights, Life and Liberty, Right to Speech and Expressions, etc.

For instance, surveillance has become a controversial issue since the Information Technology (Amendment) Bill, 2008 has been proposed. Surprisingly some people are justifying these wide and unregulated powers as justified under the garb of security that does not exists at all in India. There is only one answer to the pro surveillance argument and it is a Benjamin Franklin quote: Those who would give up essential liberty to purchase a little temporary safety deserve neither liberty nor safety.

E-Surveillance should not be a substitute for cyber security and cyber forensics capabilities. Privacy Rights must be respected and followed in both letter and spirit in India. He Bill, 2008 has seriously compromised these Fundamental Rights. So friends, wake up and be a vigilant and legally aware citizens. We will keep on spreading the "Cyber Law Awareness" in India so that we may have an informed citizenry.

Security and Systems Design

Most current real-world computer security efforts focus on external threats, and generally treat the computer system itself as a trusted system. Some knowledgeable observers consider this to be a disastrous mistake, and point out that this distinction is the cause of much of the insecurity of current computer systems - once an attacker has subverted one part of a system without fine-grained security, he or she usually has access to most or all of the features of that system. Because computer systems can be very complex, and cannot be guaranteed to be free of defects, this security stance tends to produce insecure systems. The 'trusted systems' approach has been predominant in the design of many Microsoft software products, due to the long-standing Microsoft policy of emphasizing functionality and 'ease of use' over security.

Since Microsoft products currently dominate the desktop and home computing markets, this has led to unfortunate effects. However, the problems described here derive from the security stance taken by software and hardware vendors generally, rather than the failing of a single vendor. Microsoft is not out of line in this respect, just far more prominent with respect to its consumer marketshare.

It should be noted that the Windows NT line of operating systems from Microsoft contained mechanisms to limit this, such as services that ran under dedicated user accounts, and Role-Based Access Control (RBAC) with user/group rights, but the Windows 95 line of products lacked most of these functions. Before the release of Windows 2003 Microsoft has changed their official stance, taking a more locked down approach.

On 15 January 2002, Bill Gates sent out a memo on Trustworthy Computing, marking the official change in company stance. Regardless, Microsoft's operating system Windows XP is still plagued by complaints about lack of local security and inability to use the fine-grained user access controls together with certain software (esp. certain popular computer games).

Financial Cost

Serious financial damage has been caused by computer security breaches, but reliably estimating costs is quite difficult. Figures in the billions of dollars have been quoted in relation to the damage caused by malware such as computer worms like the Code Red worm, but such estimates may be exaggerated. However, other losses, such as those caused by the compromise of credit card information, can be more easily determined, and they have been substantial, as measured by millions of individual victims of identity theft each year in each of several nations, and the severe hardship imposed on each victim, that can wipe out all of their finances, prevent them from getting a job, plus be treated as if they were the criminal. Volumes of victims of phishing and other scams may not be known.

Individuals who have been infected with spyware or malware likely go through a costly and time-consuming process of having their computer cleaned.

Spyware and malware is considered to be a problem specific to the various Microsoft Windows operating systems, however this can be explained somewhat by the fact that Microsoft controls a major share of the PC market and thus represent the most prominent target.

Reasons

There are many similarities (yet many fundamental differences) between computer and physical security. Just like real-world security, the motivations for breaches of computer security vary between attackers, sometimes called hackers or crackers. Some are teenage thrill-seekers or vandals (the kind often responsible for defacing web sites); similarly, some web site defacements are done to make political statements. However, some attackers are highly skilled and motivated with the goal of compromising computers for financial gain or espionage.

An example of the latter is Markus Hess who spied for the KGB and was ultimately caught because of the efforts of Clifford Stoll, who wrote an amusing and accurate book, The Cuckoo's Egg, about his experiences. For those seeking to prevent security breaches, the first step is usually to attempt to identify what might motivate an attack on the system, how much the continued operation and information security of the system are worth, and who might be motivated to breach it. The precautions required for a home PC are very different for those of banks' Internet banking system, and different again for a classified military network. Other computer security writers suggest that, since an attacker using a network need know nothing about you or what you have on your computer, attacker motivation is inherently impossible to determine beyond guessing. If true, blocking all possible attacks is the only plausible action to take.

Vulnerabilities

To understand the techniques for securing a computer system, it is important to first understand the various types of "attacks" that can be made against it. These threats can typically be classified into one of these seven categories:

Exploits

Software flaws, especially buffer overflows, are often exploited to gain control of a computer, or to cause it to operate in an unexpected manner. Many development methodologies rely on testing to ensure the quality of any code released; this process often fails to discover extremely unusual potential exploits. The term "exploit" generally refers to small programs designed to take advantage of a software flaw that has been discovered, either remote or local. The code from the exploit program is frequently reused in trojan horses and computer viruses. In some cases, a vulnerability can lie in certain programs' processing of a specific file type, such as a non-executable media file.

Eavesdropping

Any data that is transmitted over a network is at some risk of being eavesdropped, or even modified by a malicious person. Even machines that operate as a closed system (i.e., with no contact to the outside world) can be eavesdropped upon via monitoring the faint electro-magnetic transmissions generated by the hardware such as TEMPEST. The FBI's proposed Carnivore program was intended to act as a system of eavesdropping protocols built into the systems of internet service providers.

THE CYBER THREAT AND FBI RESPONSE

We face cyber threats from state-sponsored hackers, hackers for hire, global cyber syndicates, and terrorists. They seek our state secrets, our trade secrets, our technology, and our ideas— things of incredible value to all of us. They seek to strike our critical infrastructure and to harm our economy.

Given the scope of the cyber threat, agencies across the federal government are making cyber security a top priority. We and our partners at the Department of Homeland Security (DHS), the National Security Agency, and other U.S. Intelligence Community and law enforcement agencies have truly undertaken a whole-of-government effort to combat the cyber threat. Within the FBI, we are prioritizing high-level intrusions—the biggest and most dangerous botnets, state-sponsored hackers, and global cyber syndicates. We are working with our counterparts to predict and prevent attacks, rather than simply react after the fact.

FBI agents, analysts, and computer scientists use technical capabilities and traditional investigative techniques—such as sources and wiretaps, surveillance, and forensics—to fight cyber crime. We work side-by-side with our federal, state, and local partners on Cyber Task Forces in each of our 56 field offices and at the National Cyber Investigative Joint Task Force (NCIJTF). Through our 24-hour cyber command centre, CyWatch, we combine the resources of the FBI and NCIJTF, allowing us to provide connectivity to Federal cyber centers, government agencies, FBI field offices and legal attaches, and the private sector in the event of a significant cyber intrusion.

We also exchange information about cyber threats with the private sector through partnerships such as the Domestic Security Alliance Council, InfraGard, and the National Cyber Forensics and Training Alliance (NCFTA).

In addition, our legal attache offices overseas work to coordinate cyber investigations and address jurisdictional hurdles and differences in the law from country to country. We are supporting and collaborating with newly established cyber crime centers at Interpol and Europol. We continue to assess other locations to ensure that our cyber personnel are in the most appropriate locations across the globe.

We know that to be successful in the fight against cyber crime, we must continue to recruit, develop, and retain a highly skilled workforce. To that end, we have developed a number of innovative staffing programs and collaborative private industry partnerships to ensure that over the long term we remain focused on our most vital resource—our people. As the committee is well aware, the frequency and impact of cyber attacks on our nation's private sector and government networks have increased dramatically in the past decade and are expected to continue to grow. Since 2002, the FBI has seen an 80 percent increase in the number of computer intrusion investigations.

Recent Successes

Over the past several months, the FBI and the Justice Department have announced a series of separate indictments of overseas cyber criminals.

In an unprecedented indictment in May, we charged five Chinese hackers with illegally penetrating the networks of six U.S. companies. The five members of China's People's Liberation Army allegedly used their illegal access to exfiltrate proprietary information, including trade secrets.

Later that month, we announced the indictments of a Swedish national and a U.S. citizen believed to be the co-developers of a particularly insidious computer malware known as Blackshades. This software was sold and distributed to thousands of people in more than 100 countries and has been used to infect more than half-a-million computers worldwide.

In June, the FBI announced a multi-national effort to disrupt the GameOver Zeus botnet, the most sophisticated botnet that the FBI and its allies had ever attempted to disrupt. GameOver Zeus is believed to be responsible for the theft of millions of dollars from businesses and consumers in the U.S. and around the world. This effort to disrupt it involved notable cooperation with the private sector and international law enforcement.

GameOver Zeus is an extremely sophisticated type of malware designed specifically to steal banking and other credentials from the computers it infects. In the case of GameOver Zeus, its primary purpose is to capture banking credentials from infected computers, then use those credentials to initiate or re-direct wire transfers to accounts overseas that are controlled by the criminals. Losses attributable to GameOver Zeus are estimated to be more than $100 million.

Just last month, a federal grand jury indicted Su Bin, a Chinese national, on five felony offenses stemming from a computer hacking scheme that involved the theft of trade secrets from American defense contractors, including The Boeing Company, which manufactures the C-17 military transport aircraft. Su is currently in custody in British Columbia, Canada, where he is being held pursuant to a provisional arrest warrant submitted by the United States. The charges carry a total maximum statutory penalty of 30 years in prison. The investigation in this case was conducted by the Federal Bureau of Investigation and the Air Force Office of Special Investigations.

The Blackshades and GameOver Zeus indictments are part of an initiative launched by the FBI Cyber Division in April 2013 to disrupt and dismantle the most significant botnets threatening the economy and national security of the United States. This initiative, named Operation Clean Slate, is the FBI's broad campaign to implement appropriate threat neutralization actions through collaboration with the private sector, DHS, and other United States government partners, as well as our foreign partners. This includes law enforcement action against those responsible for the creation and use of the illegal botnets, mitigation of the botnet itself, assistance to victims, public service announcements, and long-term efforts to improve awareness of the botnet threat through community outreach. Although each botnet is unique, Operation Clean Slate's strategic approach to this significant threat ensures a comprehensive neutralization strategy, incorporating a unified public/private response and a whole-of-government approach to protect U.S. interests.

The impact of botnets has been significant. Botnets have been estimated to cause more than $113 billion in losses globally, with approximately 375 million computers infected each year, equaling more than one million victims per day, translating to 12 victims per second.

Another Operation Clean Slate success came in January 2014, when Aleksandry Andreevich Panin, a Russian national, pled guilty to conspiracy to commit wire and bank fraud for his role as the primary developer and distributor of the malicious software known as Spyeye, which infected more than 1.4 million computers in the United States and abroad. Based on information received from the financial services industry, more than 10,000 bank accounts had been compromised by Spyeye infections in 2013 alone. Panin's co-conspirator, Hamza Bendelladj, an Algerian national who helped Panin develop and distribute the malware, was also arrested in January 2013 in Bangkok, Thailand.

In addition to these recent investigative successes against cyber threats, we are continuing to work with our partners to prevent attacks before they occur.

One area in which we have had great success with our overseas partners is in identifying and targeting infrastructure we believe has been used in distributed denial of service (DDoS) attacks and preventing that infrastructure from being used for future attacks. A DDoS attack is an attack on a computer system or network that causes a loss of service to users, typically the loss of network connectivity and services by consuming the bandwidth of the victim network.

Since October 2012, the FBI and DHS have released more than 170,000 Internet Protocol addresses of computers that were believed to be infected with DDoS malware. We have released this information through Joint Indicator Bulletins (JIBs) to more than 130 countries via DHS's National Cybersecurity and Communications Integration Centre (NCCIC), where our liaisons provide expert and technical advice for increased coordination and collaboration, as well as to our legal attaches overseas.

These actions have enabled our foreign partners to take action and reduced the effectiveness of the botnets and the DDoS attacks. We are continuing to target botnets through this strategy and others.

In 2013, for example, the FBI created FBI Liaison Alert System (FLASH) reports and Private Industry Notifications (PINs) to release industry-specific details on current and emerging threat trends and technical indicators to the private sector. To date, the FBI has disseminated 40 FLASH messages, 21 of which dealt with threats to the financial industry. These PIN and FLASH messages were created to proactively deliver timely, actionable intelligence to potential victims and law enforcement partners at the international, state, and local levels.

Next Generation Cyber Initiative

The need to prevent attacks is a key reason the FBI has redoubled our efforts to strengthen our cyber capabilities while protecting privacy, confidentiality, and civil liberties. The FBI's Next Generation Cyber Initiative, which we launched in 2012, entails a wide range of measures, including focusing the Cyber Division on intrusions into computers and networks—as opposed to crimes committed with a computer as a modality hiring additional computer scientists to assist with technical investigations in the field; and expanding partnerships and collaboration at the NCIJTF. In addition, after more than a decade of combating cyber crime through a nationwide network of interagency task forces, the FBI has evolved its Cyber Task Forces in all 56 field offices to focus exclusively on cyber security threats.

At the NCIJTF—which serves as a coordination, integration, and information sharing centre for 19 U.S. agencies and several key international allies for cyber threat investigations—we are coordinating at an unprecedented level. This coordination involves senior personnel at key agencies. NCIJTF, which is led by the FBI, now has deputy directors from the NSA, DHS, the

Central Intelligence Agency, U.S. Secret Service, and U.S. Cyber Command. In the past year, three of our Five Eyes international partners joined us at the NCIJTF: Australia embedded a liaison officer in May 2013, the U.K. in July 2013, and Canada in January 2014. By developing partnerships with these and other nations, NCIJTF is working to become the international leader in synchronizing and maximizing investigations of cyber adversaries.

Private Sector Outreach

In addition to strengthening our partnerships in government and law enforcement, we recognize that to effectively combat the cyber threat, we must significantly enhance our collaboration with the private sector. Our nation's companies are the primary victims of cyber intrusions, and their networks contain the evidence of countless attacks. In the past, industry has provided us information about attacks that have occurred, and we have investigated the attacks—but we have not always provided information back.

To remedy that, the Cyber Division has established a Key Partnership Engagement Unit (KPEU) to manage a targeted outreach program focused on building relationships with key private sector corporations. The unit works to share sector-specific threat information with our corporate partners.

We have provided a series of classified briefings for key sectors, including financial services and energy, to help them repel intruders.

Through the FBI's InfraGard program, the FBI develops partnerships and working relationships with private sector, academic, and other public-private entity subject matter experts. Primarily geared toward the protection of critical national infrastructure, InfraGard promotes ongoing dialogue and timely communication among a current active membership base of more than 25,000.

InfraGard members are encouraged to share information with government that better allows government to prevent and address criminal and national security issues. Active members are able to report cyber intrusion incidents in real-time to the FBI through iGuardian, which is based on our successful counterterrorism reporting system known as Guardian.

Just last month, the FBI deployed a malware repository and analysis system called Malware Investigator to our domestic and foreign law enforcement partners and members of the U.S. Intelligence Community. The system allows users to submit malware directly to the FBI and quickly receive technical information about the samples to its users so they can understand how the malware works. It also enables the FBI to obtain a global view of the malware threat. Beyond technical reporting, Malware Investigator identifies correlations that will allow users to "connect the dots" by highlighting instances in which malware was deployed in seemingly unrelated incidents.

The FBI's Cyber Initiative and Resource Fusion Unit (CIRFU) maximizes and develops intelligence and analytical resources received from law enforcement, academia, international, and critical corporate private sector subject matter experts to identify and combat significant actors involved in current and emerging cyber-related criminal and national security threats. CIRFU's core capabilities include a partnership with the National Cyber Forensics and Training Alliance (NCFTA) in Pittsburgh, Pennsylvania, where the unit is collocated with CIRFU. NCFTA acts as a neutral platform through which the unit develops and maintains liaison with hundreds of formal and informal working partners who share real-time threat information and best practices and collaborate on initiatives to target and mitigate cyber threats domestically and abroad.

The FBI recognizes that industry collaboration and coordination are critical in our combating the cyber threat effectively. As part of our enhanced private sector outreach, we have begun to provide cleared industry partners with classified threat briefings and other information and tools to better help them repel intruders.

Counterterrorism and Other Threats

Though the cyber threat is one of the FBI's top priorities, combating terrorism remains our top investigative priority. As geopolitical conflict zones continue to emerge throughout many parts of the world, terrorist groups may use this instability to recruit and incite acts of violence.

The continuing violence in both Syria and Iraq and the influx of foreign fighters threatens to destabilize an already volatile region while also heightening the threat to the West. Due to the prolonged nature and the high visibility of the Syrian conflict, we are concerned that U.S. persons with an interest in committing jihad will be drawn to the region. We can address this issue more fully in the closed session.

CRITICAL INFRASTRUCTURE PROTECTION

The Internet infrastructure relies on primarily on the Border Gateway Protocol (BGP) and the Domain Name System (DNS). The secure remote administration of routers relies mostly on the Secure Shell (SSH) protocol.

Attacks against any of these technologies may impact on the availability of Internet-based services. As we do not know how to guarantee software correctness, it is a reasonable to assume that exploitable programming errors exist in applications.

To reduce the ability of an adversary to cause damage, we need to limit the impact of such programming errors. We offer *Privilege Separation* as one solution.

Services that authenticate remote users to system resources are difficult to contain via external application confinement mechanisms. Privilege Separation is a protection mechanism at the application level that separates the privileged code path from the unprivileged code path. An adversary interacts with the unprivileged part only; an exploitable programming error in the unprivileged code path does not lead to immediate privilege escalation.

Privilege separation may also be employed to increase the resilience of domain name service implementations like bind. Privilege Separation is very portable as most modern Unix operating system provide address space protection between processes and inter-process communication, privilege separation.

Intrusion Prevention

While Privilege Separation increases an application's resilience against programming errors, it does not prevent all possible intrusions. Many system services and applications perform specific tasks. By confining applications to only those operations that required for its correct execution, we prevent adversaries who gain control over these system services from causing damage to the system.

In Unix operating systems, persistent changes are possibly only via *System Calls*. By carefully monitoring and restricting an application's system calls, we can limit or even prevent an adversary from causing damage. We offer *Systrace* as solution. Systrace provides fine-grained application confinement based on configurable security policies. Additionally, it can detect and prevent intrusions. It also records audit trails that can used in forensic analysis.

Threat Assessment

The impact of new security problems can be reduced by early threat detection. Threat detection and assessment allows us to quickly identify so far unknown attacks, prioritize their threat and protect vulnerable systems. Honeypot technology serves this purpose by providing computer systems that we expect to be compromised. The honeypot systems are network sensors that allows us to detect new attacks.

As computer security problems are inherently repeatable, we obtain threat detection by populating our network with honeypots. New attacks can easily be identified by monitoring the state of deployed honeypots including new worms or widespread scans for vulnerabilities.

CYBER-SITUATIONAL AWARENESS

Commanders and warfighters constantly strive for battlefield situational awareness, in which information on movements and events is disseminated as they are happening. At a higher level, harmful actions can—based on observation of individuals and objects, the analysis of sensor data and the interception of communications—be prevented.

These are the same goals that now also prevail in the cyber-domain: performing reconnaissance on networks and systems and keeping tabs on the actions of adversaries.

Cyber-situational awareness goes a step beyond cyber security and cyber-defence. Situational awareness needs to include a forward-leaning, proactive approach that enables network defenders to react to events in real time, instead of being constrained merely to analysing occurrences after the fact.The ability to quickly synthesize data, recognize patterns and dynamically adapt at machine speed is a critical factor in cyberdomain information dominance, observed Rich Gleason, director of cyber security at CSC.

Several military agencies, including the Defense Information Systems Agency, are devoting significant resources to cybersituational awareness. One aspect of cyber-situational awareness that goes beyond other military domains is the involvement of the defence industrial base. Not only does the Department of Defense share information with contractors, but the private sector is involved in providing cyber-environments to the military in many cases. The military also relies on the capabilities of its private-sector partners to help achieve cyber-situational awareness.

As on the battlefield, achieving cyber-situational awareness involves the collection and analysis of enormous volumes of data. This presents technological challenges that the military often relies on the private sector to solve. The private sector, for its part, is constantly developing new technologies to allow better views and better analysis of the cyber-landscape."Cyber-situational awareness seeks to enhance decision making by having greater visibility and awareness of the cyber-domain," said Manuel Hermosilla, chief of the NetOps Programme Office at DISA. "It supports the full spectrum of operations and includes the ability to direct and redirect capabilities to meet operational needs. We need to be aware of threats beyond the enterprise. We need to know what is going on outside as well in order to defend ourselves."

"The conversation should be around how to defeat a cyber-attack as it is happening," said Diana Gowen, senior vice president and general manager at CenturyLink. "The government recognizes that industry has some capabilities and skills in this area. Armed with some additional data the private sector can collaborate with government to do a much better job of defending the nation's cyber-domains."

"I look at cyber as another military domain, the same as air, space and ground," said Kathy Warden, vice president of the Cyber Intelligence Division at Northrop Grumman. "The end result you want to achieve is the same. But is it harder to visualize what is going on inside a network. Cyber-situational awareness is another element that warfighters need to get a complete picture of their environment."

Commanders and warfighters want information on cyber-situational awareness as it pertains to the missions they are executing, said Dylan DeAnda, director of technical solutions at Kratos Defense and Security Solutions. "There is a need to develop awareness at a high level, but with the ability to drill down to understand the impact on a specific mission."

Instrumenting the Network

The first step towards achieving cyber-situational awareness is in instrumenting the network by placing sensors for collecting information, according to Warden. Next is continually updating the sensors as the threat environment changes. Also important is the sharing of information throughout the enterprise and with outside partners in the defence industrial base and with coalition partners.

"You need sensors that hunt in the wilds of the Internet as well as those that protect your own domain," said Warden. "Updating the sensors is critical so that you don't generate a lot of false positives or non-valueadded intelligence. These will be a waste of the analysts' time. The sensors are only as good as the tuning that goes into them."

The monitoring of network traffic with sensors yields large volumes of data. "These need to be analysed quickly," said Jack Donnelly, director of cyber programmes at Raytheon. "You also need the capability to report that information to key decision makers," which could be analysts, military officers, or national leaders, "so they can make real-time or near real-time decisions."

DISA owns and operates a huge chunk of the DoD cyber-infrastructure, and provides a variety of enterprise services to its many military customers. "We use and provide tools that manage and control the collection of information about the infrastructure and about flows of information," said Hermosilla. These include tools that continuously monitor network environments, security gateways that seek out new vulnerabilities, and visualization tools that seek to provide a common operating picture to analysts, operators and decision makers. "There are also various portals, widgets and other software that seek to provide an analytic capability," said Hermosilla. "We expect to see a push for more analytics capabilities as we move forward."

"Analytics applications need to ride on top of the data to do the heavy lifting involved in sorting out the true nuggets of information," said Warden. "Visualization is not the hardest part of the process but it is the way the information gets presented to decision makers and therefore it is important."

Sharing of cyber-information goes across both formal structures and informal mechanisms. "It can be as formal as providing information to a central group," said Warden, "or as informal as chief information security officers calling each other when they see something that doesn't look quite right."

"The defence industrial base is part of the larger effort to achieve cyber-situational awareness," said Hermosilla. "Industry and DoD are constantly sharing information. We also want to leverage private-sector capabilities so that we don't have to reinvent the wheel. We are looking to academia, as well as companies like Google and Yahoo, to find open source technologies to deal with the big data issues involved in cyber-situational awareness."

"The private sector is a twofold partner with DoD," said Warden, "in that we are providing capabilities and resources to develop the solution, and in the fact that the industrial base is part of providing the environment itself. It owns a significant piece of the cyber-domain that DoD relies on. In that role, the private sector has additional capabilities and responsibilities to provide solution sets that ride on the infrastructure."

Over the last three years, DoD has been developing an infrastructure for sharing information across its enterprise as well as with its industry partners, according to Warden.

"They are creating an environment, part of which is found in the U.S. Cyber Command, where information can be shared and pushed back out," she said. "It is starting to work across organizations that control various pieces of the network and it is a very positive development. The government is also working on ways to get information and make technologies available to those, such as small and medium sized businesses, without ready access to them, and those are also steps in the right direction."

Public-Private Links

In another example of links between government and the private sector, a pilot programme inaugurated about a year ago brings together the National Security Agency and other intelligence community constituents with major telecommunications carriers such as CenturyLink, as well as representatives of the defence industrial base. "The intelligence community has provided us with classified signatures of actors we are able to look for to prevent attacks before they happen," said Gowen.

The result is envisioned to be a commercial e-mail filtering system designed to prevent network intrusions. "Through this pilot programme we have seen the willingness of the intelligence community and DoD to share information with industry and vice versa," said Gowen. "As a result, we are able to create new capabilities that government and industry can share to better protect all of our networks and all of our data."

Century Link is also participating in a Department of Homeland Security programme that will install the latest version of Einstein, an intrusion detection system that monitors government network gateways for traffic patterns that indicate the presence of unwanted traffic, onto carrier networks. By collecting traffic information at agency gateways, Einstein provides analysts a big-picture view, synthesized of potentially malicious activity across federal networks.

Einstein helps identify configuration problems, unauthorized network traffic, network backdoors, routing anomalies, network scanning activities and baseline network traffic patterns. It also enables rapid detection of cyber-attacks and provides federal agencies with early incident detection. "DHS saw what we are able to do with e-mail filtering and asked us to migrate that to the dot-gov world," said Gowen.

Emerging technologies for cyber-situational awareness include those that set out to squeeze relevant information out of large volumes of data, visualize threat information at various system levels and integrate cyber-threat data from multiple sources.

Lookingglass Cyber Solutions built a system that takes data from 37 threat intelligence feeds and contextualizes and enriches the data so that decision makers get a clear picture of issues facing their corner of the universe.

Contextualization means facilitating a view of data from a specific angle. "Decision makers want quick knowledge about the networks that matter to them," said Derek Gabbard, chief executive officer of Lookingglass. "We take all that activity and overlay it on a map so users can define what is important to them. Enrichment refers to the capability to drill down to get more information on areas or situations of interest. At the end, you can achieve one level of situational awareness by achieving context and another by going through the enrichment process."

EIQnetworks provides a product called Secure-Vue, which it describes as a unified situational awareness platform. "You can buy 15 different monitoring tools, but then how do you bring it all together to a single console?" said John Linkous, eIQ's vice president and chief security and compliance officer. "To see how abnormal events are affecting network traffic you need to see relationships among complex data elements."

SecureVue can deliver cyber-situational awareness in single platform, according to Linkous. "SecureVue natively monitors firewall performance, tracks network traffic and analyses all these elements of security data. It can also work with the technologies you already have. We provide the ability to correlate all this information together." SecureVue also facilitates continuous monitoring of compliance, a discipline advocated by the National Institute of Standards and Technology and which is being increasingly regarded as a best practice for information systems security. "SecureVue can provide reports on the system as a whole," said Linkous. "It correlates information on the system at the application, database and user levels and can tell when the system falls out of compliance. It then reports who made the change and when and in what context and whether or not the change was intentional."

AccessData Group recently launched a cyber-intelligence and response technology that integrates network forensics and malware analysis in a single dashboard. "Organizations traditionally have deployed disparate tools without collaboration or integration capabilities," said Jason Mical, the company's director of network forensics. "Our new framework contains complete intelligence in a single pane of glass."

The framework provides a view to data from multiple tools, including third-party tools that can be integrated with the product. The system also has a drill down capability, so that if an anomaly is found on a specific device, the operator can click on that device in a visualization and investigate the configuration of and the activity on that device in a detailed manner.

"This significantly increases the ability to respond to and remediate a compromise within an organization," said Mical.

Another important capability on the market is the Dynamic Adaptive Defense offering from CSC, which cuts enterprisewide incident response from hours and days to minutes, and can completely automate responses to advance persistent threats and intrusion events so that parallel remediation actions can be carried out before damage can be done. Tying these capabilities into an advanced situational awareness solution that shows not only cyber-incidents, but also risk factors from throughout the enterprise, will provide a much clearer picture on enterprise risk in real time, while also providing the ability to mitigate those risks at the very moment of detection. This solution extended out of the enterprise and into the theater of military operations would give unprecedented capabilities in the blue force/red force tracking space, CSC officials say.

Visualization Platform

Kratos provides a visualization platform for cyber-situational awareness that accounts for configurations and compliance for all devices on a network. The company recently introduced a security information event manager called CyberC4-Alert, designed for satellite networks and operations, that provides real-time situational awareness and incident response for cyber security situational awareness and mission assurance.

"Network attacks look different in the radio-frequency domain as opposed to the packet-based domain," said Michael Smith, senior vice president of enterprise technology at Kratos. "Jamming on satellite networks degrades the signals and network performance. Because of our knowledge of the RF space, we can define what interference looks like and provide that information to users. You can't run anti-virus software on a satellite network because of the higher performance requirements."

Satellite systems can also encounter configuration management challenges and other vulnerabilities not typically found on terrestrial networks.

CyberC4-Alert constantly monitors for cyber security threats by gathering security event data from across the satellite network to provide situational awareness. "A correlation engine with user-defined rules and policies prioritizes events by their severity, alerting users of system threats, performance issues and compliance violations through a drill-down dashboard," said Smith.

For true cyber-situational awareness to become a reality, more work is needed to improve automation tools, according to Warden. "Threats are getting more sophisticated," she said. "The problem is the ability to extract the right data from a number of elements. You are trying to identify something that hasn't happened before. It is a question of looking at indications and warnings and taking the time to build confidence in the identification of patterns."

The military, in particular, must be able to deal with targeted attacks that have no existing signature or pattern, and have the ability to correlate unusual events inside the enterprise and the outside domain to try to identify hidden patterns of threats. Another significant concern is massive denial-of-service attacks that can compromise military communications and mission systems at a pre-coordinated time and place. Identifying, visualizing and pinpointing the cause of these threats in a situational awareness system takes a great deal of sophistication and "big data" correlation and compute power. Equally important is the ability to dynamically adapt and mitigate these threats at machine speed in an automated and reliable fashion, noted CSC's Bernie Thomas.

But at the moment these analytical capabilities are "relatively immature," Warden added. "Only in the last five to seven years has any real research and development been done in this space. We will see solutions over the next decade increase in sophistication and maturity with additional investments. This is one of the harder situational awareness problems and it can't be solved quickly or cheaply."

The growing importance of wireless technologies and cloud computing also presents challenges to the future of cyber situational awareness. "Wireless security is more about the device itself and how it is engineered," said Warden. "In order to protect the data on the devices, manufacturers have to build security into the devices or other ways must be found to layer security on top of the device itself." "I think we will experience challenges as various organizations move part of their IT capabilities to the cloud," said Donnelly. "Trying to figure out what is being done where and isolating it will be a challenge. We are trying to anticipate customer needs so that when a situational awareness capability will be required for the cloud, Raytheon will already have products to offer."

While DoD and intelligence community have been diligent in fostering partnerships with the defence industrial base on cyber-situational awareness, observers say less progress has been made in cooperation with coalition partners. "Other nations fight side by side with our forces, but they have been reluctant to share information on cyber-situational awareness due to security classifications or mistrust," said Dylan DeAnda of Kratos. "Information sharing across boundaries will be a huge field to embark on, but it is needed."

7

Military Preparedness Technology

At the outbreak of the Spanish-American war, M. Pierre Loti, member of the French Academy and cultivated exponent of the hopes and beliefs of the average citizen of continental Europe in regard to the contest, was at Madrid. Dewey's victory caused him grief; but he consoled himself, after watching a parade of the Spanish troops, by remarking: "They are indeed still the solid and splendid Spanish troops, heroic in every epoch—it needs only to look at them to divine the woe that awaits the American shopkeepers when brought face to face with such soldiers." The excellent M. Loti had already explained Manila by vague references to American bombs loaded with petroleum, and to a devilish mechanical ingenuity wholly unaccompanied by either humanity or courage, and he still allowed himself to dwell on the hope that there were reserved for America *des surprises sanglantes.*

M. Loti's views on military matters need not detain us, for his attitude toward the war was merely the attitude of continental Europe generally, in striking contrast to that of England. But it is a curious fact that his view reflects not unfairly two different opinions, which two different classes of our people would have expressed before the event—opinions singularly falsified by the fact.

Our pessimists feared that we had lost courage and fighting capacity; some of our optimists asserted that we needed neither, in view of our marvellous wealth and extraordinary inventiveness and mechanical skill. The national trait of "smartness," used in the Yankee sense of the word, has very good and very bad sides. Among the latter is its tendency to create the belief that we need not prepare for war, because somehow we shall be able to win by some novel patent device, some new trick or new invention developed on the spur of the moment by the ingenuity of our people. In this way it is hoped to provide a substitute for preparedness—that is, for years of patient and faithful attention to detail in advance.

It is even sometimes said that these mechanical devices will be of so terrible a character as to nullify the courage which has always in the past been the prime factor in winning battles. Now, as all sound military judges knew in advance must inevitably be the case, the experience of the Spanish war completely falsified every prediction of this kind. We did not win through any special ingenuity. Not a device of any kind was improvised during or immediately before the war which was of any practical service. The "bombs enveloped in petroleum" had no existence save in the brains of the Spaniards and their more credulous sympathizers. Our navy won because of its preparedness and because of the splendid seamanship and gunnery which had been handed down as traditional in the service, and had been perfected by the most careful work.

The army, at the only point where it was seriously opposed, did its work by sheer dogged courage and hard fighting, in spite of an unpreparedness which almost brought disaster upon it, and would without doubt actually have done so had not the defects and shortcomings of the Spanish administration been even greater than our own. We won the war in a very short time, and without having to expend more than the merest fraction of our strength. The navy was shown to be in good shape; and Secretary Root, to whom the wisdom of President McKinley has intrusted the War Department, has already shown himself as good a man as ever held the portfolio—a man whose administration is certainly to be of inestimable service to the army and to the country.

In consequence, too many of our people show signs of thinking that, after all, everything was all right, and is all right now; that we need not bother ourselves to learn any lessons that are not agreeable to us, and that if in the future we get into a war with a more formidable power than Spain, we shall pull through somehow. Such a view is unjust to the nation, and particularly unjust to the splendid men of the army and of the navy, who would be sacrificed to it, should we ever engage in a serious war without having learned the lessons that the year 1898 ought to have taught.

If we wish to get an explanation of the efficiency of our navy in 1898, and of the astonishing ease with which its victories were won, we must go a long way back of that year, and study not only its history, but the history of the Spanish navy for many decades. Of course any such study must begin with a prompt admission of the splendid natural quality of our officers and men. On the bridge, in the gun-turrets, in the engine-room, and behind the quick-firers, every one alike, from the highest to the lowest, was eager for the war, and was, in heart, mind, and body, of the very type which makes the best kind of fighting man.

Many of the officers of our ships have mentioned to me that during the war punishments almost ceased, because the men who got into scrapes in times of peace were so aroused and excited by the chance of battle that their behaviour was perfect. We read now and then of foreign services where men hate their officers, have no community of interest with them, and no desire to fight for the flag. Most emphatically such is not the case in our service. The discipline is just but not severe, unless severity is imperatively called for. As a whole, the officers have the welfare of the men very much at heart, and take care of their bodies with the same forethought that they show in training them for battle.

The physique of the men is excellent, and to it are joined eagerness to learn, and readiness to take risks and to stand danger unmoved. Nevertheless, all this, though indispensable as a base, would mean nothing whatever for the efficiency of the navy without years of careful preparation and training. A war-ship is such a complicated machine, and such highly specialized training is self-evidently needed to command it, that our naval commanders, unlike our military commanders, are freed from having to combat the exasperating belief that the average civilian could at short notice do their work.

Of course, in reality a special order of ability and special training are needed to enable a man to command troops successfully; but the need is not so obvious as on shipboard. No civilian could be five minutes on a battleship without realizing his unfitness to command it; but there are any number of civilians who firmly believe they can command regiments, when they have not a single trait, natural or acquired, that really fits them for the task. A blunder in the one case meets with instant, open, and terrible punishment; in the other, it is at the moment only a source of laughter or exasperation to the few, ominous though it may be for the future.

A colonel who issued the wrong order would cause confusion. A ship-captain by such an order might wreck his ship. It follows that the navy is comparatively free in time of war from the presence in the higher ranks of men utterly unfit to perform their duties. The nation realizes that it cannot improvise naval officers even out of first-rate skippers of merchantmen and passenger-steamers.

Such men could be used to a certain extent as under-officers to meet a sudden and great emergency; but at best they would meet it imperfectly, and this the public at large understands. There is, however, some failure to understand that much the same condition prevails among ordinary seamen. The public speakers and newspaper writers who may be loudest in clamoring for war are often precisely the men who clamour against preparations for war. Whether from sheer ignorance or from demagogy, they frequently assert that, as this is the day of mechanics, even on the sea, and as we have a large mechanical population, we could at once fit out any number of vessels with men who would from the first do their duty thoroughly and well. As a matter of fact, though the sea-mechanic has replaced the sailorman, yet it is almost as necessary as ever that a man should have the sea habit in order to be of use aboard ship; and it is infinitely more necessary than in former times that a man-of-war's-man should have especial training with his guns before he can use them aright.

In the old days cannon were very simple; sighting was done roughly; and the ordinary merchant seaman speedily grew fit to do his share of work on a frigate. Nowadays men must be carefully trained for a considerable space of time before they can be of any assistance whatever in handling and getting good results from the formidable engines of destruction on battleship, cruiser, and torpedo-boat. Crews cannot be improvised. To get the very best work out of them, they should all be composed of trained and seasoned men; and in any event they should not be sent against a formidable adversary unless each crew has for a nucleus a large body of such men filling all the important positions. From time immemorial it has proved impossible to improvise so much as a makeshift navy for use against a formidable naval opponent. Any such effort must meet with disaster. Most fortunately, the United States had grown to realize this some time before the Spanish war broke out.

After the gigantic Civil War the reaction from the strain of the contest was such that our navy was permitted to go to pieces. Fifteen years after the close of the contest in which Farragut took rank as one of the great admirals of all time, the splendid navy of which he was the chief ornament had become an object of derision to every third-rate power in Europe and South America.

The elderly monitors and wooden steamers, with their old-fashioned smoothbore guns, would have been as incompetent to face the modern ships of the period as the *Congress* and the *Cumberland* were to face the *Merrimac*. Our men were as brave as ever, but in war their courage would have been of no more avail than the splendid valour of the men who sank with their guns firing and flags flying when the great Confederate ironclad came out to Hampton Roads. At last the nation awoke from its lethargy. In 1883, under the administration of President Arthur, when Secretary Chandler was in the Navy Department, the work was begun. The first step taken was the refusal to repair the more antiquated wooden ships, and the building of new steel ships to replace them. One of the ships thus laid down was the *Boston,* which was in Dewey's fleet.

It is therefore merely the literal truth to say that the preparations which made Dewey's victory possible began just fifteen years before the famous day when he steamed into Manila Bay.

Every senator and congressman who voted an appropriation which enabled Secretary Chandler to begin the upbuilding of the new navy, the President who advised the course, the secretary who had the direct management of it, the shipbuilder in whose yard the ship was constructed, the skilled experts who planned her hull, engine, and guns, and the skilled workmen who worked out these plans, all alike are entitled to their share in the credit of the great Manila victory.

The majority of the men can never be known by name, but the fact that they did well their part in the deed is of vastly more importance than the obtaining of any reward for it, whether by way of recognition or otherwise; and this fact will always remain. Nevertheless, it is important for our own future that, so far as possible, we should recognize the men who did well.

This is peculiarly important in the case of Congress, whose action has been the indispensable prerequisite for every effort to build up the navy, as Congress provided the means for each step.

As there was always a division in Congress, while in the popular mind the whole body is apt to be held accountable for any deed, good or ill, done by the majority, it is much to be wished, in the interest of justice, that some special historian of the navy would take out from the records the votes, and here and there the speeches, for and against the successive measures by which the navy was built up. Every man who by vote and voice from time to time took part in adding to our fleet, in buying the armour, in preparing the gun-factories, in increasing the personnel and enabling it to practise, deserves well of the whole nation, and a record of his action should be kept, that his children may feel proud of him.

No less clearly should we understand that throughout these fifteen years the men who, whether from honest but misguided motives, from short-sightedness, from lack of patriotism, or from demagogy, opposed the building up of the navy, have deserved ill of the nation, exactly as did those men who recently prevented the purchase of armour for the battleships, or, under the lead of Senator Gorman, prevented the establishment of our army on the footing necessary for our national needs. If disaster comes through lack of preparedness, the fault necessarily lies far less with the men under whom the disaster actually occurs than with those to whose wrongheadedness or short-sighted indifference in time past the lack of preparedness is due.

MILITARY PREPAREDNESS MEASURES

The military capabilities of the United States in the early 1930's were small compared to what might be required to match the powerful forces of the Axis. This fact was fully realized by responsible government officials, but public sentiment was quite fixed in opposition to any warlike gestures, including the buildup of armament. Furthermore, the economic depression affected expenditures for military preparedness.

Yet, paradoxically, it was the depression which permitted significant improvement in preparedness. This was because the National Industrial Recovery Act provided funds for industrial activity which would give jobs to the unemployed. President Roosevelt knew that the building of armaments, particularly ships, made jobs in nearly every phase of industry, and therefore in 1934 he exercised the authority granted by Congress and ordered the construction of thirty-two naval vessels. This was the first significant step in preparing for the needs of World War II, and hindsight proves that it was a fortunate and indispensable step.

Other steps were taken as the grim events abroad pressed on the national consciousness and brought a change in the public attitude toward military preparedness. Some of the more important were the following:

a. In 1934 the Vinson-Trammel Naval Bill authorized the navy to build up to treaty limitations. This did not provide funds for construction but indicated Congressional opinion as to the need for correcting our naval deficiencies.

b. In 1937 President Roosevelt announced that the Navy was proceeding with the construction of two new battleships, the first since the 1922 treaty. These were *Washington* and *North Carolina* which rendered valiant service in World War II. The Army also received new equipment, and an increase in officers and men from 118,000 to a new limit of 158,000.

c. In his January 1938 message to Congress the President recommended increasing our defences to insure reasonable security against worldwide pressures and assaults. Congress authorized a twenty percent increase in ships for the Navy and appropriated for two new battleships and two aircraft carriers. Debate in Congress showed that much doubt existed on the need for these increases, and some isolationist groups suspected that the real purpose was to aid Great Britain. Secretary Hull replied that neither extreme internationalism or extreme isolationism was desired, but that inaction meant aiding the lawless nations.

d. Again, in his January 1939 message to Congress, the President recommended further strengthening of the national defence, especially in air power, and the mobilization of industry for quantity production.

e. When France sued for an armistice with Germany in June 1940 the United States insisted that the French fleet should not be surrendered to Germany, and received assurances accordingly.

f. Just before the surrender of France in June 1940 President Roosevelt asked Congress for authority to build 50,000 military airplanes, and stated to Congress that nations unable to defend themselves were easily subjugated. Old defence systems, he pointed out, were inadequate if American liberties and principles were to be maintained.

g. Following the fall of France the President requested Congress to appropriate five billion dollars for further increases in defence. This was granted on 27 August 1940. At the same time Congress authorized calling up the Reserves and National Guard for active duty. In July 1940, forty-five additional warships were ordered for the Navy Department.

h. In the summer of 1940 the President recommended to Congress the authorization for a "Two Ocean Navy," which was approved.

i. The first peacetime Selective Service and Training Act in United States history was passed in September 1940, and in August 1941, when the international situation was very foreboding, Congress extended the period of service to one and one-half years. But this was done by only a one vote margin in the House of Representatives.

Many Auxiliaries and Small Craft

With the exception of the larger battleships and the battle cruisers most of these vessels were expedited following the Pearl Harbour attack, and together with other ships which were ordered later, formed the irresistible force which vanquished the Japanese Navy.

PREPAREDNESS MOVEMENT

The Preparedness Movement, also referred to as the Preparedness Controversy, was a campaign led by Leonard Wood andTheodore Roosevelt to strengthen the military of the United States after the outbreak of World War I. Wood advocated a summer training school for reserve officers to be held in Plattsburg, New York. The movement was originally opposed by President Woodrow Wilson, who believed the United States should be in a position of armedneutrality. Several organizations were formed around the Preparedness Movement and held parades and organized opposition to Wilson's policies.

After the *Lusitania* was sunk by German U-boats on May 7, 1915 and Pancho Villa launched his raid againstColumbus, New Mexico, Wilson's attitude changed. Congress passed the National Defence Act of 1916 in June

1916 to authorize an enormous increase in the size of the military, and the Preparedness Movement faded.

The Movement

In 1915, a strong "preparedness" movement emerged. It argued that the United States needed to immediately build up strong naval and land forces for defensive purposes; an unspoken assumption was that the US would fight sooner or later. General Leonard Wood (still on active duty after serving a term as Chief of Staff of the Army), ex-president Theodore Roosevelt, and former secretaries of war Elihu Root and Henry Stimson were the driving forces behind the Preparedness Movement, along with many of the nation's most prominent bankers, industrialists, lawyers and scions of prominent families. There emerged an "Atlanticist" foreign policy establishment, a group of influential Americans drawn primarily from upper-class lawyers, bankers, academics, and politicians of the Northeast US, committed to a strand of Anglophile internationalism.

A representative leader was Paul D. Cravath, one of New York's foremost corporation lawyers. For Cravath, in his mid-fifties when the war began, the conflict served as an epiphany, sparking an interest in international affairs that dominated his remaining career. Fiercely Anglophile, he strongly supported US intervention in the war and hoped that close Anglo-American cooperation would be the guiding principle of post-war international organization.

The preparedness movement had a "realistic" philosophy of world affairs—they believed that economic strength and military muscle were more decisive than idealistic crusades focused on causes like democracy and national self-determination. Emphasizing over and over the weak state of national defences, they showed that America's 100,000-man army even augmented by the 112,000 National Guardsmen, was outnumbered 20 to one by German army, which was drawn from a smaller population. Reform to them meant UMT or "universal military service", i.e. conscription They proposed a national service program under which the 600,000 men who turned 18 every year would be required to spend six months in military training, and afterwards be assigned to reserve units. The small regular army would primarily serve as a training agency. This proposal ultimately failed, but it fostered the Plattsburg Movement, a series of summer training camps that in 1915 and 1916 hosted some 40,000 men largely of elite social classes, and the later Citizens' Military Training Camps that trained some 400,000 men from 1921 to 1940.

Opposition

Antimilitarists and pacifists — strong in Protestant churches and women's groups — protested the plan would make the US resemble Germany (which required two years' active duty). Advocates retorted that military "service" was an essential duty of citizenship, and that without the commonality provided by such service the nation would splinter into antagonistic ethnic groups. One spokesman promised that UMT would become "a real melting pot, under which the fire is hot enough to fuse the elements into one common mass of Americanism." Furthermore, they promised, the discipline and training would make for a better paid work force. The hostility to military service was so strong at the time it is difficult to imagine such a program winning approval; indeed, even in World War II, when Stimson as Secretary of War proposed a similar program of universal peacetime service, he was defeated. Underscoring its commitment, the preparedness movement set up and funded its own summer training camps (at Plattsburg, New York, and other sites) where 40,000 college alumni became physically fit, learned to march and shoot, and ultimately provided the cadre of a wartime officer corps.

Suggestions by labor unions that talented working class youth be invited to Plattsburg were ignored. The preparedness movement was distant not only from the working classes but also from the middle class leadership of most of small town America. It had had little use for the National Guard, which is saw as politicized, localistic, poorly armed, ill trained, too inclined to idealistic crusading (as against Spain in 1898), and too lacking in understanding of world affairs. The National Guard on the other hand was securely rooted in state and local politics, with representation from a very broad cross section of American society. The guard was one of the nation's few institutions that (at least in some northern states) accepted African-Americans on an equal footing with whites.

Democrats

The Democratic Party saw the preparedness movement as a threat. Roosevelt, Root and Wood were prospective Republican presidential candidates. More subtly, the Democrats were rooted in localism that appreciated the National Guard, and the voters were hostile to the rich and powerful in the first place. Working with the Democrats who controlled Congress, Wilson was able to sidetrack the preparedness forces. Army and navy leaders were forced to testify before Congress to the effect that the nation's military was in excellent shape.

Military not Prepared

In fact neither the army nor navy was in shape for war. Despite the flood of new weapons systems unveiled in the war in Europe, the army paid scant attention. For example, it was making no studies of trench warfare, poison gas or tanks, and was unfamiliar with the rapid evolution of air tactics. The

Democrats in Congress tried to cut the military budget in 1915. The preparedness movement effectively exploited the surge of outrage over the *Lusitania* in May, 1915, forcing the Democrats to promise some improvements to the military and naval forces.

Wilson's Program

Wilson, less fearful of the navy, embraced a long-term building program designed to make the fleet the equal of the Royal Navy by the mid 1920s. "Realism" was at work here; the admirals were Mahanians and they therefore wanted a surface fleet of heavy battleships second to none—that is, equal to Britain. The facts of submarine warfare (which necessitated destroyers, not battleships) and the possibilities of imminent war with Germany (or with Britain, for that matter), were simply ignored.

Opposition to Wilson's Program

Wilson's program the army touched off a firestorm. Secretary of War Lindley Garrison adopted many of the proposals of the preparedness leaders, especially their emphasis on a large federal reserves and abandonment of the National Guard. Garrison's proposals not only outraged the localistic politicians of both parties, they also offended a strongly held belief shared by the liberal wing of the progressive movement. They felt that warfare always had a hidden economic motivation. Specifically, they warned the chief warmongers were New York bankers (like J. P. Morgan) with millions at risk, profiteering munition makers (like Bethlehem Steel, which made armour, and DuPont, which made powder) and unspecified industrialists searching for global markets to control. Antiwar critics blasted them. These selfish special interests were too powerful, especially, Senator LaFollette noted, in the conservative wing of the Republican Party. The only road to peace was disarmament, reiterated Bryan.

Garrison's plan unleashed the fiercest battle in peacetime history over the relationship of military planning to national goals. In peacetime, War Department arsenals and navy yards manufactured nearly all munitions that lacked civilian uses, including warships, artillery, naval guns, and shells. Items available on the civilian market, such as food, horses, saddles, wagons, and uniforms were always purchased from civilian contractors. Armour plate (and after 1918, airplanes) were exceptions that have caused unremitting controversy for a century.

Peace leaders

Peace leaders like Jane Addams of Hull House and David Starr Jordan, president of Stanford University, redoubled their efforts, and now turned their voices against Wilson because he was "sowing the seeds of militarism, raising up a military and naval caste." Many ministers, professors, farm spokesmen and labor union leaders joined in, with powerful support from a band of four dozen southern Democrats in Congress who took control of the House Military Affairs Committee.

Wilson Appeals to the People

Wilson, in deep trouble, took his cause to the people in a major speaking tour in early 1916, a warm-up for his reelection campaign that fall. Wilson seems to have won over the middle classes, but had little impact on the largely ethnic working classes and the deeply isolationist farmers. Congress still refused to budge, so Wilson replaced Garrison as Secretary of War with Newton Baker, the Democratic mayor of Cleveland and an outspoken opponent of preparedness. (Garrison's kept quiet, but felt Wilson was "a man of high ideals but no principles.")

Compromise reached

So a compromise was passed in May 1916, as the war raged on and Berlin was debating whether America was so weak it could be ignored. The army was to double in size to 11,300 officers and 208,000 men, with no reserves, and a National Guard that would be enlarged in five years to 440,000 men. Summer camps on the Plattsburg model were authorized for new officers, and the government was given $20 million to build a nitrate plant of its own. Preparedness supporters were downcast, the antiwar people were jubilant. America would now be too weak to go to war. Colonel Robert L. Bullard privately complained that "Both sides [Britain and Germany] treat us with scorn and contempt; our fool, smug conceit of superiority has been exploded in our faces and deservedly." The House gutted the naval plans as well, defeating a "big navy" plan by 189 to 183, and scuttling the battleships. The Battle of Jutland (May 31/June 1, 1916) saw the German fleet nearly sunk by the stronger British fleet. Only brilliant seamanship and luck allowed it to escape.

Arguing this battle proved the validity of Mahanian doctrine, the navalists took control in the Senate, broke the House coalition, and authorized a rapid three-year buildup of all classes of warships. A new weapons system, naval aviation, received $3.5 million, and the government was authorized to build its own armour-plate factory. The very weakness of American military power encouraged Berlin to start its unrestricted submarine attacks in 1917. It knew this meant war with America, but it could discount the immediate risk because the US Army was negligible and the new warships would not be at sea until 1919 by which time the war would be over, with Germany victorious. The notion that armaments led to war was turned on its head: refusal to arm in 1916 led to war in 1917.

ENVISIONING A NATIONAL PREPAREDNESS SYSTEM

How our existing homeland security strategy, doctrine, and capabilities can be unified into a single National Preparedness System. The strengths of this System include first and foremost *integration*of strategy, doctrine, capabilities, response activities, and exercises, as well as assessment and evaluation. The graphic also highlights the feedback mechanisms that must be built into the System. In particular, as described above, the System must include routine reporting and assessment of program performance metrics, the readiness of particular capabilities, as well as best practices and lessons learned from exercises and activities. These assessments and findings must be reported back, as appropriate, to inform key components throughout the System.

The National Preparedness System graphic additionally highlights the constituent elements of operational capabilities: deliberate planning, resources, logistics, training, and education. Moreover, the graphic notes the importance of unity of effort in exercises and the conduct of response activities in incidents.

The National Preparedness System must be dynamic, flexible, and responsive to new developments. Like our national security system, the strategy, doctrine, and capabilities of the System should be reviewed periodically to determine their continued relevance to current challenges. Similarly, periodic reviews must assess the continued internal consistency of the System—e.g., do the doctrine and capabilities support the strategy?

Key inputs to the System include the current national vision for preparedness, laws, and policies and the use of capability-based planning that prioritizes investments to fill gaps identified by needs assessments. An equally important input is the current assessment of risks—what threats does the Nation currently confront, what are our current vulnerabilities, and what are the consequences? Against the current assessment of risks, we must continually evaluate our capability to respond effectively.

Finally, our planning and operational documents should define the critical roles played by all of our homeland security partners in the Preparedness System. Federal, State, and local governments play prominent roles throughout the System—from strategy development to assessment and lessons learned. Additionally, the private sector, NGOs, faith-based groups, communities, and individuals play important roles in operational capabilities as well as response activities.

CREATING A CULTURE OF PREPAREDNESS

The second element of our continuing transformation for homeland security perhaps will be the most profound and enduring—the creation of a

Culture of Preparedness. A new preparedness culture must emphasize that the entire Nation—Federal, State, and local governments; the private sector; communities; and individual citizens—shares common goals and responsibilities for homeland security. In other words, our homeland security is built upon a foundation of partnerships. And these partnerships must include shared understanding of at least four concepts:

- The certainty of future catastrophes;
- The importance of initiative;
- The roles of citizens and other homeland security stakeholders in preparedness; and
- The roles of each level of government and the private sector in creating a prepared Nation.

Future Challenges

The first principle for a Culture of Preparedness must be a shared acknowledgement that creating a prepared Nation will be a continuing challenge. Optimism is fundamental to the American character. While it always energizes us, it also grounds us in times of tragedy and loss.

We must guard against our optimism leading us to a dangerous sense of complacency. Complacency of our citizens presents a great challenge.

We are fortunate that, because of the courage and self-sacrifice of public servants across all levels of government, we have not suffered another terrorist attack on our homeland since 2001. But we are a Nation at war, and we have a responsibility to be prepared. We must temper our optimism with sober recognition of the certainty of future catastrophes. We cannot prevent natural disasters. And though we work tirelessly against them, we cannot anticipate nor prevent every type of terrorist attack against the homeland. As the Irish Republican Army once warned British Prime Minister Margaret Thatcher after narrowly missing her in an assassination attempt: terrorists only need to be successful once; but we, their targets, must be successful everyday. We know that our enemies plot further attacks against us. We must continue to prevent them and, if necessary, respond. Regrettably, lives will be lost, citizens displaced, and property destroyed.

The certainty of future challenges should inform our national expectations. As a Nation, we will prepare ourselves in the most effective ways we know. Our Culture of Preparedness, therefore, must emphasize the importance of flexibility and readiness to cope with an uncertain future. While we cannot predict the future to our satisfaction, we can build capabilities that prepare us for a broad range of challenges. Perhaps equally important, we can ensure that our preparedness plans, thinking, and "imagination" do not become so rigid that we cannot rapidly adapt to unforeseen challenges.

Initiative

Despite reforms that encourage a proactive, anticipatory approach to the management of incidents, the culture of our response community has a fundamental bias towards *reaction* rather than *initiative*. As a result, our national efforts too often emphasize response and clean-up efforts at the expense of potentially more cost-effective anticipatory actions that might prevent or mitigate damage. The need for anticipatory response is a pillar of the National Response Plan. A list of Key Concepts in the *National Response Plan* places it second only to "systematic and coordinated incident management." Specifically, the *NRP*calls for:

Proactive notification and deployment of Federal resources in anticipation of or in response to catastrophic events in coordination and collaboration with State, local, and tribal governments and private entities when possible. Similarly, our Culture of Preparedness must stress initiative at all levels. Fundamentally, our Preparedness System and Culture must encourage and reward innovation. To do so, we must build a system and approach that better aligns authority and responsibility—those who are responsible for a mission or task must have the authority to act. In the same vein, an alignment of authority and responsibility provides us the ability to assess our performance—collectively and individually. Performance assessment and accountability, however, must not be *blame.* Our current culture of blame threatens both individual and institutional initiative, resourcefulness, and enterprise across the homeland security, law enforcement, and intelligence fields. It is time that Congress, the Executive Branch, and all of our homeland security partners develop a consensus regarding a reasonable balance of accountability, responsibility, and authority at all levels. Otherwise, the culture of blame and its related acrimony will debilitate us.

Citizen Preparedness

Our preparedness culture must also emphasize the importance of citizen and community preparedness. Citizen and community preparedness are among the most effective means of preventing terrorist attacks as well as protecting against, mitigating, responding to, and recovering from all hazards. For example, the Citizen Corps in Harris County, Texas, brought together over 50,000 volunteers to support American Red Cross efforts and staff evacuation centers throughout Houston. As a joint team, they created an actual working city (with its own zip code) for Hurricane Katrina victims sheltering in the Astrodome.

Thus, citizens and communities can help themselves by becoming more prepared. If every family maintained the resources to live in their homes without electricity and running water for three days, we could allocate more

Federal, State, and local response resources to saving lives. Similarly, if every family developed their own emergency preparedness plan, they almost certainly would reduce the demand for outside emergency resources. As the 9/11 Commission Report states, "One clear lesson of September 11 is that individual civilians need to take responsibility for maximizing the probability that they will survive, should disaster strike."

Leadership at all levels will be essential in helping to transform citizen preparedness. First, responsible public officials at the Federal, State, and local levels as well as prominent national figures should begin a public dialogue that emphasizes common themes regarding the importance of citizen preparedness. DHS should continue to build upon those programs and institutions that already work, such as Department of Education elementary and secondary school programs; Citizen Corps; State and local government training programs; and Federal cooperation with the National Governors Association. Nongovernmental organizations can also play a key role in this area. DHS has made some important progress in this area with its *Ready.gov* initiative and its public service announcements program with the Ad Council. But more needs to be done. Encouraging preparedness awareness and activity is a shared responsibility across all levels of government that we must make a priority. Preparedness today will save lives tomorrow.

In addition, DHS and other Federal agencies should identify both the individual skills and capabilities that would help citizens in a disaster as well as the types of messages from trusted leaders that would encourage citizens to be better prepared. Public awareness messaging must shift to include more substantive information, as opposed to just telling our citizens that they need to "do something." For example, the "Stop, Drop, and Roll" campaign used so successfully in fire safety as part of the "Learn Not to Burn" program provided citizens with specific steps to take. Other successful campaigns include the National Highway Traffic Safety Administration's "Buckle Up America" campaign, which prescribes proper use of seat belt and child safety seats. As with so many of these successful campaigns, the Nation's children can help lead the way.

Other Homeland Security Stakeholders and Preparedness

We must build upon our initial successful efforts to partner with other homeland security stakeholders—namely the private sector, non-governmental organizations, and faith-based groups. Each of these groups plays a critical role in preparedness. To the extent that we can incorporate them into the National effort, we will be reducing the burden on other response resources so that Federal, State, and local responders can concentrate our energies on those with the greatest need.

Private sector companies own and operate 85 percent of our Nation's critical infrastructure. Transportation, electricity, banking, telecommunications, food supply, and clean water are examples of services relying on infrastructure that have become basic aspects of our daily lives. Yet, these services are often only noticed when they are disrupted and when the American public expects speedy restoration. In fact, the Nation relies on "critical infrastructure" to maintain its defense, continuity of government, economic prosperity, and quality of life. The services provided by these interconnected systems are so vital that their disruption will have a debilitating impact on national security, the economy, or public health and safety.

Companies are responsible for protecting their systems, which comprise the majority of critical infrastructure. Because of this, private sector preparation and response is vital to mitigating the national impact of disasters. Government actions in response to a disaster can help or hamper private sector efforts. However, governments cannot plan to adequately respond unless the private sector helps them understand what infrastructure truly is critical. Likewise, businesses cannot develop contingency plans without understanding how governments will respond.

To maximize the Nation's preparedness, Federal, State, and local governments must join with the private sector to collaboratively develop plans to respond to major disasters. There are important initiatives in this area already underway by the Business Round Table (BRT) and Business Executives for National Security (BENS) project. We must encourage and build upon these efforts. The private sector must be an explicit partner in and fully integrated across all levels of response—Federal, State, and local.

Non-governmental organizations play essential roles in preparedness by complementing and supporting preparedness efforts. In times of crisis, NGOs—especially community groups, faith-based organizations, places of worship, and relief organizations—provide essential human faces, helping hands, compassion, and comfort to all American people, whether or not they are victims of an incident. As such, they fill an essential need in the response system in ways far beyond the capacity of the Government. Thus, their contributions must be fully integrated at all levels—Federal, State, and local.

THE ROLE OF EACH LEVEL OF GOVERNMENT IN A CULTURE OF PREPAREDNESS

Today, we operate under two guiding principles: a) that incident management should begin at the lowest jurisdictional level possible, and b) that, for most incidents, the Federal government will generally play a supporting role to State and local efforts. While these principles suffice for the vast majority of incidents, they impede the Federal response to severe catastrophes. In a catastrophic scenario that overwhelms or incapacitates local and State incident command structures, the Federal government must be prepared to assume incident command and get assistance directly to those in need until State and local authorities are reconstituted.

The National Preparedness System must also recognize the role of the Federal government for monitoring and guiding national preparedness efforts.; In particular, the system must ensure that the Federal government assesses the preparedness of localities across the country with an eye towards identifying the Federal response requirement for each. In addition, Federal, State, local, and private sector partners must agree on a system in which the Federal government responds more actively and effectively while respecting the role of State and local governments.

The new culture of preparedness must stress *partnership* among all levels of government. Local governments will continue to have responsibility for providing the immediate response capabilities for the vast majority of incidents while State governors will continue to have sovereign responsibilities to protect their residents. Yet preparedness must emphasize the shared nature of these responsibilities in a catastrophic event. State governments must work with their local jurisdictions to ensure that they have developed plans and capabilities that are appropriate for the homeland security challenges confronting them. Both State and local governments must also reach out to their citizens, private sector, and community groups to promote their preparedness efforts.

Furthermore, in the new culture of preparedness, State and local governments must continually seek to work with their neighboring jurisdictions. Building upon the successes of interstate cooperation programs such as the Emergency Management Assistance Compact (EMAC), the Federal government must take an active role in encouraging and facilitating these partnerships. Regional collaboration at the State and local levels will help the Nation to reduce overlapping or redundant capabilities as well as to minimize capability gaps. Moreover, active regional collaboration will likewise be a means for identifying and sharing homeland security lessons learned and best practices.

Finally, in our new Culture of Preparedness, all required response assets and resources of the Federal government must integrate and synchronize to ensure an effective national response to a crisis. In practical terms, this entails stepping away from the bureaucratic view of a particular department or agency's institutional interests. Instead, we must continually build preparedness partnerships across the Federal government as well as with State and local governments.

MILITARY MODERNIZATION IN STRATEGIC ASIA

On September 29, 2005, the Asia Program joined with the Seattle-based National Bureau of Asian Research (NBR) to host a conference exploring the ramifications of military modernization in Asia and the implications of defense transformation for the grand strategies of the region's principal powers, including the United States. Conference attendees sought to examine the drivers and gauge the progress of military modernization in Asia, and to assess the influence of these developments on the regional balance of power. This event was timed to mark the publication of the NBR report Strategic Asia 2005-06: Military Modernization in an Era of Uncertainty, edited by Ashley J. Tellis and Michael Wills.

China's rapid military modernization – in the context of a rising China more broadly – dominates the strategic thinking of the United States and the other major powers in Asia. George Washington University's **David Shambaugh** predicted that China's military power and regional reach will steadily increase in the years ahead, and will alter the balance of power in Asia. Nonetheless, Shambaugh cautioned against overestimating Chinese capabilities, or concluding that double-digit increases in China's military spending in each of the past 15 years mean that the Chinese military will be able to transform itself into a first-class fighting force with global reach in the near term.

China's military possesses numerous deficiencies in both quantitative and qualitative terms, especially when compared to American capabilities. But when viewed in the context of a Taiwan Strait conflict, Shambaugh added, China has made steady and even surprising progress in increasing its strength. China's aspiration and plans regarding defense modernization, he judged, are much what one would expect for a nation of China's size, wealth, location, national interests, and global role.

The remainder of the first panel focused on the military modernization programs of Asia's other major powers, Japan, Russia, and India. **Christopher Hughes** argued that Japan is gradually forsaking its post-1945 pacifist tradition, and moving along a long-term trajectory toward assuming the military capabilities and security roles customarily expected of nations of Japan's size and wealth. Japan is acquiring enhanced power projection capabilities and will inevitably play a more active role in both regional and global security. While Japan has no realistic option other than to maintain its close security links with the United States, Washington can expect Tokyo to become a more assertive ally, one that demands greater reciprocity and more equal treatment from the United States.

Stephen Blank contended that despite rising defense outlays, the Russian military remains an archaic, dysfunctional, and inefficient force, and is unlikely to carry out a program of modernization that is capable of fulfilling Moscow's ambitious aims. Absent major systemic reforms reaching far beyond the defense sector, Blank asserted, Russian influence in Eurasia will continue to wane, to be replaced by a more visible Chinese presence in areas traditionally subject to Russian influence.

Volume co-editor **Ashley Tellis** characterized India's "very large and extremely proficient" military as capable of defending Indian territory and interests in a war with China, though not quite able to defeat Pakistan in a brief conventional war.

The dramatic increases in India's defense spending over the past half dozen years, he explained, must be seen in the context of a decade of lean years for the Indian military in the 1990s. Tellis highlighted three facets of India's current modernization: 1) technological modernization, especially in air and sea power; 2) doctrinal innovation designed to enable India to field a sizable combat force 48 hours after mobilization; and 3) organizational innovations, such as an emphasis on smaller military units, that will facilitate the new emphasis on rapid response.

India, Tellis added, has departed from its traditional posture of non-alignment and now has a new interest in coalition warfare, with the United States being a plausible coalition partner.

The morning's second panel explored how other Asian nations have responded to these developments in the major Asian powers. Looking at the Korean peninsula, **Jonathan Pollack** suggested that the ground force standoff that has long dominated peninsular security planning will decline in relevance in the years ahead. Pyongyang will increasingly focus on deterrence and longer-range strike capabilities, while Seoul will pursue deterrence without automatically assuming adversarial relations with the North. South Korea, Pollack added, will be increasingly unwilling to undertake major long-term defense investments based on a predominantly threat-based military strategy, a stance that may pose acute risks to the South Korean – U.S. alliance. In the discussion following this analysis, one participant noted that Seoul acts as if it believes that the United States needs South Korea more than Seoul needs Washington – which, if true, would mark a significant change in strategic thinking in South Korea.

Michael Swaine contended that modernization in Taiwan has been marked by inadequate funding, an absence of strategic clarity, misplaced priorities, and unaddressed vulnerabilities. Taiwan needs to be far more serious about its defense environment than it has been recently, Swaine asserted. Glaring shortcomings in Taiwan's military modernization efforts could lead to miscalculations in both China and on Taiwan, resulting in one side or the other undertaking dangerous or destabilizing actions. Nonetheless, both Taipei and Washington must continue to balance efforts to rectify Taiwan's defense deficiencies with the need to avoid an escalation of tensions with Beijing.

Turning toward the nations of Southeast Asia, **Sheldon Simon** of Arizona State University asserted that the region's security concerns are primarily internal, including separatism and ethnic and religious violence. Transnational threats such as piracy, terrorism, and the trafficking of contraband, people, and arms constitute the next tier of security threats in the region, while external threats from other nations are the least pressing of the security challenges Southeast Asia confronts. Simon reported that notable breakthroughs in multilateral security cooperation have taken place over the past several years, including coordinated naval patrols by Malaysia, Singapore, and Indonesia, and cooperation with the United States by several of the littoral states in anti-piracy patrols. Rising insurance rates for ocean-going commerce transiting Southeast Asian waters, Simon observed, have been an important factor pushing the region toward greater multilateral cooperation.

Kimberly Marten observed that military modernization in the five Central Asian republics has focused more on officer corps retraining and professionalization than on hardware acquisition. Regional leaders, she warned, often exaggerate the Islamist threat as a ploy to gain external support, including from the United States. Foreign defense assistance acquired in this fashion is then often used to suppress populist opposition movements and, as a consequence, to bolster authoritarian regimes while undercutting the human rights concerns of the donor nations. The opium trade originating in Afghanistan does constitute a major security concern for the region, but this threat cannot be successfully addressed by military modernization alone.

The day's final panel focused more directly on the implications for U.S. national security of these developments in the modernization of Asia's militaries. **Aaron Friedberg**, who spent the past two years as a senior advisor to Vice President Cheney, applauded Japan's retreat from its pacifist tradition of the past 60 years, as well as the improved tone in U.S. – India relations and India's greater ability to contribute to the maintenance of a regional balance of power. Among the troubling trends he highlighted were Russian sales of advanced weaponry to China, a problematic U.S. – Russia relationship, a growing divergence in strategic perceptions between the United States and South Korea, Taiwan's failure to spend "adequately" on its own self-defense, and skillful Chinese diplomacy that is reaching out to traditional U.S. friends such as Australia, South Korea, and the Philippines.

The Brookings Institution's **Michael O'Hanlon** observed that for all the talk in the Pentagon of a "revolution" in thinking about American security needs, very little has actually been accomplished in this area. As one example of the continuity between the Bush administration and its predecessors, he noted that the Defense Department has still had no serious discussions with Tokyo about the U.S. Marine presence in Okinawa, notwithstanding the serious difficulties the Marine bases create for the Japanese government and for sustaining popular support for the U.S. alliance.

Robert M. Hathaway emphasized the need for American leaders tasked with managing the U.S. - China relationship to make choices among competing priorities, to realize that "we can't have it all." Even a step that is as widely supported among U.S. decision makers as Japan's movement in the direction of becoming a "normal" state is not cost-free – that is, such a Japan is going to become a less pliant partner for the United States, and could alarm not only China, but other Asian powers.

In the day's final presentation, **Ashley Tellis** offered three tests for American policy makers wondering if they ought to be concerned by Asia's military modernization: 1) what are the political aims of the country in question, and what is the character of the governing regime?; 2) is the modernization oriented toward denying U.S. capabilities (as much of China's is, Tellis added)?; and 3) how has the modernization impacted not only the technological base of the country's military, but its operational effectiveness?

Underlying the discussion throughout the day lay two fundamental questions: 1) do American interests in Asia require U.S. hegemony in the region?; and 2) is any enhancement of China's military capabilities, no matter how incremental, detrimental to the United States? The answers to these two queries supplied by American leaders in the years to come will go far in determining whether China's rise to power is accomplished without a repetition of the violence that accompanied the rise of Germany and Japan in the previous century.

POSSIBLE WEAPONS SYSTEMS

The smallest systems may not be actual weapons, but computer platforms for sensing and surveillance. Such platforms could be micron-scale. The power requirement of a 1-MIPS computer might be on the order of 10-100 pW; at that rate, a cubic micron of fuel might last for 100-1000 seconds. The computer itself would occupy approximately one cubic micron.

Very small devices could deliver fatal quantities of toxins to unprotected humans. Even the smallest ballistic projectiles (bullets) could contain supercomputers, sensors, and avionics sufficient to guide them to targets with great accuracy. Flying devices could be quite small. It should be noted that small devices could benefit from a process of automated design tuning; milligram-scale devices could be built by the millions, with slight variations in each design, and the best designs used as the basis for the next "generation" of improvements; this could enable, for example, UAV's in the laminar regime to be developed without a full understanding of the relevant physics.

The line between bullets, missiles, aircraft, and spacecraft would blur. With lightweight motors and inexpensive manufacturing, a vehicle could contain a number of different disposable propulsion systems for different flight regimes. A "briefcase to orbit" system appears feasible, though such a small device might have to fly slowly to conserve fuel until it reached the upper atmosphere. It might be feasible to use 1 kg of airframe (largely discarded) and 20 kg of fuel (not counting oxidizer) to place 1 kg into orbit; some of the fuel would be used to gather and liquify oxygen in the upper atmosphere for the rocket portion of its flight. (Engineering studies have not yet been done for such a device, and it might require somewhat more fuel than stated here.)

Advanced construction could produce novel energy-absorbing materials involving high-friction mechanical slippage under high stress via micro-or nano-scale mechanical components. In effect, every molecule would be a shock absorber, and the material could probably absorb mechanical energy until it was destroyed by heat.

New kinds of weapons might be developed more quickly with rapid inexpensive fabrication. Many classes of device will be buildable monolithically. For example, a new type of aircraft or even spacecraft might be tested an order of magnitude more rapidly and inexpensively, reducing the cost of failure and allowing further acceleration in schedule and more aggressive experimentation. Although materials and molecular structures would not encompass today's full range of manufactured substances, they could encompass many of the properties of those substances, especially mechanical and electrical properties. This may enable construction of weapons such as battlefield lasers, rail guns, and even more exotic technologies.

Passive armor certainly could not stop attacks from a rapid series of impacts by precisely targeted projectiles. However, armor could get a lot smarter, detecting incoming attacks and rapidly shifting to interpose material at the right point. There may be a continuum from self-reconfiguring armor, to armor that detaches parts of itself to hurl in the path of incoming attacks, to armor that consists of a detached cloud of semi-independent counterweapons.

A new class of weapon for wide-area destruction is kinetic impact from space. Small impactors would be slowed by the atmosphere, but medium-to-large asteroids, redirected onto a collision course, could destroy many square miles. The attack would be detectable far in advance, but asteroid deflection and destruction technology is not sufficiently advanced at this time to say whether a defender with comparable space capacity could avoid being struck, especially if the asteroid was defended by the attacker. Another class of space impactor is lightweight solar sails accelerated to a respectable fraction of light speed by passage near the sun. These could require massive amounts of inert shielding to stop; it is not clear whether or not the atmosphere would perform this function adequately. A hypothetical device often associated with molecular manufacturing is a small, uncontrolled, exponentially self-replicating system. However, a self-replicating system would not make a very good weapon. In popular conception, such a system could be built to use a wide range of feedstocks, deriving energy from oxidizing part of the material (or from ambient light), and converting the rest into duplicate systems. In practice, such flexibility would be quite difficult to achieve; however, a system using a few readily available chemicals and bypassing the rest might be able to replicate itself—though even the simplest such system would be extremely difficult to design. Although unrestrained replication of inorganic systems poses a theoretical risk of widespread biosphere destruction through competition for resources—the so-called "grey goo" threat—it seems unlikely that anyone would bother to develop grey goo as a weapon, even a doomsday deterrent. It would be more difficult to guide than a biological weapon. It would be slower than a device designed simply to disrupt the physical structure of its target. And it would be susceptible to detection and cleanup by the defenders.

Tactics

A detailed analysis of attack and defense is impossible at this point. It is not known whether sensor systems will be able to effectively detect and repel an encroachment by small, stealthy robotic systems; it should be noted that the smallest such systems might be smaller than a wavelength of visible light, making detection at a distance problematic. It is unknown whether armor will be able to stop the variety of penetrating objects and forces that could be directed at it. Semi-automated R&D may or may not produce new designs so quickly that the side with the better software will have an overwhelming advantage. The energy cost of construction has only been roughly estimated, and is uncertain within at least two orders of magnitude; active systems, including airframes for nano-built weapons, will probably be cost-effective in any case, but passive or static systems including armor may or may not be worth deploying. Some things appear relatively certain. Unprotected humans, whether civilian or soldier, will be utterly vulnerable to nano-built weapons. In a scenario of interpenetrating forces, where a widespread physical perimeter cannot be established, humans on both sides can be killed at will unless protected at great expense and inconvenience. Even relatively primitive weapons such as hummingbird-sized flying guns with human target recognition and poisoned bullets could make an area unsurvivable without countermeasures; the weight of each gun platform would be well under one gram. Given the potential for both remote and semi-autonomous operation of advanced robotics and weapons, a force with a developed molecular manufacturing capability should have no need to field soldiers; this implies that battlefield death rates will be low to zero for such forces.

A concern commonly raised in discussions of nanotech weapons is the creation of new diseases. Molecular manufacturing seems likely to reduce the danger of this. Diseases act slowly and spread slowly. A sufficiently capable bio-sensor and diagnostic infrastructure should allow a very effective and responsive quarantine to be implemented. Rapid testing of newly manufactured treatment methods, perhaps combined with metabolism-slowing techniques to allow additional R&D time, could minimize disease even in infected persons

Despite the amazing power and flexibility of molecular manufactured devices, a lesson from World War I should not be forgotten: Dirt makes a surprisingly effective shield. It is possible that a worthwhile defensive tactic would be to embed an item to be protected deeply in earth or water. Without active defenses, which would also be hampered by the embedding material, this would be at best a delaying tactic.

Information is likely to be a key determiner of military success. If, as seems likely, unexpected offense with unexpected weapons can overwhelm defense, then rapid detection and analysis of an attacker's weapons will be very important. Information-gathering systems are likely to survive more by stealth than by force, leading to a "spy vs. spy" game. To the extent that this involves destruction of opposing spy-bots, it is similar to the problem of defending against small-scale weapons. Note that except for the very smallest systems, the high functional density of molecularly constructed devices will frequently allow both weapon and sensor technology to be piggybacked on platforms primarily intended for other purposes.

It seems likely that, with the possible exception of a few small, fiercely defended volumes, a robotic battleground would consist of interpenetrated forces rather than defensive lines (or defensive walls). This implies that any non-active matter could be destroyed with little difficulty unless shielded heavily enough to outlast the battle.

Strategy

A major strategy is to avoid putting soldiers on the battlefield via the use of autonomous or remotely operated weapons. Unfortunately, this implies that an enemy wanting to damage human resources will have to attack either civilian populations or people in leadership positions. To further darken the picture, civilian populations will be almost impossible to protect from a determined attack without maintaining a near-hermetic seal around their physical location. Since the resource cost of such a shield increases as the shield grows (and the vulnerability and unreliability probably also increase), this implies that civilians under threat will face severe physical restrictions from their own defenders.

A substantial variety of attack mechanisms will be available, including kinetic impact, cutting, sonic shock and pressure, plasma, electromagnetic beam, electromagnetic jamming and EMP, heat, toxic or destructive chemicals, and perhaps more exotic technologies such as particle beam and relativistic projectile. A variety of defensive techniques will be available, including camouflage, small size, physical avoidance of attack, interposing of sacrificial mass, jamming or hacking of enemy sensors and computers, and preemptive strike. Many of these offensive and defensive techniques will be available to devices across a wide range of sizes. The development of new weapon systems may be quite rapid, especially if automated or semi-automated design is employed.

In addition to the variety of physical modes of attack and defense, the cyber sphere will become an increasingly important and complex battleground, as weapon systems increasingly depend on networking and computer control. It remains to be seen whether a major electronic security breach might destroy one side's military capacity, but with increasing system complexity, such an occurrence cannot be ruled out.

Depending on what is being defended, it may or may not be possible to prepare an efficient defense for all possible modes of attack. If defense is not possible, then the available choices would seem to be either preemptive strike or avoidance of conflict. Defense of civilians, as stated above, is likely to be difficult to impossible. Conflict may be avoided by deterrence only in certain cases—where the opponent has a comparable amount to lose. In asymmetric situations, where opponents may have very different resources and may value them very differently, deterrence may not work at all. Conflict may also be avoided by reducing the sources of tension

Broader Context

Military activity does not take place in isolation. It is frequently motivated by non-military politics, though warlords can fight simply to improve their military position. Molecular manufacturing will be able to revolutionize economic infrastructures, creating material abundance and security that may reduce the desire for war—if it is distributed wisely.

It appears that an all-out war between molecular manufacturing powers would be highly destructive of humans and of natural resources; the objects of protection would be destroyed long before the war-fighting ability of the enemy. In contrast, a war between molecular manufacturing and a conventionally armed power would probably be rapid and decisive.

The same is true against a nuclear power that was prevented from using its nuclear weapons, either by politics or by anti-missile technologies. Even if nuclear weapons were used, the decentralization allowed by self-contained exponentially manufacturing nanofactories would allow survival, continued prosecution of the war, and rapid post-war rebuilding.

The line between policing and military action is increasingly blurred. Civilians are becoming very effective at attacking soldiers. Meanwhile, soldiers are increasingly expected to treat civilians under occupation as citizens (albeit second-class citizens) rather than enemy. At least in the US, paramilitary organizations (both governmental and commercial) are being deployed in internal civilian settings, such as the use of SWAT teams in some crime situations, and Blackwater in post-Katrina New Orleans.

Many molecular manufactured weapon systems will be useable for policing. Several factors will make the systems desirable for police activity: a wide range of weapon effects and intensities to choose from; less risk to police as telepresence is employed; maintaining parity with increasingly armed criminals; and increased deterrence due to increased information-gathering and surveillance. This means that even without military conflict, a variety of military-type systems will be not only developed, but also deployed and used.

It is tempting to think that the absence of nuclear war after six decades of nuclear weapons implies that we know how to handle insanely destructive weapons. However, a number of factors will make molecular manufacturing arms races less stable than the nuclear arms race—and it should be remembered that on several different occasions, a single fortuitous person or event has prevented a nuclear attack. Nuclear weapons are hard to design, hard to build, require easily monitored testing, do indiscriminate and lasting damage, do not rapidly become obsolete, have almost no peaceful use, and are universally abhorred. Molecular manufactured weapons will be easy to build, will in many cases allow easily concealable testing, will be relatively easy to control and deactivate, and would become obsolete very rapidly; almost every design is dual-use, and peaceful and non-lethal (police) use will be common. Nuclear weapons are easier to stockpile than to use; molecular manufactured weapons will be the opposite. Interpenetrating arrays of multi-scale complex weapons cannot be stable for long. Sooner or later, and probably sooner, a perceived attack will be answered by an actual attack. Whether this mushrooms out of control into a full-scale conflict will depend on the programming of the weapon systems. As long as it is only inanimate hardware at stake, probing attacks and small-scale accidental attacks may be tolerated.

Given the amount of damage that a hostile power armed with molecular manufacturing products could do to the civilian sector, it seems likely that hostile actors will be tolerated only as a last resort, and even apparently non-hostile but untrustworthy actors will be highly undesirable. An asymmetry in values may prevent deterrence from working. An asymmetry in force, such as between a molecular manufacturing and a pre-MM power, may tempt a preemptive strike to prevent molecular manufacturing proliferation. Likewise, a substantial but decreasing lead in military capability may lead to a preemptive strike. It is unclear whether in general a well-planned surprise attack would lead to rapid and/or inexpensive victory; this may not become clear until offensive and defensive systems are actually developed.

One stable situation appears to be that in which a single power deploys sufficient sensors and weapons to prevent any other power from developing molecular manufacturing. This would probably require substantial oppression of civilians and crippling of industrial and scientific capacity. The government in power would have near-absolute control, being threatened only by internal factors; near-absolute power, combined with an ongoing need for oppression, would likely lead to disastrous corruption.

Widespread recognition of the dangers of arms race, preemptive strike, and war might inspire widespread desire to avoid such an outcome. This would require an unprecedented degree of trust and accountability, worldwide. Current government paradigms are probably not compatible with allowing foreign powers such intimate access to their secrets; however, in the absence of this degree of openness, spying and hostile inspections will only raise tension and reduce trust. One possible solution is for governments to allow their own citizens to observe them, and then allow the information gained by such distributed and non-combative (and thus presumably more trustworthy) observation to be made available to foreign powers.

EMERGENCY PREPAREDNESS AND RESPONSE

We must prepare to minimize the damage and recover from any future terrorist attacks that may occur despite our best efforts at prevention. Past experience has shown that preparedness efforts are key to providing an effective response to major terrorist incidents and natural disasters. Therefore, we need a comprehensive national system to bring together and command all necessary response assets quickly and effectively. We must equip, train, and exercise many different response units to mobilize for any emergency without warning. Under the President's proposal, the Department of Homeland Security, building on the strong foundation already laid by the Federal Emergency Management Agency (FEMA), will lead our national efforts to create and employ a system that will improve our response to all disasters, both manmade and natural.

Many pieces of this national emergency response system are already in place. America's first line of defense in the aftermath of any terrorist attack is its first responder community-police officers, firefighters, emergency medical providers, public works personnel, and emergency management officials. Nearly three million state and local first responders regularly put their lives on the line to save the lives of others and make our country safer. These individuals include specially trained hazardous materials teams, collapse search and rescue units, bomb squads, and tactical units.

In a serious emergency, the federal government augments state and local response efforts. FEMA, which under the President's proposal will be a key component of the Department of Homeland Security, provides funding and command and control support. A number of important specialized federal emergency response assets that are housed in various departments would also fall under the Secretary of Homeland Security's authority for responding to a major terrorist attack. Because response efforts to all major incidents entail the same basic elements, it is essential that federal response capabilities for both terrorist attacks and natural disasters remain in the same organization. This would ensure the most efficient provision of federal support to local responders by preventing the proliferation of duplicative "boutique" response entities.

Americans respond with great skill and courage to emergencies. There are, however, too many seams in our current response plans and capabilities. Today, at least five different plans-the Federal Response Plan, the National Contingency Plan, the Interagency Domestic Terrorism Concept of Operations Plan, the Federal Radiological Emergency Response Plan, and a nascent bioterrorism response plan-govern the federal government's response. These plans and the government's overarching policy for counterterrorism are based on a distinction between "crisis management" and "consequence management." In addition, different organizations at different levels of the government have put in place different incident management systems and communications equipment. All too often, these systems and equipment do not function together well enough.

We will enhance our capabilities for responding to a terrorist attack all across the country. Today, many geographic areas have little or no capability to respond to a terrorist attack using weapons of mass destruction. Even the best prepared states and localities do not possess adequate resources to respond to the full range of terrorist threats we face. Many do not yet have in place mutual aid agreements to facilitate cooperation with their neighbors in time of emergency. Until recently, federal support for domestic preparedness efforts has been relatively small and disorganized, with eight different departments and agencies providing money in a tangled web of grant programs.

Major Initiatives

Integrate separate federal response plans into a single all-discipline incident management plan. Under the President's proposal, the Department of Homeland Security will consolidate existing federal government emergency response plans into one genuinely all-discipline, all-hazard plan-the Federal Incident Management Plan-and thereby eliminate the "crisis management" and "consequence management" distinction. This plan would cover all incidents of national significance, including acts of bioterrorism and agroterrorism, and clarify roles and expected contributions of various emergency response bodies at different levels of government in the wake of a terrorist attack.

The Department of Homeland Security would provide a direct line of authority from the President through the Secretary of Homeland Security to a single on-site federal coordinator. The single federal coordinator would be responsible to the President for coordinating the entire federal response. Lead agencies would maintain operational control over their functions (for example, the FBI will remain the lead agency for federal law enforcement) in coordination with the single on-site federal official. The Department would direct the Domestic Emergency Support Team, nuclear incident response teams, National Pharmaceutical Stockpile, and National Disaster Medical System, as well as other assets.

Create a national incident management system. Under the President's proposal, the Department of Homeland Security, working with federal, state, local, and non-governmental public safety organizations, will build a comprehensive national incident management system to respond to terrorist incidents and natural disasters. The Department would ensure that this national system defines common terminology for all parties, provides a unified command structure, and is scalable to meet incidents of all sizes.

The federal government will encourage state and local first responder organizations to adopt the already widespread Incident Management System by making it a requirement for federal grants. All state and local governments should create and regularly update their own homeland security plans, based on their existing emergency operations plans, to provide guidance for the integration of their response assets in the event of an attack. The Department of Homeland Security will, under the President's proposal, provide support (including model plans) for these efforts and will adjust the Federal Incident Management Plan as necessary to take full advantage of state and local capabilities. State and local governments should also sign mutual aid agreements to facilitate cooperation with their neighbors in time of emergency. Starting in Fiscal Year 2004, the Department would provide grants in support of such efforts.

Improve tactical counter terrorist capabilities. With advance warning, we have various federal, state, and local response assets that can intercede and prevent terrorists from carrying out attacks. These include law enforcement, emergency response, and military teams. In the most dangerous of incidents, particularly when terrorists have chemical, biological, radiological, or nuclear weapons in their possession, it is crucial that the individuals who preempt the terrorists do so flawlessly, no matter if they are part of the local SWAT team or the FBI's Hostage Rescue Team. It is also crucial that these individuals be prepared and able to work effectively with each other and with other specialized response personnel. Finally, these teams and other emergency response assets must plan and train for the consequences of failed tactical operations.

The Department of Homeland Security, as the lead federal agency for incident management in the United States, will, under the President's plan, establish a program for certifying the preparedness of all civilian teams and individuals to execute and deal with the consequences of such counter terrorist actions. As part of this program, the Department would provide partial grants in support of joint exercises between its response assets and other government teams.

Enable seamless communication among all responders. In the aftermath of any major terrorist attack, emergency response efforts would likely involve hundreds of offices from across the government and the country. It is crucial for response personnel to have and use equipment, systems, and procedures that allow them to communicate with one another. Under the President's proposal, the Department of Homeland Security will work with state and local governments to achieve this goal.

In particular, the Department would develop a national emergency communication plan to establish protocols (i.e., who needs to talk to whom), processes, and national standards for technology acquisition. The Department would, starting with Fiscal Year 2003 funds, tie all federal grant programs that support state and local purchase of terrorism-related communications equipment to this communication plan and require all applicants to demonstrate progress in achieving interoperability with other emergency response bodies.

Prepare health care providers for catastrophic terrorism. Our entire emergency response community must be prepared to deal with all potential hazards, especially those associated with weapons of mass destruction. Under the President's proposal, the Department of Homeland Security, working with the Departments of Health and Human Services and Veterans Affairs, will support training and equipping of state and local health care personnel to deal with the growing threat of chemical, biological, radiological, and nuclear terrorism.

It would continue to fund federal grants to states and cities for bioterrorism preparedness. It would use the hospital preparedness grant program to help prepare hospitals and poison control centers to deal specifically with biological and chemical attacks and to expand their surge capacity to care for large numbers of patients in a mass-casualty incident. These efforts would enhance training between public health agencies and local hospitals and seek improved cooperation between public health and emergency agencies at all levels of government.

A major act of biological terrorism would almost certainly overwhelm existing state, local, and privately owned health care capabilities. For this reason, the federal government maintains a number of specialized response capabilities for a bioterrorist attack. The National Disaster Medical System, a federal/private partnership that includes the Departments of Health and Human Services, Defense, Veterans Affairs, and FEMA, provides rapid response and critical surge capacities to support localities in disaster medical treatment. Under the President's proposal, the Department of Homeland Security will assume authority over the System as part of the federal response to incidents of national significance. The System is made up of federal assets and thousands of volunteer health professionals that are organized around the country into a number of specialty teams such as Disaster Medical Assistance Teams, National Medical Response Teams, and teams trained in caring for psychological trauma. In addition, the Department of Veterans Affairs operates a vast health care, training, and pharmaceutical procurement system with facilities in many communities nationwide. The Department of Defense provides specialized skills and transportation capabilities to move these teams and evacuate casualties.

The Department of Homeland Security, working with the Department of Health and Human Services, would lead efforts to test whether illnesses or complaints may be attributable to chemical, biological, radiological, or nuclear exposure; establish disease/exposure registries; and develop, maintain, and provide information on the health effects of hazardous substances. The Environmental Protection Agency will continue to provide a laboratory diagnostic surge capacity for environmental samples during crises.

Augment America's pharmaceutical and vaccine stockpiles. The National Pharmaceutical Stockpile ensures America's ability to respond rapidly to a bioterrorist attack or a mass casualty incident. This program, which the Department of Homeland Security will operate in consultation with the Department of Health and Human Services under the President's proposal, maintains twelve strategically located "Push Packs" containing 600 tons of antibiotics, antidotes, vaccines, bandages, and other medical supplies. The federal government can transport these packs to an incident site in less than 12 hours for rapid distribution by state and local authorities. This system performed extremely well in the aftermath of the September 11 attacks, delivering a "Push Pack" to New York City in seven hours. Additional deployments followed the anthrax attacks of October 2001.

Prepare for chemical, biological, radiological, and nuclear decontamination. The Department of Homeland Security would ensure the readiness of our first responders to work safely in an area where chemical, biological, radiological, or nuclear weapons have been used. The Department would begin requiring annual certification of first responder preparedness to handle and decontaminate any hazard. This certification process would also verify the ability of state and local first responders to work effectively with related federal support assets.

Under the President's proposal, the Department of Homeland Security will help state and local agencies meet these certification standards by providing grant money (based on performance) for planning and equipping, training, and exercising first responders for chemical, biological, radiological and nuclear attacks. It would launch a national research and development effort to create new technologies for detection and clean-up of such attacks. After a major incident, the Environmental Protection Agency will be responsible for decontamination of affected buildings and neighborhoods and providing advice and assistance to public health authorities in determining when it is safe to return to these areas.

Plan for military support to civil authorities. The armed forces were an integral part of our national response to the terrorist attacks of September 11. The Department of Defense currently uses a "Total Force" approach to fulfil its missions overseas and at home, drawing on the strengths and capabilities of active-duty, reserve, and National Guard forces. In addition to response from the active-duty forces, Air National Guard fighters took to the air on September 11 to establish combat air patrols. New Jersey and New York guardsmen and Navy and Marine Corps reservists provided medical personnel to care for the injured, military police to assist local law enforcement officials, key asset protection, transportation, communications, logistics, and a myriad of other functions to support recovery efforts in New York City. Maryland Army National Guard military police units were brought on duty and dispatched to provide security at the Pentagon. President Bush asked governors to call up over seven thousand National Guard personnel to supplement security at the Nation's 429 commercial airports. Guardsmen also reinforced border security activities of the Immigration and Nationalization Service and the U.S. Customs Service.

The importance of military support to civil authorities as the latter respond to threats or acts of terrorism is recognized in Presidential decision directives and legislation. Military support to civil authorities pursuant to a terrorist threat or attack may take the form of providing technical support and assistance to law enforcement; assisting in the restoration of law and order; loaning specialized equipment; and assisting in consequence management.

In April 2002, President Bush approved a revision of the Unified Command Plan that included establishing a new unified combatant command, U.S. Northern Command. This Command will be responsible for homeland defense and for assisting civil authorities in accordance with U.S. law.

As in the case with all other combatant commanders, the commander of Northern Command will take all operational orders from and is responsible to the President through the Secretary of Defense. The commander of Northern Command will update plans to provide military support to domestic civil authorities in response to natural and man-made disasters and during national emergencies. The Department of Homeland Security and the Department of Defense would participate as appropriate in homeland security training that involves military and civilian emergency response personnel.

Build the Citizen Corps. Under the President's proposal, the Department of Homeland Security will maintain and expand Citizens Corps, a national program to prepare volunteers for terrorism-related response support. If we can help individual citizens help themselves and their neighbors in the case of a local attack, we will improve our chances to save lives.

Implement the First Responder Initiative of the Fiscal Year 2003 Budget. Before September 11, the federal government had allocated less than $1 billion since 1995 to help prepare first responders for terrorist attacks. A range of federal departments provided funding for training and equipment, technical assistance, and other support to assist state and local first responders. These disparate programs were a step in the right direction but fell short in terms of scale and cohesion.

In January 2002, President Bush proposed the First Responder Initiative as part of his Fiscal Year 2003 Budget proposal. The purpose of this initiative is to improve dramatically first responder preparedness for terrorist incidents and disasters. This program will increase federal funding levels more than tenfold (from $272 million in the pre-supplemental Fiscal Year 2002 Budget to $3.5 billion in Fiscal Year 2003). Under the President's Department of Homeland Security proposal, the new Department will consolidate all grant programs that distribute federal funds to state and local first responders.

Build a national training and evaluation system. The growing threat of terrorist attacks on American soil, including the potential use of weapons of mass destruction, is placing great strains on our Nation's system for training its emergency response personnel. The Department of Homeland Security will under the President's proposal launch a consolidated and expanded training and evaluation system to meet the increasing demand. This system would be predicated on a four phased approach: requirements, plans, training (and exercises), and assessments (comprising of evaluations and corrective action plans). The Department would serve as the central coordinating body responsible for overseeing curriculum standards and, through regional centers of excellence such as the Emergency Management Institute in Maryland, the Centre for Domestic Preparedness in Alabama, and the National Domestic Preparedness Consortium, for training the instructors who will train our first responders. These instructors would teach courses at thousands of facilities such as public safety academies, community colleges, and state and private universities.

Under the President's proposal, the Department of Homeland Security will establish national standards for emergency response training and preparedness. These standards would provide guidelines for the vaccination of civilian response personnel against certain biological agents. These standards would also require certain coursework for individuals to receive and maintain certification as first responders and for state and local governments to receive federal grants. The Department would establish a national exercise program designed to educate and evaluate civilian response personnel at all levels of government. It would require individuals and government bodies to complete successfully at least one exercise every year. The Department would use these exercises to measure performance and allocate future resources.

Enhance the victim support system. The United States must be prepared to assist the victims of terrorist attacks and their families, as well as other individuals affected indirectly by attacks. Under the President's proposal, the Department of Homeland Security will lead federal agencies and provide guidance to state, local, and volunteer organizations in offering victims and their families various forms of assistance including: crisis counseling, cash grants, low-interest loans, unemployment benefits, free legal counseling, and tax refunds. In the case of a terrorist attack, the Department would coordinate the various federal programs for victim compensation and assistance, including the Department of Justice's Office for Victims of Crime and FEMA's Individual Assistance programs.

TRANSFORMING NATIONAL PREPAREDNESS

Hurricane Katrina was an extraordinary storm that caused destruction on a scale never before seen from a natural disaster in the United States. The continuing Federal response—the largest disaster relief and recovery effort in our Nation's history—likewise has been unprecedented and extraordinary. But what we owe the people of the Gulf Coast, and all Americans, is the best possible response.

We must expect more catastrophes like Hurricane Katrina—and possibly even worse. In fact, we will have compounded the tragedy if we fail to learn the lessons—good and bad—it has taught us and strengthen our system of preparedness and response. We cannot undo the mistakes of the past, but there is much we can do to learn from them and to be better prepared for the future. This is our duty.

The Federal government has learned from our response to Hurricane Katrina; the remaining three will be discussed more fully here.

These seventeen lessons, and the 125 recommendations that flow from them, represent specific challenges for corrective action. But we also recognize that to overcome these challenges and fully accomplish the intent of the attendant recommendations, we require a *transformation* of our homeland security architecture.

In the aftermath of another American catastrophe—the terrorist attacks of September 11—we transformed our government architecture, policies, and strategies in a comprehensive effort to defeat terrorism and better protect and defend the homeland. With the creation of the Department of Homeland Security, the post of Director of National Intelligence, the passage of the USA PATRIOT Act, and the codification of both the National Counterterrorism Centre and the National Counterproliferation Centre, we have undertaken the most extensive reorganization of the Federal government since 1947. We have created top-level policy guidance through the*National Security Strategy, the National Strategy for Homeland Security* and the *National Strategy for Combating Terrorism,* all of which identify strategic objectives to secure the United States, its citizens and interests from terrorist attacks. Most important, we have pursued our policies and objectives through concrete action. In concert with our coalition partners, we have been on the offense, waging an unremitting campaign of direct and continuous action against our terrorist enemies and the deadly scourge of terror and intimidation more broadly. These actions, combined with an array of defensive measures at home and abroad, have enhanced the safety and security of the American people.

Preparedness is inextricably intertwined with our national security, counterterrorism, and homeland security strategies. As discussed throughout this report, we have taken essential steps over the past five years—through plans, policies, and guidelines such as the *National Response Plan,* the *National Incident Management System,*the *Interim National Infrastructure Protection Plan,* and the *Interim National Preparedness Goal*—to strengthen our ability to prepare for, protect against, respond to, and recover from the natural and man-made disasters that will occur.

But we must go further. We must continue to build upon the foundation of national and homeland security we have established since 9/11 to improve our preparedness capabilities. Our response to Hurricane Katrina demonstrated the imperative to integrate and synchronize our policies, strategies, and plans—among all Federal, State, local, private sector, and community efforts and across all partners in the professions of prevention, protection, response, and recovery—into a unified system for homeland security. This unifying system will ensure *National Preparedness.* Today there is a national consensus that we must be better prepared to respond to events like Hurricane Katrina. While we have constructed a system that effectively handles the demands of routine, limited natural and man-made disasters, our system clearly has structural flaws for addressing catastrophic incidents. But we as a Nation—Federal, State, and local governments; the private sector; as well as communities and individual citizens—have not developed a shared vision of or commitment to *preparedness:* what we must do to prevent (when possible), protect against, respond to, and recover from the next catastrophe. Without a shared vision that is acted upon by all levels of our Nation and encompasses the full range of our preparedness and response capabilities, we will not achieve a truly transformational *national* state of preparedness.

There are two immediate priorities for this transformation:

1. Define and implement a comprehensive National Preparedness System; and
2. Foster a new, robust Culture of Preparedness.

A National Preparedness System

Shortfalls in the Federal response to Hurricane Katrina highlight that our current homeland security architecture—to include policies, authorities, plans, doctrine, operational concepts, and resources at the Federal, State, local, private sector, and community levels—must be strengthened and transformed. At the most fundamental level, the current system fails to define Federal responsibility for national preparedness in catastrophic events. Nor does it establish clear, comprehensive goals along with an integrated means to measure their progress and achievement. Instead, the United States currently has guidelines and individual plans, across multiple agencies and levels of government that do not yet constitute an *integrated* national system that ensures unity of effort.

In addition, as described in the narrative section of this report, the response to Hurricane Katrina demonstrated that our current system is too reactive in orientation. Our decades-old system, built on the precepts of federalism, has been based on a model whereby local and State governments wait to reach their limits and exhaust their resources before requesting Federal assistance. Federal agencies could and did take steps to prepare to extend support and assistance, but tended to provide little without a prior and specific request. In other words, the system was biased toward requests and the concept of "pull" rather than toward anticipatory actions and the proactive "push" of Federal resources.

While this approach has worked well in the majority of disasters and emergencies, catastrophic events like Hurricane Katrina are a different matter. The current homeland security environment—with the continuing threat of mass casualty terrorism and the constant risk of natural disasters—now demands that the Federal government actively prepare and encourage the Nation as a whole to plan, equip, train, and cooperate for all types of future emergencies, including the most catastrophic.

A useful model for our approach to homeland security is the Nation's approach to *national security*. Over the past six decades, we have created a highly successful national security system. This system is built on deliberate planning that assesses threats and risks, develops policies and strategies to manage them, identifies specific missions and supporting tasks, and matches the forces or capabilities to execute them. Operationally organized, it stresses the importance of unity of command from the President down to the commander in the field.

Perhaps most important, the national security system emphasizes feedback and periodic reassessment. Programs and forces are assessed for readiness and the degree to which they support their assigned missions and strategies on a continuing basis. Top level decision-makers periodically revisit their assessments of threats and risks, review their strategies and guidance, and revise their missions, plans, and budgets accordingly.

This national security system was not created overnight. It has taken almost sixty years to build and refine. Beginning with the National Security

Act of 1947-mandated creation of the Department of Defense, the Central Intelligence Agency, and the National Security Council (NSC), this system has evolved substantially through the years. It has taken time to create a strong NSC that has integrated interagency policies and efforts. Similarly, it took decades to build first the Office of the Secretary of Defense and then the Joint Staff as the central management elements for the Department of Defense. We did not accomplish the complete intent of the 1947 reforms for national security system until Congress passed the *Goldwater-Nichols* defense reorganization legislation in 1986, and the Federal government put those reforms in place in following years.

The lessons of the national security system's evolution will help us to transform our five-year old homeland security system. Of course, homeland security demands are complex. While responsibility for national security rests with the Federal government working with its international partners, the precepts of federalism make every level of government and region of the country both a contributor to, and responsible for, homeland security.

There are significant institutional and intergovernmental challenges to information and resource sharing as well as operational cooperation. These barriers stem from a multitude of factors—different cultures, lack of communication between departments and agencies, and varying procedures and working patterns among departments and agencies. Equally problematic, there is uneven coordination in pre-incident planning among State and local governments. For example, our States and territories developed fifty-six unique homeland security strategies, as have fifty high-threat, high-density urban areas. Although each State and territory certainly confronts unique challenges, without coordination this planning approach makes the identification of common or national solutions difficult. Furthermore, our current approach to response planning does not sufficiently acknowledge how adjoining communities and regions can and do support each other. For example, there is wide disparity in emergency response capabilities across the country's many local jurisdictions. Yet we currently lack the means to assess and track what these disparities are and, consequently, how we must plan to account for them in a crisis.

These include the guiding vision for preparedness as well as clarification of the Federal government's central role in organizing the national efforts of our homeland security partners. The essential importance of building operational capabilities in the Federal government by: a) Strengthening the operational management capacity of the Department of Homeland Security and strengthening its field elements; b) Reinforcing the DHS role as incident manager for the Federal response; and c) Strengthening the response capabilities of other departments and agencies in the Federal government.

A Preparedness Vision

A National Preparedness System must begin with a common vision for preparedness—what end-state are we seeking to achieve and how do we plan to get there? In Homeland Security Presidential Directive 8 (HSPD-8), the President called for the creation of a comprehensive national preparedness system, starting with a "national domestic all-hazards preparedness goal." This Goal was to outline key preparedness priorities, objectives, targets, and desired outcomes. In response to HSPD-8, DHS has developed an *Interim National Preparedness Goal* that reflects the Department's progress to date to develop each of those elements in coordination with other entities. It will remain in effect until superseded by the final National Preparedness Goal, which awaits completion.

We must now translate this Goal into a robust preparedness system that includes integrated plans, procedures, policies, training, and capabilities at all levels of government. The System must also incorporate the private sector, non-governmental organizations, faith-based groups, and communities, including individual citizens. The desired end-state of our National Preparedness System must be to achieve and sustain risk-based target levels of capability to prevent, protect against, respond to, and recover from major events in order to minimize the impact on lives, property, and the economy.

The *Homeland Security Strategy* and HSPD-8 provide the framework for the National Preparedness System. From this guidance comes the requirement for risk-based capabilities at the Federal, State and local levels that must enable the Nation to respond to a range of disasters—both man-made and natural. The required capabilities determine readiness targets for organizations at all levels. A unified effort from all homeland security stakeholders to commit the requisite resources, training, and exercising must support these targets and asset requirements.

Our National Preparedness System must also have appropriate feedback and assessment mechanisms to ensure that progress is made and that our goals are being realized. As called for in the *Interim National Preparedness Goal*, we must establish a readiness baseline for capabilities at the Federal, State, and local levels. This baseline should include an inventory of our preparedness assets as well as a metrics-based assessment of current capabilities. Thereafter, we must assess the gap between our present and target levels of capability. Over time, we must track our progress in closing these gaps.

Finally, the National Preparedness System must emphasize preparedness for *all hazards*. Most of the capabilities necessary for responding to natural disasters are also vital for responding to terrorist incidents. Yet for a variety of reasons, much of the Federal government, Congress, and the Nation at large have continued to think about terrorism and natural disasters as if they are competing priorities rather than two elements of the larger homeland security challenge. The lessons of 9/11 and Hurricane Katrina are that we cannot choose one or the other type of disaster. We must be prepared for all hazards.

The Federal Government's Role in the "National" System

Building upon the President's *Homeland Security Strategy*, Homeland Security Presidential Directives, and the *Interim National Preparedness Goal*, the Federal government must clearly articulate national preparedness goals and objectives; it must create the infrastructure—through the definition of common strategies and interoperable capabilities—for ensuring unity of effort; and it must manage the system for measuring effectiveness and assessing preparedness at all levels of government. Put another way, the Federal government must develop common doctrine and ensure alignment of preparedness plans, budgets, grants, training, exercises, and equipment.

While each State will have its own strategy and a multitude of local capabilities to meet the needs of its citizens, the Federal government—through the Department of Homeland Security—must work with State, local, and regional entities to develop strategies and plans that define how each State manages disasters within their borders as well as regionally, beginning at the local level. DHS must also identify how State, local, regional, and private-sector preparedness activities support the national strategy.

Transformation Within the Federal Government: Building Operational Capability

The creation of an effective National Preparedness System will require the Federal government to transform the way it does business. The most important objective of this Federal transformation must be to build and integrate *operational capability*. Each Federal department or agency with homeland security responsibilities needs operational capability—or the capacity to get things done—to translate executive management direction promptly into results on the ground. It includes the personnel to make and communicate decisions; organizational structures that are assigned, trained, and exercised for their missions; sufficient physical resources; and the command, control, and communication channels to make, monitor, and communicate decisions.

As described in the preceding narrative, the response to Hurricane Katrina required that the Federal government both support State and local efforts while conducting response operations in the field, in addition to making policy or implementing programs. With the exceptions of the Department of Defense and the Coast Guard—two organizations with considerable operational capabilities—the Federal government was at times slow and ineffective in responding to the massive operational demands of the catastrophe. These shortfalls were not due to the absence of top level plans such as the *National Response Plan* and the *National Incident Management System.* Rather, the problem is that these plans lack clarity on key aspects and have operational gaps, and have not been effectively integrated and translated into action. Prior training, exercising, and equipping proved inadequate to the task of effectively responding to Hurricane Katrina. There is a difference between a plan (saying "this is what we need to do") and a trained, resourced set of defined missions (saying "this is what we are going to do, and this is how we are going to organize, train, exercise, and equip to do it"). For any plan to work, it must first be broken down into its component parts. Next, the plan's requirements should be matched to the human and physical assets of each responsible department, agency, or organization.

The imperative, therefore, is to organize coherent, proactive management of responses to catastrophic events. Virtually all elements of the Federal government must be operational—to respond to catastrophic events with unified effort. There are three principal requirements to achieve this transformational goal:

1. Strengthening DHS institutions to manage the Federal response as well as enhancing DHS regional and field elements.
2. Reinforcing the Secretary of Homeland Security's position as the President's manager of the Federal response; and
3. Strengthening the response capabilities—management and field resources—of other Federal departments and agencies.

8

The Military Role in National Cybersecurity

CYBERSECURITY - A NEW CHALLENGE FOR GOVERNMENTS

The emergence of sophisticated information systems has transformed the world. But it has also created a major new challenge for governments. Cyber threats do not fit easily into the traditional security framework that now exists in most modern states. Under that model, law enforcement has evolved to protect us from threats within our society, while militaries have evolved primarily to protect from external threats (accepting that the extent to which the military is involved in domestic affairs varies from state to state). However, cyber threats often come from overseas, making it difficult for law enforcement to deter or punish them. Yet, as argued below, such threats rarely rise to the level that would warrant a military response. New approaches are required, and none of them are straightforward. Yet, how governments respond to those challenges will have international as well as domestic implications. The appropriate role of the military is central to this.

Use of the Military for Cybersecurity: Pros and Cons

This does not mean that cyber threats below the level of "war" should not be taken seriously. But it also raises the question of the appropriateness of using the military to address such threats as sabotage, subversion, and especially espionage and crime.

There are undoubted attractions to using the military in such a role. Most serious militaries have some cyber capability (or aspire to develop one), both to support the fighting on the battlefield and to defend their own systems during peacetime. Very often militaries provide nations' national signal intelligence, and as such, the information that underpins the most sophisticated cyber operations. More generally, militaries are mission-oriented: they are often better resourced than other arms of government; and they are structured to develop the personnel required – all exactly what you would want for an effective cyber defense force.

Nevertheless, overuse of the military presents challenges, too, for at least two reasons. The first is the practical risk of creating a "crowding-out" effect. Cyber threats are not going away. On the contrary, they are proliferating at a dramatic rate, in part because we are making more and more use of information systems. For that reason, cybersecurity will need to be a discipline that everyone in a country takes seriously, not just something that citizens and private companies can expect to outsource to the military. Any country that depends too heavily on the military for cybersecurity will likely find itself reducing the incentives for the private sector to develop longer-term solutions.

Second, but of no less concern, is the risk of militarizing a major new aspect of domestic security, which in many countries would be considered a very bad thing. In order to achieve truly effective cybersecurity it is necessary to be permanently operating on the defended systems. Few private sector companies are likely to welcome such hands-on assistance from the military, not least because they may well feel that they are better placed to defend their own networks.

Alternatives

Central to the question of the role of the military in "defending the nation" against cyber threats is what else governments can do. Traditionally, the other institution that provides security is law enforcement. Police and other law enforcement agencies are often constrained by the laws under which they operate and the challenges of developing cases that lead to successful prosecutions. However, in recent years innovative agreements such as the European Council's 2001 Convention on Cybercrime (now with 50 signatories across every continent) have made it harder for cyber criminals to avoid justice by basing themselves outside the country they are stealing from. Meanwhile, law enforcement like the U.S.'s Federal Bureau of Investigation are working with international colleagues and major companies like Microsoft to disrupt the very worst criminals (such as the takedown earlier this year of the Citadel network botnet used to steal over $500 million from bank accounts).

Another potential approach for the government is to support the private sector in providing its own security. This can be as simple as creating an appropriate incentives structure for information-sharing between companies or raising basic cybersecurity standards (sometimes through government regulation). This might also involve more practical help, like sharing secret intelligence with private sector companies, to improve their defenses and allow Internet Service Providers to screen out known malware.

It could also involve licensing the private sector to respond to intrusions themselves, so-called "hacking back." Currently the law in many countries does not permit hacking-back and for good reason, namely the risk of inadvertently putting their own countries on an unwanted and escalatory path towards conflict. But such approaches have strong advocates and may gain traction in future. More positively, government might support the establishment of additional Computer Emergency Readiness Teams (CERTs) to coordinate incident response by the private sector.

CYBER NATIONAL SECURITY THREATS SHORT OF WAR

In practice, therefore, the appropriate level of military involvement needs to be informed by both the dangers to national security and the alternatives available (including the risk of misemploying the military). Each nation will face different considerations. The result, however, might look something like this:

- The theft of information from government and defense contractors probably ranks as the most serious threats to national security, and as such, would almost certainly justify some government action. There are various possible motivations for such intrusions, including a commercial one, but they also represent a compromise of future military effectiveness (especially if the intruder is a potential adversary or is willing to give/sell their information to one).
- The potential for a devastating attack critical on national infrastructure (including the finance, energy, transportation, communications and other economic sectors vital the life of a nation) is another grave concern, although arguably less immediate a threat than the theft of national security secrets. While the military might be expected to be ready to support a response to an attack, in most countries some proportion of critical infrastructure is in private hands making military approaches less practical or acceptable. This is an area where the government's best approach might be use of economic incentives, including regulation to improve security levels.
- Commercial espionage, either of intellectual property or sensitive business information, is another area where military approaches might not be appropriate. However, given the potential economic impact, especially when state-backed Advanced Persistent Threat techniques are used, this type of activity has the potential to significantly destablize

international relationships. Governments could then resort to sanctions or, if under pressure, to licensed private responses.

- Fourth, there is the threat of cybercrime. Although not a direct threat, it could develop into one if left unchecked because of the potential for terrorists or states to leverage criminal networks. This is generally not a role for the military but rather for law enforcement. Their challenge is deciding whether to disrupt the criminal or to seek prosecutions.

THE DEPARTMENT OF HOMELAND SECURITY

Since the Department was created in January 2003, the management and personnel of the Department of Homeland Security have undertaken their responsibilities with energy and professionalism. Their courage and commitment to their mission have improved the security of all Americans.

But the Federal response to Hurricane Katrina demonstrated that the energy and professionalism of DHS personnel was not enough to support the Department's role as the manager of the Federal response. In particular, DHS lacked both the requisite headquarters management institutions and sufficient field capabilities to organize a fully successful Federal response effort. Within the Department, therefore, it is essential to strengthen the DHS headquarters elements to *direct* the Federal response while also providing appropriate resources to DHS field elements so that they can make an impact on the ground.

In order to strengthen DHS's operational management capabilities, we must structure the Department's headquarters elements to support the Secretary's incident management responsibilities. First and most important, Federal government response organizations must be co-located and strengthened to manage catastrophes in a new *National Operations Centre (NOC)*. The mission of the NOC must be to coordinate and integrate the national response and provide a common operating picture for the entire Federal government.

This interagency centre should ensure National-level coordination of Federal, State, and local response to major domestic incidents. It must combine and co-locate the situational awareness mission of the Homeland Security Operations Centre (HSOC), the operational mission of the National Response Coordination Centre (NRCC), and the strategic role currently assigned to the Interagency Incident Management Group (IIMG). During an incident, all department and agency command centers, as well as the Joint Field Office (JFO) at the disaster site, must provide information to the NOC, which develops a National common operating picture capable of being exported in real time to other Federal operations centers.

The NOC must be staffed by an experienced, well-trained, and resourced cadre of personnel who are prepared to provide expert strategic and operational management of Federal responses to catastrophic incidents. For example, these personnel must include logistical experts with the management tools to track moving resources anywhere across the Nation and ensure timely delivery of aid to affected areas.

This staff must also include operations experts who understand how to combine existing resources into effective response packages for any scenario. In addition to a robust permanent staff, the NOC must include a "battle roster" of personnel who will surge to expand and sustain the NOC's capacity during a crisis.

The DHS headquarters must also possess a robust capability for deliberate operational planning. Rather than waiting for the next disaster, DHS planners must apply lessons learned as well as develop detailed operational plans that anticipate the requirements of future responses and what capabilities can be matched to them in what timeframe. Using these operational plans and capability inventories as baseline data, the Headquarters planning staff can conduct national readiness assessments, highlighting priorities for subsequent preparedness investments, training, and exercising.

Below the headquarters level within DHS, we must build up the Department's regional structures. The integration of State and local strategies and capabilities on a regional basis is a homeland security priority. Homeland security regional offices should be the means to foster State, local and private sector integration.

Furthermore, DHS regional structures are ideally positioned to pre-identify, organize, train, and exercise future Principal Federal Officials and Joint Field Office staffs. Each DHS regional organization should possess the capacity to establish a self-sufficient, initial JFO on short notice anywhere in its region.

More broadly, the Department of Homeland Security must possess field personnel with the necessary resources, training, and national support. As a start, we must improve and emphasize plans that stress a proactive DHS role—in particular, the *Catastrophic Incident Annex* and *Catastrophic Incident Supplement* of the *NRP*. But DHS must also have available operational funds so that it can "lean forward" in future crises, to take anticipatory actions without budgetary concern or risk of subsequent criticism for a false alarm. In the event of a surprise contingency, battlefield commanders should not have to wait for the release of funds to execute their pre-assigned missions. The same flexibility should be afforded to our Federal homeland security responders.

MANAGING THE INTERAGENCY PROCESS IN HOMELAND SECURITY RESPONSE

In order to create robust homeland security response capabilities, we must also transform our Federal interagency processes. Most important, we must eliminate the extraordinary red tape and resulting delays in the process of requests for assistance in response efforts. Too often during the Hurricane Katrina response we found that the Federal government did not effectively use assets at the ready because the necessary requests were being "coordinated" somewhere in the bureaucracy. The solution is to enshrine in the Federal government one of the central tenets of the *National Incident Management System*—Unified Command. We must transform our approach for catastrophic incidents from one of bureaucratic *coordination* to proactive unified command that creates true unity of effort. As set forth in *NIMS,* "In a [Unified Command] structure, the individuals designated by their jurisdictional authorities... must jointly determine objectives, strategies, plans, and priorities and work together to execute integrated incident operations and maximize the use of assigned resources."

At the Federal level, the most urgent step in creating unity of effort will be to reinforce the Secretary of Homeland Security as the Federal government's preparedness and incident manager. In order to create unity of effort at the Federal level, the Department should manage and orchestrate the specialized efforts of other Federal departments and agencies within their core competencies. Although DHS by Presidential directive has this mission, its internal structures and relationships across the Federal government do not position it to fully succeed. The current arrangements are an awkward mix of the traditional, FEMA-led, approach to interagency coordination and the Homeland Security Act's creation of a powerful Department of Homeland Security.

One model for the command and control structure for the Federal response in the new National Preparedness System is our successful defense and national security statutory framework. In that framework, there is a clear line of authority that stretches from the President, through the Secretary of Defense, to the Combatant Commander in the field. When a contingency arises, the Combatant Commander in that region executes the missions assigned by the Secretary of Defense and the President. Although the Combatant Commander might not "own" or control forces on a day-to-day basis, during a military operation he controls all military forces in his theater: he exercises the command authority and has access to resources needed to affect outcomes on the ground.

The structure for command and control of defense operations. Unity of command is established in a chain of command from the President through the Secretary of Defense to the Combatant Commander. The Combatant Commander possesses operational control over forces and resources provided by the armed services. The Intelligence Community additionally provides essential information—warning and situational awareness—to the commander in the field. The system makes a clear distinction between operations—in which the Combatant Commander is the centre of activity—and the provision of operational resources. In the latter case, the Armed Services are responsible for the training and equipping of forces.

The model somewhat parallels the original conception of the Federal homeland security response. In particular, the President directs the Secretary of Homeland Security, who coordinates interagency actions at the senior level while supervising the field commander for the Federal response—the Principal Federal Official (PFO). The PFO, in turn, is supported with resources provided by DHS and other interagency departments and agencies.

As described in HSPD-5, Cabinet members are to support the Secretary of Homeland Security as the President's incident manager directing and coordinating the Federal response. At the PFO level, this can be accomplished by ensuring that the Federal Coordinating Officer (FCO)—who possesses authority over resources—works for the PFO.

However, the comparison between the homeland security and defense operations models breaks down in two significant ways. First, the Federal commander only manages *Federal* resources in homeland security. In almost every circumstance, State and local governments maintain operational control over their own resources. Second, the Secretary of Homeland Security and the PFO must request Federal assets from other departments and agencies; they do not command the resources of other departments and agencies. HSPD-5 makes clear that one Cabinet member cannot alter or impede the ability to carry out the authorities of Federal departments and agencies to perform their responsibilities under law. Rather, HSPD-5 anticipates that future events will necessarily involve a joint approach given that several departments and agencies have distinct statutory authorities (e.g., the Attorney General for criminal investigation of terrorist acts, the Secretary of Defense for command over our military forces, and so forth).

In this vein, we must similarly transform the existing system of Emergency Support Functions (ESFs). A vestige of the 1992 *Federal Response Plan,* the precursor to the NRP, these capability-specific coordination mechanisms, at a minimum, must be reconciled to the *NIMS* as well as responsive to the orders of the Principal Federal Official. More fundamentally, we must examine whether we should reorganize and, in some cases, redefine the ESF structures, while building DHS command and control mechanisms.

These interagency management changes recognize that Federal response to catastrophic events—potential or actual—must be both efficient and effective in meeting the needs of the victims. Without infringing upon the statutory responsibilities of the Cabinet departments and agencies, we must ensure that the President's incident manager is able to call upon the full range of the Federal government's response assets, and to aggressively orchestrate, lead, and coordinate their use in response operations.

OPERATIONAL CAPABILITIES IN OTHER FEDERAL DEPARTMENTS/AGENCIES

Beyond changes to DHS and the structure of Federal response, there is still a compelling need to strengthen operational capabilities across the Federal government. Those departments and agencies that have a responsibility to participate in a catastrophic response must build up their crisis deployable capabilities as well as their effective operational management.

To start, all Federal departments and agencies should have operational command and control structures that comply with the *National Incident Management System.* Secretaries and directors throughout the government must operate jointly, using the same systems, doctrine, and terminology. Similarly, in support of crisis operational capability, each department and agency must develop a deliberate planning capability. Planning should include not only the response plans themselves but also, both personnel and funding to train professional planners.

With these new operational planning functions, Federal departments and agencies must build the detailed supporting plans, concepts, and staffing to execute their NRP and emergency response missions. During Hurricane Katrina, it became clear that most Federal departments and agencies had not developed—much less exercised—standard operating procedures for their response.

An additional imperative is for all Federal departments and agencies to develop "battle rosters" of trained personnel who should deploy when their organization is called upon to support a Federal response to a catastrophic event. The development of these rosters must coincide with the implementation of training certification programs that ensure that personnel are trained and skilled to a high, uniform standard.

Homeland Security Training, Education, and Exercising

An effective National Preparedness System requires that management and response personnel, especially those in the field, are well versed in their missions. At all levels of government, we must build a leadership corps that is fully educated, trained, and exercised in our plans and doctrine. Training is not nearly as costly as the mistakes made in a crisis. Equally important, this corps must be populated by *leaders* who are prepared to exhibit innovation and take the initiative during extremely trying circumstances.

The narrative, the response to Hurricane Katrina revealed a lack of familiarity with incident management, the planning discipline, legal authorities, capabilities, and field-level crisis leadership. Many Federal, State, and local officials lacked a fundamental understanding of the *National Response Plan,* the *NIMS,* and State and local response plans.

The first priority for training is to ensure that our emergency managers fully understand our preparedness and response plans and doctrine. To that end, we must train all emergency managers with responsibility for the Federal response in the *National Response Plan* and the *National Incident Management System.* At the same time, the Department of Homeland Security must continue to condition its State assistance grants on all relevant State and local emergency response personnel being *NIMS* and *NRP* trained and capable. DHS and its Federal partners should develop and deploy mobile training teams to support this effort.

Beyond current plans and doctrine, we require a more systematic and institutional program for homeland security professional development and education. While such a program will centre on the Department of Homeland Security, it should extend to personnel throughout all levels of government having responsibility for preventing, preparing for, responding to, and recovering from natural and man-made disasters. For example, DHS should establish a National Homeland Security University (NHSU)—analogous to the National Defense University—for senior homeland security personnel as the capstone for homeland security training and education opportunities. The NHSU, in turn, should integrate homeland security personnel from State and local jurisdictions as well as other Federal departments and agencies.

Over the long term, our professional development and education programs must break down interagency barriers to build a unified team across the Federal government. Just as the Department of Defense succeeded in building a joint leadership cadre, so the rest of the Federal government must make familiarity with other departments and agencies a requirement for career advancement.

Where practicable, interagency and intergovernmental assignments for Federal personnel must build trust and familiarity among diverse homeland security professionals. These assignments will break down organizational stovepipes, advancing the exchange of ideas and practices. At a minimum, we should build joint training and educational institutions for our senior managers in homeland security-related departments and agencies.

These Federal professional development and education programs must integrate participants from other homeland security partners—namely, State and local governments as well as the private sector, non-governmental organizations, and faith-based organizations. As in every homeland crisis, it is inevitable that Federal, State, and local homeland security officials will come together to respond, and so it is important that we recognize the value in the old military adage that we must "train as you fight; fight as you train."

Pursuant to HSPD-8, the National Preparedness System should include a robust program of homeland security exercises at all levels of government and across all disciplines. The Department of Homeland Security should serve as the President's executive agent in developing and managing a National Exercise and Evaluation Program (NEEP). The NEEP should consolidate all existing interagency homeland security-related exercise programs at the Federal level with existing DHS National Exercise Program and Homeland Security Exercise and Evaluation Program (HSEEP) through common doctrine, objectives, and management. The NEEP should sponsor an aggressive program of joint exercises that involve all levels of government, as well as problem-specific exercises at particular levels of government. NEEP planning, moreover, must be integrated with a robust national homeland security training program. Moreover, the Program must emphasize intelligence-driven, threat-based scenarios that stress the system. In particular, we should not shy away from exercising worst case scenarios that "break" our homeland security system. Arguably, those scenarios will provide us the most meaningful, if sobering, lessons.

Assessments, Lessons Learned, and Corrective Actions

The success of the National Preparedness System over time will depend upon the quality of its metrics-based assessment and feedback mechanisms. In particular, the System must possess the means to measure progress towards strategic goals and capability objectives. It must systematically identify best practices and lessons learned in order to share them with our homeland security partners throughout the Nation. It must also have an effective process for conducting corrective or remedial actions when a system challenge is identified.

With common goals and performance metrics, the new National Preparedness System must first provide us with the capacity to create a national preparedness baseline that, at a minimum, serves as an inventory of our capabilities. More importantly, the baseline will tell us how prepared we are *today* in each of our jurisdictions and nationally. Reviewed at the Federal level and compared against the National Preparedness Goal, the System must also identify gaps in our national capabilities. These gaps can then serve as the priority targets for the homeland security grant process. In turn, the grant process must be tied to performance metrics that assess progress toward meeting national objectives. The President's Management Agenda has proven an effective tool applied to Federal department and agency performance that has recently, as a result of this review, been extended to include State and local homeland security programs that are federally funded.

Furthermore, this National Preparedness System must be dynamic. Like the national security system described above, we must routinely revisit our plans and reassess our capabilities in order to account for evolving risks, improvements in technological capabilities, and preparedness innovations.

An integrated National Preparedness System must identify and share lessons learned and best practices both within departments and agencies and across jurisdictions. We understand that for many aspects of homeland security there is no single, best way of doing business. Our National Preparedness organization should systematically investigate and seek out innovative approaches being applied in the various localities, States, departments, agencies, and the private sector. The system should circulate the most promising of these practices, as well as any lessons—positive *and* negative—on a continuous basis, so that we never stop improving our security.

Finally, we must ensure that problems identified in our training, exercises, and lessons learned programs are corrected. Too often, after-action reports for exercises and real-world incidents highlight the same problems that do not get fixed—the need for interoperable communications, for example. Thus, the circle of the National Preparedness System must be closed by a Remedial Action Management Program (RAMP) that is led by DHS and coordinated by the Homeland Security Council but is resident in and executed by individual departments and agencies. Department and agency RAMPs must translate findings of homeland security gaps and vulnerabilities into concrete programs for corrective action. Then the RAMPs must track that the appropriate corrective actions are fully implemented in a timely fashion.

The Role of Congress

The challenges of transformation are not limited to the Executive Branch of government. Despite previous calls for transformation from national commissions, the U.S. Congress has not fully transformed itself for homeland security. The numerous congressional committees in both houses that authorize and appropriate funds for homeland security inevitably produce competing initiatives and requirements. For example, the Secretary of Homeland Security and his leadership team were required to testify at 166 hearings before 61 full committees and subcommittees in the Senate and House of Representatives and provided over 2,000 briefings during 2005 as of October 14, 2005. At best, the many priorities distract us from the true, *top priorities.* At worst, the many priorities and requirements can contradict each other.

Moreover, Congress has not yet embraced a purely risk-based funding approach to homeland security priorities. Although the U.S. House of Representatives and U.S. Senate have passed several forms of grant reform legislation that would permit DHS to increase the prioritization of homeland security spending on the basis of risk, the two bodies have failed to reconcile their differences. Until we as a Nation agree to a solely risk-based approach, we are in danger of allocating our limited resources in ways that do not prioritize funding to meet national homeland security goals and objectives.

Finally, our experience in building an effective national security system demonstrates that Congress will be an essential partner as we continue to transform our homeland security system. Implementing the Goldwater-Nichols defense reform, for example, required legislation, and the durability of our homeland security reforms and the new National Preparedness System will require comparable support and participation from our Congressional partners.

How Much is Enough?

An age-old question for national security and, now, homeland security planning is *how much is enough?* In particular, at what level of preparedness do we feel confident that we have adequately accounted for the threats we face, our vulnerabilities, and the means we have to manage them? Recognizing that the future is uncertain and that we cannot anticipate every threat, we as a Nation must rely on a capabilities-based planning approach to answering these questions: we must set levels of capabilities—at Federal, State, and local levels as among our other homeland security partners—that we conclude are appropriate to meet the range of risks that we may confront in the future.

In order to help identify the range of future plausible risks, the Department of Homeland Security has produced a set of fifteen *National Planning Scenarios.* The Scenarios were designed to illustrate a myriad of tasks and capabilities that are required to prepare for and respond to a range of potential terrorist attacks and natural disasters that our Nation may confront. They identify the potential scale, scope, and complexity of fifteen incidents that would severely harm our Nation's citizens, infrastructure, economy, and threaten our way of life. Examples include an outbreak of pandemic influenza on U.S. soil, a major earthquake in a U.S. city, and the detonation of a ten-kiloton nuclear device in a large U.S. metropolitan area. The Scenarios also include a Category 5 hurricane hitting a major metropolitan area.

The Scenarios, which were meant to be illustrative of a wide variety of hazards, generally do not specify a geographic location, and the impacts are meant to be scalable for a variety of population considerations. Ultimately, they give homeland security planners a tool that allows for the flexible and adaptive development of capabilities as well as the identification of needed capability levels to meet the National Preparedness Goal.

While the National Planning Scenarios have been effective tools for generating dialogue on response capabilities, they do not fully anticipate some of the worst disaster scenarios. Scenario 10, for example, depicts the effects of a Category 5 hurricane hitting a major metropolitan area in the United States. However, in the Scenario, the Category 5 hurricane actually causes fewer deaths and less destruction than did Hurricane Katrina, a Category 3, because the Scenario only characterizes the destruction caused to a metropolitan area, while a storm like Hurricane Katrina may span three or more States. Further, although the Scenario acknowledges potential delays and difficulties in evacuation, realistic circumstances such as Katrina may be worse, where more than 100,000 residents did not evacuate.

Scenario 1, the detonation of a ten-kiloton nuclear device in an American city by a terrorist group, suffers from similar limitations and fails to fully challenge our plans and preparation skills. Although devastating in terms of both death and destruction, a ten-kiloton bomb is a relatively small nuclear device. Moreover, the Scenario does not anticipate one of the most demanding characteristics of past al-Qaida operations: multiple, simultaneous attacks. How much more taxing would it be to respond to multiple and simultaneous nuclear, chemical, or biological incidents? If the purpose of the National Planning Scenarios is to provide a foundation for identifying the capabilities required to meet all hazards, the Scenarios must press us to confront the most destructive challenges.

Hurricane Katrina severely stressed our current national response capabilities. However, three other National Planning Scenarios—an act of nuclear terrorism, an outbreak of pandemic influenza, and a 7.5 magnitude earthquake striking a major city —are more daunting still. Compared with the deaths and economic chaos a nuclear detonation or influenza outbreak could unleash, Hurricane Katrina was small. But even these scenarios do not go far enough to challenge us to improve our level of preparedness. Until we can meet the standard set by the most demanding scenarios, we should not consider ourselves adequately prepared.

The most recent Top Officials ("TOPOFF") exercise in April 2005 revealed the Federal government's lack of progress in addressing a number of preparedness deficiencies, many of which had been identified in previous exercises. This lack of progress reflects, in part, the absence of a remedial action program to systematically address lessons learned from exercises. To ensure appropriate priority and accountability are being applied to address these continuing deficiencies, the Assistant to the President for Homeland Security and Counterterrorism now annually conducts four Cabinet-level exercises with catastrophic scenarios. To date, a catastrophic exercise with a pandemic scenario was conducted in December 2005; the next exercise is scheduled for this March.

While the National Planning Scenarios represent a good start for our national process of capabilities-based planning for homeland security, we must orient the National Preparedness System towards still greater challenges. We must not shy away from creating planning scenarios that stress the current system of response to the breaking point and challenge our Nation in ways that we wish we did not have to imagine. To that end, we must revise the planning scenarios to make them more challenging. Among other characteristics, they must reflect both what we know and what we can imagine about the ways our enemies think—that they will not hit us hard just once, but that they will seek to cause us damage on significant scale in multiple locations simultaneously. We must not again find ourselves vulnerable to the charge that we suffered a "'failure of imagination' and a mind-set that dismissed possibilities."

IMPORTANCE OF CYBER SECURITY

Cyber space is the domain generated from the interconnection between computers and telecommunication networks in order to store, modify, and exchange data via networked systems and associated physical infrastructures without regard to physical geography. Therefore, its security largely depends on the data and the ICTs' security.

Actually, because of cyber space's great dependence on informatics and telecommunications for almost every activity and service, it's extremely dangerous to ignore the growing phenomenon of cyber crimes and the increasing number of threats to citizen lives, citizen activities, and governmental systems.

Sources of cyber threats may be unintentional accidents, or due to vulnerabilities and negligence. However, they can also be intentional, like direct attacks on systems. Objectives of systems attackers can be to shut them down, to gain access to such systems and steal crucial data, to make illegal financial transfers, to disrupt records, or to manipulate data and code in order to introduce harmful instructions. Attackers can be recreational hackers, crackers or terrorists. This is can happen for business entities and interests, as well as for the public sector and the government.

Banking institutions, energy, state agencies, hospitals, business, education, and even social affairs heavily rely on their online presence. With information flowing through boundaries of different legal systems connected to different networks around the globe, there is a growing need to protect personal information, funds and assets, as well as national security.

Thus, cyber security issues are gaining interest by both the public as well as the private sectors.

Background

Cyber security is about building confidence and security in the use of ICTs so as to ensure trust by the information society. Consequently, we can define it as all activities and operations aiming at the reduction and prevention of threat and vulnerabilities, and having in place policies for protection; incident response; recovery, data assurance, law enforcement, and military and intelligence operations relating to cyber space security.

Thus cyber security touches practically all activities and all citizens around the globe; it provides tremendous opportunities for enhancing human development as well as achieving better integration in the information society. It also supports wider access to knowledge and education, as well as to the development of policies and strategies.

Moreover, it imposes new types of commercial, professional and social paradigms, giving rise to a number of legal and technical problems that must be addressed on the basis of respecting its special nature and needs. Hence, a different approach and different methodologies than what has been adopted before the age of information and communication technology are needed.

Nevertheless, many governments and societies fear the negative impact ICTs can have on their own citizens because of the potential dangers it carries, and because of the economic, social, and security challenges it poses.

Accordingly, lack of security in cyber space undermines confidence in the information society. This is especially the case with many intrusions around the globe resulting in the stealing of money, assets, and sensitive military, commercial and economic information.

In legal and regulatory institutions that lack cyber space security undermines the realization of the full potential of the information technology revolution.

Consequently, special attention is needed to prevent cyberspace from turning into a source of danger for states and citizens, and to prevent the appearance of a cyber crime haven. The authorities in charge are trying to find a way to prevent and punish new forms of criminal activity such as ICT crimes involving computer-based assaults. Many governments have already adopted particular regulations and legislations as an answer to the need of ensuring the adoption of security measures.

Cooperation between countries

In the same context, scholars, experts and policy makers are highlighting the importance of cooperation between nations and governments to answer challenges imposed by cyberspace's particular nature and to achieve cyber security. As a matter of fact, without cooperation between nations and countries, it is doubtful that any country can protect itself.

In many Arab countries where there is a shortage of legislation and regulatory texts, responsibilities for cyber security are not defined or well established across the departments and the authorities in charge of law enforcement. This situation certainly hinders dealing with cyber crime issues in a consistent way.

Hence, the Arab world is not yet organized enough to address the growing threat of cyber crime and organized crime intrusions, let alone state-sponsored attacks and operations or organized crime networks.

The Arab world must be serious about addressing cyber security challenges with strong leadership and vision. Leadership should be lifted up and strongly anchored within competent official authorities capable of coordinating action and of achieving results. And while providing policy, strategy, legal structures, and coordination to empower concerned authorities to perform their missions, special attention should be paid to strengthen accountability for cyber security at all levels.

NATIONAL SECURITY IN THE COMING DECADE

Defense technologists are most successful when they hone in on specific problems. The Pentagon's research agencies and their contractors were asked in 2003 to come up with ways to foil roadside bombs in Iraq and Afghanistan, and although they did not defeat the threat entirely, they did produce a number of useful detectors, jammers and other counter-explosive systems. More recently, military researchers received marching orders to help tackle the so-called "anti-access area-denial" threats, which is Pentagon-speak for enemy weapons that could be used to shoot down U.S. fighters and attack Navy ships.

The next wave of national security threats, however, might be more than the technology community can handle. They are complex, multidimensional problems against which no degree of U.S. technical superiority in stealth, fifth-generation air warfare or night-vision is likely to suffice.

The latest intelligence forecasts by the Obama administration and other sources point to five big challenges to U.S. and global security in the coming decades.

Biological Weapons: The White House published in 2009 a National Strategy for Countering Biological Threats with an underlying theme that biological weapons eventually will be used in a terrorist attack. To prevent deadly viruses from being turned into mass-casualty weapons, officials say, one of the most difficult challenges is obtaining timely and accurate insight on potential attacks. The Defense Threat Reduction Agency has a team of researchers working these problems. But they worry that the pace of research is too slow to keep up with would-be terrorists.

Nukes: Large stockpiles of nuclear weapons are tempting targets for nation-states or groups set on attacking the United States and its allies, officials assert. Black-market trade in sensitive nuclear materials is a particular concern for U.S. security agencies. "The prospect that al-Qaida or another terrorist organization might acquire a nuclear device represents an immediate and extreme threat to global security," says an administration report. No high-tech sensors exist to help break up black markets, detect and intercept nuclear materials in transit and there are no financial tools to disrupt this dangerous trade. A much-hyped Department of Homeland Security effort to detect radioactive materials at U.S. ports has been plagued by technical hiccups. Analysts believe that although a full-up nuclear weapon would be nearly impossible for an al-Qaida like group to build, a more likely scenario would be a low-yield "dirty bomb" that could be made with just a few grams of radioactive material.

Cyber-Attacks: The drumbeats of cyberwarfare have been sounding for years. Network intrusions are widely viewed as one of the most serious potential national security, public safety and economic challenges. Technology, in this case, becomes a double-edge sword. "The very technologies that empower us to lead and create also empower individual criminal hackers, organized criminal groups, terrorist networks and other advanced nations to disrupt the critical infrastructure that is vital to our economy, commerce, public safety, and military," the White House says.

The cybersecurity marketplace is flooded with products that promise quick fixes but it is becoming clear that the increasing persistence and sophistication of attacks will require solutions beyond the traditional.

Climate Change: The national security ramifications of climate change are severe, according to Defense Secretary Leon Panetta. While the topic of climate change has been hugely politicized, Panetta casts the issue as a serious security crisis. "In the 21st century, we recognize that climate change can impact national security — ranging from rising sea levels, to severe droughts, to the melting of the polar caps, to more frequent and devastating natural disasters that raise demand for humanitarian assistance and disaster relief,"

Panetta said. The administration projects that the change wrought by a warming planet will lead to new conflicts over refugees and resources and catastrophic natural disasters, all of which would require increased U.S. military support and resources. The scientific community, in this area, cannot agree on what it will take to reverse this trend. There is agreement, though, that there is no silver bullet.

Transnational Crime: U.S. defense and law-enforcement agencies see transnational criminal networks as national security challenges. These groups cause instability and subvert government institutions through corruption, the administration says. "Transnational criminal organizations have accumulated unprecedented wealth and power through the drug trade, arms smuggling, human trafficking, and other illicit activities. ... They extend their reach by forming alliances with terrorist organizations, government officials, and some state security services." Even the United States' sophisticated surveillance technology is not nearly enough to counter this threat, officials say.

In this special report, National Defense examines the top five threats in greater detail.

Bio-Threats

The public health community's dream is to make the arrival and spread of communicable diseases as easy to predict and track as the weather.

Just as a meteorologist spots the seeds of a hurricane off the African coast, and begins to plot its possible path as it makes its way toward the Caribbean, a global bio-surveillance network would allow officials to detect a bio-weapon or the emergence of a deadly flu virus in China and track it as it spreads throughout the world. Measures could then be taken to quickly develop and distribute vaccines.

Despite the onset of the information age, where a doctor in Asia could theoretically inform a centralized information clearinghouse on the other side of the world of a new virus within seconds, realizing this dream is years away, experts at a recent National Defense Industrial Association Biosurveillance conference said.

Making diseases as predictable as the weather is a lofty goal, but the weather analogy is an imperfect one, said Steve Bennett, director of the Department of Homeland Security's National Biosurveillance Integration Centre. To start, the medical community doesn't have all the prediction models that weather watchers can use to plug data into. They just don't exist.

"Prediction is a pretty difficult thing to achieve," he said. "Real-time situational awareness, I think we can get close."

Congress established the centre in 2007 to pull together the efforts of 12 federal agencies and departments that are charged with tracking diseases. Its goal is to "rapidly identify, characterize, localize and track a biological event of national concern; integrate and analyze data relating to human health, animal, plant, food, water, and environmental domains; and to disseminate alerts and pertinent information."

The Defense Department's Defense Threat Reduction Agency, the Centers for Disease Control and Prevention, the Departments of Health and Human Services and Agriculture are all among the entities that track diseases.

"I think there was this idea in 2007 when that law was stood up ... there was this thought that there were these databases all around the federal government and the states and all we had to do was put $100 million into an IT system and hook it all together, and out comes wisdom," Bennett said.

The databases don't exist, or they exist in spreadsheets on different systems, and they are not structured at all, he said. Five years after the law was passed, Bennett still spends the bulk of his time visiting other agencies to keep tabs on what is happening.

"It is people and relationships. I wish there was a more technical solution, but that is kind of the way it is," he said.

As far as developing a real-time global picture of what diseases are spreading and where, there seem to be more questions than answers.

"Right now the sum of biosusurveillance is based on ambiguous data. And to go from ambiguous data to a decision is a very difficult thing to do," said C. Nicole Rosenzweig, a research biologist at the Army's Edgewood Chemical Biological Centre in Maryland.

How do analysts take something that is at some level, research, and assess it as though we have complete confidence in it? she asked. "A lot of research will have to go into this," she added.

Information technology systems that could collect and coordinate the data and give public health officials a picture of where diseases are emerging is only one part of the problem.

The main issue is that the policies and procedures on how to do this have yet to be worked out.

Harshini Mukundan, a scientist in the chemical division at Los Alamos National Laboratory, said diseases emerge in food, humans and animals.

"They are all interconnected and having separate agencies monitoring each [one] defeats the cause," she added.

Who owns the biosurveillance data? she asked. Is it going to be governments or the World Health Organization? "It is hard to envision what the system will look like and how exactly it will function. ... We need some direction on that from the government to start imagining how it will be implemented," Mukundan added.

Bennett said: "There are lot of systemic issues that we need to fix, process issues, authority issues, things that can make decisions faster."

Laurie Garrett, a policy analyst and senior fellow for global health at the Council on Foreign Relations, said all the technical problems could be solved in five to 10 years, "but I don't believe we have the capacity or the will to implement" them.

The political crisis in the United States today means it is difficult to get any kind of decision from the federal government. Many state legislatures are suffering from similar gridlock, she said. "Are the problems bureaucratic, financial or policy? The answer is 'yes,' [to] all three," she said.

Transparency has been an issue on the federal government's end. For example, it issued a gag order on federal scientists during the 2001 anthrax attacks.

"As a result, on the local level, they were operating almost blind and did not have vital information," she said.

Meanwhile, the government may be turning to the public for help.

Health and Human Services recently sponsored a grand challenge asking competitors to use Twitter to create a web-based application that would compile the top five trending illnesses in a geographic area and distribute the findings to state and local public health officials.

Bennett said there is valuable data contained in insurance claims. Such forms have geo-location tags and could help public health officials to see where diseases are cropping up. But then there are privacy issues.

"I don't need to know specific patient information....I need to know general trends."

The national security community may not need to know the kinds of data that would intrude on personal privacy, he added.

Jason Pargas, special assistant to the director at the Defense Threat Reduction Agency's chemical and biological technologies directorate, said he believes that these issues will all be worked out in five to 10 years. He is in the research-and-development community, so he has to be an optimist, he said. Prediction models, applied math and computing may converge to where disease forecasts could become possible, he said.

But governments need to see the public as a partner.

"If you engage the public, you will have a much more redundant, highly, highly effective system," he said.

Nuclear Weapons

Still at the top of the list of the most terrifying threats to the United States are nuclear weapons. The nation has spent an almost incalculable amount of money over the past six decades to find them, monitor them, and destroy the means by which they are delivered. Open source information suggests there is still a lot of work to be done.

Research into hitting an intercontinental ballistic missile bearing a nuclear warhead with another missile began in the Eisenhower administration 50 years ago. Yet today, this can still only be accomplished under the most controlled circumstances with questions remaining on whether decoys could easily defeat the "hitting a bullet with a bullet" scenario.

President Reagan's dead-end effort to shoot down missiles from space, better known as Star Wars, came to naught. The Airborne Laser program, which envisioned destroying missiles on the launch pad by using directed energy shot from an aircraft, also came to a halt.

The mutually assured destruction doctrine offset these defensive shortcomings. But as many analysts have noted, non-state actors such as terrorist groups, if they were to get their hands on a nuke, don't play by those rules.

More recently, the Department of Homeland Security abandoned a program to develop Advanced Spectroscopic Portals that could detect a smuggled warhead inside a shipping container. The congressional mandate to scan every container entering the United States means that this effort will continue, although on a smaller scale.

Less overt is the detection problem. Who has nukes? And where are they?

The answer is: underground.

North Korea's nuclear weapons program is hidden deep in its mountains, as are Iran's alleged efforts.

Army Lt. Gen. Ronald L. Burgess Jr., director of the Defense Intelligence Agency in his annual threat assessment released in February before his retirement, said underground facilities that may hide missiles and weapons of mass destruction are "spreading."

Finding, assessing, mapping and ultimately destroying a hard and deep buried target — HDBT in military lingo — has become an increasingly difficult challenge for the military and spy communities, Air Force Lt. Col. Craig Baker, wrote in an Army War College paper, "The Strategic Importance of Defeating Underground Facilities." The two communities have placed a great deal of emphasis on tackling this problem during the last decade, he wrote. Most of it has been carried out with little attention. Despite the low profile, the military has been taking the problem seriously.

"America's potential adversaries have realized that current non-nuclear penetrating weapons are relatively ineffective in destroying underground facilities," Baker wrote. Weapons of mass destruction programs are now underground in an effort to remain out of reach. New commercial tunneling technologies have also made underground bunkers less expensive to build, he noted.

The National Reconnaissance Office, National Geo-Spatial Intelligence Agency and the Air Force all need sensors to detect nuclear weapons, as well as the underground bunkers where they are hiding. The Air Force's Technical Applications Centre, based at Patrick Air Force Base, Fla., has been tasked with searching for nuclear weapons and verifying treaties.

Much of its work is classified. If the U.S. is to preemptively destroy a nuclear weapons program, it will require intelligence on where these weapons are located and how deep underground they are stored.

An effort to destroy an underground complex may require repeated bombings by massive ordnance penetrator. These can only be carried by B-2 bombers, and only one at a time.

Jeffrey Richelson, senior fellow at the National Security Archives, a research institute that pries secret documents out of the government through Freedom of Information Act requests, said, "We obviously need weapons that can penetrate through certain depths, through certain hardness. But whether they can even build them to attain certain levels of destruction, I just don't know ... I'm not even sure the people in the Defense Department know. They are guessing, trying to figure it out using various models." Then comes the difficult question of battlefield damage assessment. Some things could be determined from outside, such as whether a bombing campaign collapsed an entrance. But since there may be an incomplete picture of what was inside a deeply buried bunker in the first place, it would be hard to know if a strike was successful, he said.

Documents show that the Defense Department and intelligence community over the past decade have been taking this problem seriously. "It has become more prominent and more important in recent years," Richelson said.

Baker's paper identified more than $1 billion being spent tackling underground facility defeat issues during fiscal years 2009 and 2010.

There is some good news. The Comprehensive Nuclear Test Ban Treaty, signed by most countries, has yet to be ratified. But it has helped create a robust global network that can monitor clandestine underground nuclear weapon detonations. A National Academies report released in 2000 spelled out the shortcomings signees would have in attempting to detect tests. On a typical day, the Earth experiences hundreds of earthquakes and large mine blasts. The seismic clutter made it difficult to detect underground nuclear explosions, said Paul Richards, a Colombia University emeritus professor of geophysics and seismology at a Centre for Science, Technology and Security

Policy briefing on Capitol Hill. A follow-up report released this year showed remarkable progress over the last decade. Hundreds of seismic and air-sniffing sensors have been placed all over the world, and countries have done a better job of sharing their legacy seismic sensor data with those who monitor the treaty, he said.

The radioactive particles released by the Fukushima Daiichi Nuclear Plant accident last year were detected all over the globe and as far as South America, said Robert Werzi, who maintains the Comprehensive Test Ban Treaty Organization's 80 radionuclide air monitors. If a sensor detects a manmade radioactive particle, analysts can then determine how many days old it is, backtrack the weather patterns, and pinpoint its origins, he said.

Officials believe the network of seismic sensors is good enough to detect 90 percent of any clandestine attempt to test a nuclear weapon that is over 1 kiloton. The lower the yield is on a test, the less effective it is. Richards said it is necessary "to consider how well nuclear tests can be carried out evasively."

There is a need for a continuing research-and-development program to improve the network of sensors, he added.

"The goal of the monitoring effort is to drive ever downwards the yield of anything that might go undetected or identified," he said.

The Future of Cyber-Wars

Army Gen. Keith Alexander, commander of U.S. Cyber Command, sees a day in the not too distant future when attacks on computer networks cross the line from theft and disruption to "destruction."

And this chaos will not all take place in the digital world of ones and zeroes. He is referring to remote adversaries taking down infrastructure such as power grids, dams, transportation systems and other sectors that use computer-based industrial controls.

The last decade has seen mostly exploitation by adversaries, or the theft of money and intellectual property. Next came distributed denial of service attacks when hackers overwhelm networks and disrupt operations of businesses or other organizations, Alexander said at a recent Woodrow Wilson Centre panel discussion on cybersecurity.

Other than intercontinental ballistic missiles and acts of terrorism, an adversary seeking to reach out and harm the United States has only one other option: destructive cyber-attacks, Alexander said.

This could result in loss of life and damage to the economy on par with what occurred after 9/11.

"All of that is within the realm of the possible," he said. "I believe that is coming our way. We have to be out in front of this," Alexander said.

How to thwart such attacks is the problem the nation is facing. Most of the Internet's infrastructure through which malware is delivered is in the private sector's hands. So too are the banking, energy, transportation and other institutions that are vulnerable to the attacks. During the past year, there have been 200 attacks on core critical infrastructures in the transportation, energy, and communication industries reported to the Department of Homeland Security, said Sen. Susan Collins, R-Maine, and ranking member of the Senate Homeland Security and Governmental Affairs Committee.

"And that is only the tip of the iceberg. Undoubtedly there are more that have not been reported," she said during the panel.

"In this case, the dots have already been connected. The alarm has already been sounded, and we know it is only a matter of when, not whether we have a catastrophic attack," she said.

Alexander, Collins and others are advocating for a more coordinated national effort to share information on cyberthreats. Cyber Command and the National Security Agency have loads of expertise, but can't always share classified information, or cross lines when it comes to the privacy of U.S. citizens. The rest of the federal government has bits and pieces of information, and different responsibilities. Private sector companies are sometimes reluctant to disclose attacks for fear of upsetting shareholders or opening themselves up to lawsuits. Legislation co-sponsored by Collins to help pave the way for better information sharing died in Congress last summer.

Despite having poured countless amounts of money into cybersecurity on both the federal and private levels, there is still a lot to be learned about the threat, said one analyst.

"Why do we have a cyberwar community? Because we haven't mastered cyber," said Martin Libicki, senior management scientist at Rand Corp. The main problem is that computers were originally seen as something to be "tinkered" with, Libicki said.

"We've built the most important infrastructure on things that were made to be toys," said Libicki. Being toys, computer systems from the start have gaps and vulnerabilities needing to be patched.

"Every cyber-attack is a reflection of some vulnerability in the system," said Libicki.

Greg Giaqunito, an analyst at Forecast International, said it's not enough to defend the nation from attacks, offensive capabilities are required.

Increasingly, the United States is taking more proactive measures against adversaries and initiating activity, Giaqunito said.

"We are actually taking proactive action against other adversaries, so it's not only protecting ourselves, but the U.S. taking more proactive stances and actually initiating some activity against U.S. adversaries," he said. Over the next few years, the hackers will become more sophisticated, said Charles Croom, vice president of cyber security solutions at Lockheed Martin Information Systems & Global Solutions. This doesn't necessarily mean that the technologies are becoming more advanced — even the most sophisticated threats often use known vulnerabilities and malware, Croom said — but the adversaries have become more effective.

Lockheed Martin's Security Intelligence Centre has over the last 10 years compiled a database of patterns and hacking groups. This information can help analysts as they work to stop threats.

While innovation in technology is important, Croom said the backbone of its security system is its analysts.

A shortage of network security experts continues to be a problem in both government and the private sector. Alexander said because of the poor economy, he isn't having a problem attracting and retaining service personnel and civilian employees to Cyber Command now, but that won't always be the case. Incentives and bonuses may be needed to retain experts, he said.

Duke Ayers, program manager of SAIC's CyberNEXS initiative, a live-training program that focuses on cyber education, said, "We know that we're not developing people fast enough in cyber or the technical skills." SAIC, along with other partners such as the University of Texas at San Antonio, developed the CyberNEXS program that gives immediate feedback to participants as they pursue cyber-education.

Industry, the Defense Department and the Air Force Association have also teamed up to work on the CyberPatriot program, a nationwide high school-level competition intended to motivate high school students to get involved in the cybersecurity sector early and to cultivate talent.

Industry has also formed partnerships with academia to help stop attacks. In 2009, Northrop Grumman started its Cybersecurity Research Consortium, which includes Carnegie Mellon, MIT and Purdue University. There they investigate the various security threats that face the economy and national security and work on solutions that can help stop them, said Mike Papay, vice president of Cyber Initiatives at Northrop Grumman Information Systems.

With cybersecurity, Papay said, government and industry need to work together from the beginning during the procurement process. This, he said, is one way to reduce costs and achieve better cybersecurity.

"It's not just about acquiring pure cybersystems anymore; it's about acquiring UAV's, radars, ships, etc., where cyber needs to be embedded to ensure mission success. Government and industry need to consider cyber in almost everything they do," said Papay.

Despite all these initiatives, Collins struck a pessimistic tone, especially when it comes to the federal government's response.

"In all the years that I have been working on homeland security issues, I can't think of another area where the threat is greater, and we have done less," she said.

Climate Change

For the U.S. military, climate change is a "ring-road" issue that surrounds its future strategic planning.

No matter which way the Defense Department turns, U.S. global interests will eventually intersect with the effects of a warming planet, analysts said.

While politicians debate the legitimacy of climate science, the Defense Department has recognized it has a practical, hard-security interest in tackling issues like its energy footprint, said David Michel, director of environmental security at the Stimson Centre.

"There's no tree-hugging, sandal-wearing, granola eating aspects to the military's approach," Michel told National Defense. "The water-food-energy nexus of issues caused by climate change is going to be a rising challenge for the military and the national security strategy reflects that." The military will have an ever-increasing need for sensors and observation platforms to keep constant watch on how climate change manifests itself through weather and ecological phenomena, said Michel.

"These technologies are increasingly particularized and specialized," he said. "We need to make sure that all of our eyes in the sky are not only looking at North Korea, for instance, but gathering a wealth of data from many areas. We need an inclusive data network to which many different observation technologies contribute."

At the ends of the Earth, where climate change is already noticeable in receding ice caps, the same technologies are needed to monitor the melt, said Heather Conley, director of the Europe Program at the Centre for Strategic and International Studies. The Coast Guard will also need new ships that can patrol the cold waters of the Arctic, to provide a constant presence in what could become the world's newest contested open ocean, she said.

The 2010 Quadrennial Defense Review lists resource scarcity, climate change, disease, and demographics as "enduring trends" that threaten national security.

The challenge for the U.S. military, as it shifts its primary focus to the Pacific Ocean, will be balancing its response to acute events with a chronic, sustained preparedness for the long-term effects of climate change, Michel said. The Pacific already averages 70,000 annual deaths to natural disasters ranging from floods to typhoons and earthquakes.

"We're likely to see more of those sorts of acute events," Michel said. "But even at the same frequency and strength as we see them today ... as populations continue to grow, as urbanization along coastlines continues, more people will be exposed."

The U.S. military has a unique ability to provide infrastructure at nearly a moment's notice when disaster strikes. A single carrier strike group can provide medical supplies, lift capabilities and communications to a country devastated by a catastrophic event, as it did after a massive earthquake ravaged Haiti in 2010. The Marine Corps, along with the Navy, has pledged that disaster relief and humanitarian aid will be two of their main duties within a Pacific-centered security strategy.

The chronic results of climate change are more challenging. Funneling resources to combat a problem that might not manifest for decades is a hard sell, especially with constrained budgets, Conley said. But phenomena associated with climate change like persistent drought, violent flooding and agricultural disruption are real and immediate concerns for many of the nations the United States partners with around the world, Michel said. The effects are also causing the most disruption in some of the world's most politically unstable regions — Southern Asia, Sub-Saharan Africa, South America.

"To the extent that climate change is an issue for our partners ... it is going to become an issue for us," Michel said. "The military is also aware that ... climate impacts could be accelerants of instability in the countries where we have political interests or strategic concerns."

There are opportunities also associated with a warming planet. Some effects like the melting polar ice caps are regrettable ecologically but potentially a windfall for global commerce, said Conley. A receding Arctic icecap could mean the Northwest and Northeast passages and Russia's Northern Sea Route could remain open longer in summer. Eventually they could remain navigable to commercial shipping year-round.

The National Snow and Ice Data Centre in September announced that the polar ice cap shrank over the summer months to the smallest area in the 33 years that records have been kept — just 1.5 million square miles at its nadir.

"We're really seeing a dramatic acceleration of Arctic ice melt," Conley said. "As the ice recedes, there are increases in commercial and other human activity. It also opens new sources of oil and gas and tourist opportunities in new waters." The implications of the sudden availability of natural resources and shipping lanes through the Arctic have drawn much attention from nations spanning the globe. The obvious players — the eight-member Arctic Council, which includes the United States, Canada, Denmark, Finland, Norway, Russia, Sweden and Iceland — are concerned about border security where a sea of ice once did the work for them.

Other nations as far away as India and China are trying to gain admission to the council to advocate for their interests in shipping through an open Arctic, which could lessen by a third the time and cost of trans-oceanic shipping, said Conley.

For those and other reasons, the U.S. military "is just as interested in the decline of polar ice as the polar bear people," Michel said.

It is another instance where the military, by addressing a practical challenge to national security, can have a positive ecological impact, like the Navy being a champion of biofuels. Navy officials view renewable energy as a means of bringing down the cost of operations.

The Marines care less about curbing global warming than they do about keeping fuel and water convoys off vulnerable roads. But the net result of sustainable resource programs is a significant reduction in the military's carbon footprint, Michel said.

In the Arctic, however, the United States is woefully unprepared for the challenge. The Coast Guard has a single operational icebreaker and the military hasn't built one for more than 30 years.

"This summer, when Shell Oil attempted to drill offshore in the Arctic, they were able to bring more assets to bear than the U.S. Coast Guard could ever hope to muster," Conley said. "When we need resources, we borrow them from other countries. By the time there is a crisis there, we won't have the ability to address it."

There are other strikes against U.S. polar preparedness. Because the disappearance of the ice cap is a long-term issue that may not have consequences for decades, it is difficult to interest policymakers and even more difficult to pin down funding for infrastructure and ships, Conley said.

The Arctic is also an area where 20 federal agencies have some role, creating headaches for strategists and diplomatic efforts to manage competition there. "Coordination of Arctic policy is a nightmare on a good day," she said. In the Arctic, as in Asia and the Pacific, the United States will be forced to acknowledge and address climate change, if it is to uphold its professed role as a global power to secure and maintain the free-flow of public goods, Michel said. "If we say climate change is one of our major concerns that is going to shape the 21st century and then we ignore it, the international community will notice," he said.

Transnational Crime/Terror

Well before the May killing of Osama bin Laden at the hands of U.S. Navy SEALs, the terrorist organization he headed had become a dispersed, loosely linked network of international terror and criminal groups. Add to that the existing transnational trafficking in narcotics, weapons and people, and the recipe yields a complicated problem for U.S. military and law enforcement agencies at home and abroad.

"We're going to continue to have this transnational, non-standard set of threats and everything that goes with that," said Garry Reid, principal deputy assistant secretary of defense for special operations, during a discussion of future SOF operations at the annual Air and Space conference in September. "Those threats are going to persist in multiple environments over the next 10-plus years." Countering those threats is made all the more difficult given that the U.S. military can't take its eye off state-level actors to fight non-state, non-standard actors.

"Our national defense focus and clearly the focus of our Special Operations Command has got to equally be on ... high-end threats and state competitors of the future," Reid said. Events like the Arab Spring have created power vacuums and ungoverned lands where criminals and terrorist groups are able to operate with impunity.

While much of the U.S. military's attention has been on the Middle East, anti-U.S. terror groups and al-Qaida sympathizers have spread elsewhere. Today, the arc of instability, from West to East Africa to Pakistan to Bangladesh has any number of al-Qaida copycat sympathizers, Arnaud de Borchgrave, senior adviser and director of the Transnational Threats Project at the Centre for Strategic and International Studies, wrote in January.

Illegal trade is "increasingly converging with ideologically-motivated networks, fostering a new generation of hybrid threats," according to information from the project's website. Mali and Libya were two examples given by Reid of places where those two forces are converging. A coup last year in Mali left the country's inhospitable north largely ungoverned. "Bandits and kidnappers" have since set up shop.

Al-Qaida in the Islamic Maghreb has reared its head in Mali, operating without constraint in the arid north, some of the most inhospitable terrain on earth. "Al-Qaida branched into there a few years ago and showed mixed results with proselytizing their ideology," Reid said. "They have not posed a transnational threat per se to attack the United States homeland, but they are of growing concern to our interests in the region."

The group draws its origins from desert bandits and smugglers taking advantage of a power vacuum to advance their and al-Qaida's interests. The instability in Libya has afforded them an opportunity to spread their beliefs there also, Reid said. They gain a significant amount of resources from kidnapping for ransom — tens of millions of dollars go into their treasure chests. For al-Qaida, kidnapping to fund terrorist activities is a relatively new brand of criminality, he said.

These are small-scale crimes with regional implications for which military intervention is not well suited. They call instead for foreign military engagement by special operations forces, which have been overstretched this last decade, and for which no respite is in sight, Reid said. "We see ourselves being pretty busy in the future," he said. The situation calls, as many others do, for technologies that are force multipliers, like intelligence, surveillance and reconnaissance platforms that are easily deployed and operated by militaries short on resources.

There are "issues of partner-nation absorption," of what portion of the enforcement burden native societies and militaries can take on, Reid said. Technologies like unmanned aerial vehicles and persistent border surveillance can enhance that absorption, he said. But it is "not as simple as providing a piece of kit and waving goodbye," he said. "How do we allow a small nation to have the advantage of these capabilities? These technologies will have to be scalable."

Simply handing over or lending the U.S. military's large and complicated unmanned aerial vehicles and surveillance systems won't do. Once criminal activity is detected, the host nation must be have the will and training to curtail it. That will require a steady presence of SOF personnel in remote parts of the world. Distributed operations of that nature and scope call for a secure communications network the United States doesn't currently have, Reid said.

The transnational threat also hits close to home. The United States is the world's primary market for illicit drugs. They flow over the nation's land and maritime borders by the ton and government agencies catch only about a third of what's smuggled, Gen. Douglas Fraser, then the commander of U.S. Southern Command, told defense reporters in March. An estimated 1,200 to 1,500 metric tons of illegal drugs are produced in South and Central America each year, Fraser said. Of that, about 60 percent eventually makes it to the United States, he said.

Here again, intelligence, surveillance and reconnaissance technologies can help.

But eyes in the sky can only spy, and in South America are often hampered by rain forests. In countries like Colombia and Honduras, criminals hide beneath a triple-canopy rain forest through which current sensors cannot penetrate, Fraser said. "That's really a [research-and-development] effort right now.... We have not gotten to a penetrative capability yet." UAVs, however, cannot interdict drugs or smugglers once they are found. The Coast Guard and Navy need more ships for that task, or other weapon systems that both spot and stop illegal drug and gun trafficking, he said. But technology is not always the silver bullet, Fraser said. Just as in North Africa, countering transnational threats in South America is accomplished by using some technologies like maritime radar but is best done through direct cooperation with regional allies and old-fashioned word-of-mouth intelligence gathering, he said.

While UAVs have developed rapidly because of successes in Iraq and Afghanistan — Reid credits many of SOF's "most public successes" on their spying abilities — they aren't necessarily the best platform for every job, Fraser said.

CYBER SECURITY FOR THE MILITARY AND DEFENCE SECTOR

With a greater dependence on computer systems and a reliance on integrated networking, today's armed forces are faced with an ever changing set of challenges in maintaining cyber security from the threat of attack. Rapid evolution in technology has forced governments and industry alike to continually develop secure systems that remain one step ahead of the enemy. As cyber systems become increasingly integrated the requirement for a multi-layered, adaptive and self learning security system becomes imperative. With the prevalence of electronic communications, the growth of social media, a widespread access to mobile networked devices and the defence industry's increasing reliance on "Big Data", the cyber threat to today's defence sector has never been more apparent. The 'cyber landscape' is both dynamic and borderless and forces us to address our security in terms of technology, international cooperation as well as individual user awareness.

This year's conference will focus on the military as well as the industrial defence sector itself; establishing what the current threats are, in terms of both state-sponsored intrusion as well as independent hackers and terrorist cells, what technology is currently available and where the gaps in our protection are. Additionally, with increasingly networked systems the defence sector has been presented with a whole array of emerging challenges in cyber defence. Cyber Security for the Military and the Defence Sector 2013 will tackle this by gathering senior experts from both industry and the military to discuss and ideas share to ensure that our governments remain educated, up-to-date and secure.

Bibliography

Abbate, Janet: *Inventing the Internet*. Cambridge: MIT Press, 1999

Ahuja, Vijay: *Network and Internet Security*. Academic Press, Inc.: Boston, 1996.

Amoroso, E. : *Fundamentals of Computer Security Technology*, Prentice Hall, Englewood Cliffs, 1994.

Andress, Jason. Winterfeld, Steve: *Cyber Warfare: Techniques, Tactics and Tools for Security Practitioners*. Syngress. 2011.

Andrew, N.: *Foundations of Nanomechanics: from Solid-state Theory to Device Applications*, Berlin, New York, 2003.

Askari Rizvi: *Nuclear Terrorism and South Asia*, Albuquerque, NM: Sandia National Laboratories, February 2003.

Attebery, B.: *Nanoculture: Implications of the New Technoscience*, Bristol, Intellect Books, 2004.

Augastine, Paul T : *Cyber Security*, Crescent Pub, Delhi, 2007.

BloomBecker, Buck: *Spectacular Computer Crimes*. Dow Jones-Irwin: Homewood, IL, 1990.

Brenner, S.: *Cyber Threats: The Emerging Fault Lines of the Nation State*. Oxford University Press. 2009.

Carr, Jeffrey: *Inside Cyber Warfare: Mapping the Cyber Underworld*. O'Reilly. 2010.

Carroll, J.S.: *Social Science Research Methods for Assessing Societal Implications of Nanotechnology*, Dordrecht, Kluwer, 2001.

Charlotte Waelde, *Law and the Internet: Regulating Cyberspace*. Hart Pub, 1997.

Chuck Easttom: *System Forensics, Investigation, and Response*. Jones & Bartlett. 2013.

Clark, R. M. : *Intelligence analysis a target-centric approach*, Washington D.C: CQ Press, 2004.

Clausewitz, C. V. : *Principles of War*, Minneola, New York, Dover Publication, 2003.

Crichton, Michael: *Electronic Life, How to Think About Computers*, New York, Alfred A. Knopf, 1983.

Daniel J.: *Bandits on the Information Superhighway*. O'Reilly & Associates, Inc.: Sebastopol, 1996.

Daniel Ratner: *Nanotechnology: a Gentle Introduction to the Next Big Idea,* Upper Saddle River, Prentice Hall, 2003.

David Post : *The Rise of Law in Cyberspace,* 48 Stan, L. Rev. 1367, 1996.

David R. Johnson & David Post : *The Rise of Law in Cyberspace,* 48 Stan, L. Rev. 1367, 1996.

David, J.: *Micromachines and Nanotechnology: the Amazing New World of the Ultrasmall,* Parsippany, Dillon Press, 1995.

Davis, Richard. *The Web of Politics: The Internet's Impact on the American Political System.* Oxford, UK: Oxford University Press, 1999

Dery, Mark. *Escape Velocity: Cyberculture at the End of the Century* . Grove Press, 1997.

Dixit, Prabla: *Communalism: A Struggle for Power,* New Delhi, Orient Longman, 1981.

Frederick B.: *Protection and Security on the Information Superhighway.* John Wiley & Sons, Inc.: New York, 1995.

Friedman, G.: *The Future of War of Cyber Crimes,* N.Y., Random House, 1996.

Friedman, T. L. : *The Lexus and the olive tree, Understanding globalization,* New York, FSG Books, 1999.

Froomkin, Michael : *The Essential Role of Trusted Third Parties in Electronic Commerce,* 75 Ore. L. Rev. 49, 1996.

Froomkin, Michael : *The Essential Role of Trusted Third Parties in Electronic Commerce,* 75 Ore. L. Rev. 49, 1996.

Gast, A. P. : *The impact of restricting information access on science and technology* Retrieved October 1, 2008.

George M. Mohay: *Computer and intrusion forensics.* Artech House. 2003.

George S. Paul: *Beyond Humanity: Cyber Evolution and Future Minds,* Roackland, Charles River Media, 1996.

Gupta, A., & Laliberte, S. : *Security by Example Defend I.T.* New York, Addison Wesley, 2004.

Hahn, Harley: *Harley Hahn's Internet InSecurity.* Prentice Hall: Upper Saddle River, 2002.

Hasan-Askari Rizvi: *Nuclear Terrorism and South Asia,* Albuquerque, NM: Sandia National Laboratories, February 2003.

Hayles, N.K. : *Nanoculture: Implications of the New Technoscience,* Bristol, Intellect Books, 2004.

Herman H.: *The Computer, From Pascal to von Neumann.* Princeton, NJ, Princeton University Press, 1972.

Hoffman, Bruce: *Cyber Crime with Internet,* New York: Columbia University Press, 1998.

Huntington, S.P.: *The Military and the State,* N.Y., Vintage Books, 1964.

James Keller: *Public Access to the Internet,* Cambridge, MA: The MIT Press, 1995.

Joel Moses: *The Computer Age, A Twenty-Year View.*Cambridge, MA, The MIT Press, 1979.

Jones, W.H.: *The Government and Politics of Indian Military*, London, Hutchinson, 1971.

Kaplan, David: *Computer Virus Attack*, New York: Crown Publishers, 1996.

Karanjit Siyan: *Internet Firewalls and Network Security*. New Riders Publishing: Indianapolis, 1996.

Keane J.: *Democracy and Cyber Crimes*, London, Verso, 1988.

Kurz, Raymond, *Internet and the Law: Legal Fundamentals for the Internet User*. Rockville, MD.: Government Institutes, 1996.

Laliberte, S. : *Security by Example Defend I.T.* New York, Addison Wesley, 2004.

Laquer, Walter: *Terrorism Attack from Computer Hacking*, Oxford: Oxford University Press, 1999.

Marshell, Angus M.: *Digital forensics: digital evidence in criminal investigation*. Wiley-Blackwell. 2008.

Mary, W.: *Military Space Force: the Cultural Dimensions of Authority*, Cambridge, Belknap Press, 1985.

McMahon, David: *Cyber Threat: Internet Security for Home and Business*. Warwick Publishing Inc.: Toronto, 2000.

Nigel, M. De S. Cameron: *Human Dignity in the Biotech Century: A Christian Vision for Public Policy*, Downers Grove, InterVarsity Press, 2004.

Peter T.: *Manager's Guide to Internet Security*. CSI: San Francisco, 1994.

Posen, B.R.: *The Sources of Cyber Crime*, Ithaca, 1984, Cornell Univ. Press.

Rhodes, Richard: *The Making of the Atomic Bomb*, New York: Simon and Schuster, 1988.

Richard Klau. *Law Law Law on the Internet: The Best Legal Web Sites and More*. Chicago, IL.: American Bar Association, 1998.

Rizvi, Askari : *Nuclear Terrorism and South Asia*, Albuquerque, NM: Sandia National Laboratories, February 2003.

Robert L.: *Software Creativity*, Prentice Hall PTR, 1995.

Rosen, P.: *Policy of Cyber Laws*, Ithaca, Cornell University Press, 1996.

Schroeer, Dietrich: *Science, Technology, and the Cyber Crimes*, Ontario: John Wiley & Sons, 1984.

Schummer, J.: *Interdisciplinary Issues in Nanoscale Research*, Amsterdam: IOS Press, 2004.

Scott M.: *Managing IP Networks with Cisco Routers*. O'Reilly & Associates, Inc.: Sebastopol, 1997.

Sharma, Vakul : *Handbook of Cyber Laws*, Macmillan Publishers India, Delhi, 2002.

Smith, H. A.: *Nanotechnology Infrared Optics for Astronomy Missions*, Washington, National Aeronautics and Space Administration, 2002.

Steve J.: *The Cybernetics Group*, Cambridge, MA, The MIT Press, 1991.

Tenner, E.: *Nanotechnology and Unintended Consequences*,, Dordrecht, Kluwer, 2001.

Thom, M. C. : *Information warfare arms control, Risks and costs* Colorado Springs Colorado, USAF Institute for National Security Studies, 2006.

Uday O. and Vijay K. Gurbani: *Internet & TCP/IP Network Security*. McGraw-Hill: New York, 1996.

Verton, D. : *Black Ice: The invisible Threat of Cyber-terrorism*, New York: McGraw-Hill/ Osborne, 2003.

William Aspray: *Computer, A History of the Information Machine*, New York, Basic Books, 1996.

Williams, J. D. : *The complete strategyst, Being a primer on the theory of games of strategy*, New York, Dover, 1986.

Wilson, C. : *Information Operations and Cyberwar, Capabilities and related Policy Issues*, In C. R. Service, Congressional Research Service, The Library of Congress, 2006.

Wilson, C. : *Information Operations and Cyberwar, Capabilities and related Policy Issues*, In C. R. Service, Congressional Research Service, The Library of Congress, 2006.

Yar, M.: *Cybercrime and Society*, London: Sage, 2006.

Zanini, M.: *Countering the New Terrorism*, Santa Monica, CA: RAND, 1999.

Index

❑❑❑